# CARE OF THE SOUL

# CARE OF THE SOUL

## A GUIDE FOR CULTIVATING DEPTH AND SACREDNESS IN EVERYDAY LIFE

### THOMAS MOORE

Walker and Company

New York

Library of Congress Cataloging-in-Publication Data
Moore, Thomas, 1940–
    Care of the soul: a guide for cultivating depth and sacredness in
everyday life / by Thomas Moore. —1st large print ed.
      p.   cm.
    Includes bibliographical references.
    ISBN 0-8027-2674-7
    1. Spiritual life.   2. Psychology, Religious.   3. Large type
books.   I. Title.
    [BL624.M663  1993]
    158'.1—dc20                  93-13239
                                          CIP

Grateful acknowledgment is made for permission to reproduce the following material: Excerpts from "Sonnet 9," Part One, from *Sonnets to Orpheus* by Rainer Maria Rilke, translated by M. D. Herter Norton. Copyright 1942 by W. W. Norton & Company, Inc. Copyright renewed © 1970 by M. D. Herter Norton. Reprinted by permission of W. W. Norton & Company, Inc. "The Ancient Coffer of Nuri Bey" from *Tales of the Dervishes* by Idries Shah. Copyright © 1967 by Idries Shah. Reprinted by permission of Dutton, an imprint of New American Library, a division of Penguin Books USA, Inc. Excerpt from "Endymion" from *John Keats Complete Poems*, edited by Jack Stillinger. Copyright © 1978, 1982 by the President and Fellows of Harvard College. Reprinted by permission of Harvard University Press, Cambridge, Mass.

Jacket design © 1992 by Michael Katz/David Bullen
Jacket illustration *Woman Sewing Before a Garden Window*, 1895 by Edouard Vuillard, France, 1868–1940. Bequest of John T. Spaulding. Courtesy, Museum of Fine Arts, Boston. Art research: Diana Straub

First Large Print Edition, 1993
Walker and Company
720 Fifth Avenue
New York, New York 10019

Printed in the United States of America

10  9  8  7  6  5  4  3  2  1

# CONTENTS

*Acknowledgments ix*

*Introduction xi*

## I. Care of the Soul

1. Honoring Symptoms as
a Voice of the Soul  3

## II. Care of the Soul in Everyday Life

2. The Myth of Family
and Childhood  35

3. Self-love and Its Myth:
Narcissus and Narcissism  82

4. Love's Initiations  115

5. Jealousy and Envy:
Healing Poisons  146

6. The Soul and Power  178

7. Gifts of Depression  205

8. The Body's Poetics of Illness  232

9. The Economics of Soul:
   Work, Money, Failure,
   and Creativity  265

III. *Spiritual Practice and
     Psychological Depth*

10. The Need for Myth, Ritual,
    and a Spiritual Life  303

11. Wedding Spirituality
    and Soul  345

IV. *Care of the World's Soul*

12. Beauty and the Reanimation
    of Things  399

13. The Sacred Arts of Life  427

   *Notes  459*
   *Suggestions for
   Further Reading  465*

# ACKNOWLEDGMENTS

While this book is a personal statement based on many years of experience as a psychotherapist, I am unusually indebted to several gifted friends who have inspired and guided me. I would like to thank Christopher Bamford for planting and working the seeds of the initial idea. Much of the thought in this book has come from my association with original thinkers who have taught us how to think about the soul, especially James Hillman and Robert Sardello. I'd also like to thank Ben Sells, Terrie Murphy, and Sarah Jackson for reading parts of the manuscript. I am grateful to Charles Boer for his graceful translation of *The Homeric Hymns*. The Ann and Erlo Van Waveren Foundation provided funding to help me do the basic writing. Hugh Van Dusen, of HarperCollins, provided constant enthusiastic encouragement and advice. His warmth and deep culture gave soul to the sometimes challenging demands of publication. Jane Hirshfield worked very hard with amazing patience to get my sometimes esoteric use of language into shape. Michael Katz, my agent, brought a brilliant artist's touch to the business and aesthetic aspects of the book, and he was a sensitive guiding companion during the writing and publishing process. Finally, I must thank Joan Hanley for urging me to go ever deeper in my search for ways of presenting possibilities for a soulful life.

# INTRODUCTION

The great malady of the twentieth century, implicated in all of our troubles and affecting us individually and socially, is "loss of soul." When soul is neglected, it doesn't just go away; it appears symptomatically in obsessions, addictions, violence, and loss of meaning. Our temptation is to isolate these symptoms or to try to eradicate them one by one; but the root problem is that we have lost our wisdom about the soul, even our interest in it. We have today few specialists of the soul to advise us when we succumb to moods and emotional pain, or when as a nation we find ourselves confronting a host of threatening evils. But within our history we do have remarkable sources of insight from people who wrote explicitly about the nature and needs of the soul, and so we can look to the past for guidance in restoring this wisdom. In this book I will draw on that past wisdom, taking into account how we live now, to show that by caring for the soul we can find relief from our distress and discover deep satisfaction and pleasure.

It is impossible to define precisely what the soul is. Definition is an intellectual enterprise anyway; the soul prefers to imagine. We know intuitively that soul has to do with genuineness and depth, as when we say certain music has soul or a remarkable person is soulful. When you look closely at the image of soulfulness, you see that it is tied to life in all its particulars—good food, satisfying conversation, genuine friends, and experiences that stay in the memory and touch the heart. Soul is revealed in attachment, love, and community, as well as in retreat on behalf of inner communing and intimacy.

Modern psychologies and therapies often contain an unspoken but clear salvational tone. If you could only learn to be assertive, loving, angry, expressive, contemplative, or thin, they imply, your troubles would be over. The self-help book of the Middle Ages and Renaissance, which in some fashion I'm taking as a model, was cherished and revered, but was never great art and didn't promise the sky. It gave recipes for good living and offered suggestions for a practical, down-to-earth philosophy of life. I'm interested in this humbler approach, one that is more accepting of human foibles, and indeed sees dignity and peace as emerging more from that acceptance than from any method of transcending the human condition. Therefore, this book, my own imagination of what a self-help manual could be, is a guide offering a philosophy of soulful living and techniques for dealing with everyday problems without striving for perfection or salvation.

During the fifteen years I have been practicing psychotherapy, I have been surprised how much my studies in Renaissance psychology, philosophy, and medicine have contributed to the work. That influence will be evident in this book, as I follow the Renaissance penchant for turning to mythology for insight and cite authors of that time, such as Marsilio Ficino and Paracelsus. These were practical lovers of wisdom who saw patients regularly, applying their highly imagistic philosophies to the most ordinary matters.

I have also taken the Renaissance approach of not separating psychology from religion. Jung, one of our most recent doctors of the soul, said that every psychological problem is ultimately a matter of religion. Thus, this book contains both psychological advice and spiritual guidance. A spiritual life of some kind is absolutely necessary for psychological "health"; at the same time, excessive or ungrounded spirituality can also be dangerous, leading to all kinds of compulsive and even violent behavior. Therefore, I include a section on the interplay of spirituality and soul.

In his studies of alchemy, Jung says that the work begins and ends with Mercury. I think his recommendation applies to this book as well. Mercury is the god of fictions and fabrications, of trickery, thievery, and sleight-of-hand. The self-help idea lends itself to excessive sincerity. I often tell my clients that they should not strive for sincerity so earnestly; a dose of Mercury is necessary to keep our work honest. Therefore, to some extent I see this book also as a *fiction* of self-help. No one can tell you how to live your life. No one knows the secrets of the heart sufficiently to tell others about them authoritatively.

All of this leads to the heart of the book—care of the soul. Tradition teaches that soul lies midway between understanding and unconsciousness, and that its instrument is neither the mind nor the body, but imagination. I understand therapy as nothing more than bringing imagination to areas that are devoid of it, which then must express themselves by becoming symptomatic.

Fulfilling work, rewarding relationships, personal power, and relief from symptoms are all gifts of the soul. They are particularly elusive in our time because we don't believe in the soul and therefore give it no place in our hierarchy of values. We have come to know soul only in its complaints: when it stirs, disturbed by neglect and abuse, and causes us to feel its pain. It is commonplace for writers to point out that we live in a time of deep division, in which mind is separated from body and spirituality is at odds with materialism. But how do we get out of this split? We can't just "think" ourselves through it, because thinking itself is part of the problem. What we need is a way out of dualistic attitudes. We need a third possibility, and that third is soul.

In the fifteenth century, Marsilio Ficino put it as simply as possible. The mind, he said, tends to go off on its own so that it seems to have no relevance to the physical world. At the same time, the materialistic life can be so absorbing that we get caught in it and forget about spirituality. What we need, he said, is soul, in the middle, holding together mind and body, ideas and life, spirituality and the world.

What I am going to present in this book, then, is a program for bringing soul back into life. This is not a new idea. I am simply developing a very old idea in a way I hope will be intelligible and applicable to us in this particular crucial period in history. The idea of a soul-centered world goes back to the earliest days of our culture. It has been sketched out in every period of our history, in the writings of Plato, in the experiments of Renaissance theologians, in the letters and literature of the Romantic poets, and finally in Freud, who gave us a glimpse of a psychic underworld full of memory, fantasy, and emotion. Jung made explicit what was embryonic in Freud, speaking forthrightly for soul and reminding us that we have much to learn about it from our forebears. Most recently James Hillman, my mentor and colleague, and others in his circle—Robert Sardello, Rafael López-Pedraza, Patricia Berry, and Alfred Ziegler, for example—have presented a new approach to psychology that is mindful of this history and explicitly follows Ficino's advice to put soul at the very center of our lives.

This book will focus not just on the idea of soul, but on concrete ways we can foster soulfulness in our ordinary everyday lives. To describe this process, I have borrowed a key phrase from Christianity. For hundreds of years the parish priest received into his charge the souls of those who lived within the boundaries of his church. This responsibility, as well as the work he did tending the needs of his people, was known as *cura animarum,* the cure of souls. *Cure* meant "charge" as well as "care." If we take up this image and apply it to ourselves, we can imagine the responsibility we each have to our own soul. Just as the parish priest was available at life's crucial moments, not as a doctor or healer but simply to accompany and tend the soul in times of birth, illness, marriage, crisis, and death, we can respond to our own soul as it winds its way through the maze of our life's unfolding. The role of the curate, as he was called, was to provide a religious context for the larger turning points in life and also to maintain the affectional ties of family, marriage, and community. We can be the curates or curators of our own souls, an idea that implies an inner priesthood and a personal religion. To undertake this restoration of soul means we have to make spirituality a more serious part of everyday life.

You can see already that care of the soul is quite different in scope from most modern notions of psychology and psychotherapy. It isn't about curing, fixing, changing, adjusting or making healthy, and it isn't about some idea of perfection or even improvement. It doesn't look to the future for an ideal, trouble-free existence. Rather, it remains patiently in the present, close to life as it presents itself day by day, and yet at the same time mindful of religion and spirituality.

Here is another major difference between

care of the soul and psychotherapy in the usual sense: psychology is a secular science, while care of the soul is a sacred art. Although I am borrowing the terminology of Christianity, what I am proposing is not specifically Christian, nor is it tied to any particular religious tradition. It does, however, imply a religious sensibility and a recognition of our absolute need for a spiritual life.

In the modern world we separate religion and psychology, spiritual practice and therapy. There is considerable interest in healing this split, but if it is going to be bridged, our very idea of what we are doing in our psychology has to be radically re-imagined. Psychology and spirituality need to be seen as one. In my view, this new paradigm suggests the end of psychology as we have known it altogether because it is essentially modern, secular, and ego-centered. A new idea, a new language, and new traditions must be developed on which to base our theory and practice.

Our Renaissance and Romantic ancestors, as well as Freud, Jung, and Hillman and their colleagues, all turn to the past for a renewal of their imaginations. We are in grave need of just such a renaissance of our own, a rebirth of ancient wisdom and practice accommodated to our own situation. The great Renaissance thinkers made continuous efforts to reconcile medicine and magic, religion and philosophy, everyday life and meditation, ancient wisdom and the most recent discoveries and inventions. We are dealing with the same issues, except that we are farther in time from the days of magic and mythology, and for us, technology has become a burden as well as an enormous achievement.

The emotional complaints of our time, complaints we therapists hear every day in our practice, include

emptiness
meaninglessness
vague depression
disillusionment about marriage, family, and
    relationship
a loss of values
yearning for personal fulfillment
a hunger for spirituality

All of these symptoms reflect a loss of soul and let us know what the soul craves. We yearn excessively for entertainment, power, intimacy, sexual fulfillment, and material things, and we think we can find these things if we discover the right relationship or job, the right church or therapy. But without soul, whatever we find will be unsatisfying, for what we truly long for is the soul in each of these areas. Lacking that soulfulness, we attempt to gather these alluring satisfactions to us in great masses, thinking apparently that quantity will make up for lack of quality.

Care of the soul speaks to the longings we feel and to the symptoms that drive us crazy, but it is not a path away from shadow or death. A soulful personality is complicated, multifaceted, and shaped by both pain and pleasure, success and failure. Life lived soulfully is not without its moments of darkness and periods of foolishness. Dropping the salvational fantasy frees us up to the possibility of self-knowledge and self-acceptance, which are the very foundation of soul.

Several classical phrases describing care of the soul are relevant in the modern world. Plato used the expression *techne tou biou,* which means "the craft of life." When *techne* is defined with sufficient depth, it refers not just to mechanical skills and instruments but to all kinds of artful managing and careful shaping. For now, we can say that care of the soul requires a special crafting of life itself, with an artist's sensitivity to the way things are done. Soul doesn't pour into life automatically. It requires our skill and attention.

Many of our words for psychological work have religious overtones. In Plato's writing, Socrates says that "therapy" refers to service to the gods. A therapist, Socrates says, is a sacristan, someone who takes care of the practical elements in religious worship. Another phrase Plato used was *heautou epimeleisthai,* "care of oneself"; this word for care also described honoring the gods and the dead. Somehow we have to understand that we cannot solve our "emotional" problems until we grasp this mystery that honoring the divine and the departed is part of the basic care that as human beings we have to bring to life.

The later Roman writer Apuleius said, "Everyone should know that you can't live in any other way than by cultivating the soul." Care can also mean cultivation, watching, and participating as the seed of soul unfolds into the vast creation we call character or personality, with a history, a community, a language, and a unique mythology. Cultivation of the soul implies a lifelong husbanding of raw materials. Farmers cultivate their fields, all of us cultivate our souls. The aim of soul work, therefore, is not adjustment to accepted norms or to an image of the statistically healthy individual. Rather, the goal is a richly elaborated life, connected to society and nature, woven into the culture of family, nation, and globe. The idea is not to be superficially adjusted, but to be profoundly connected in the heart to ancestors and to living brothers and sisters in all the many communities that claim our hearts.

Epicurus, a much misunderstood philosopher who stressed simple pleasure as a goal of life, wrote, "It is never too early or too late to care for the well-being of the soul." Epicurus was a vegetarian who urged his followers to cultivate intimacy through letters. He held his classes in a garden, so that as he taught he was surrounded by the simple foods he ate. (Ironically, his name has since become a symbol for gourmet eating and sensuality.) This concept of the value of simple pleasure runs through the entire tradition of thinking about soul. As we try to understand what care of the soul might mean for us, we may want to keep in mind the epicurean principle that the rewards we are seeking may be quite ordinary and may exist right under our noses, even as we look to the stars for some extraordinary revelation or perfection.

These statements of our ancient teachers come from Michel Foucault's book *The Care of the Self*. But the word *self* implies an ego project. Soul is nothing like ego. Soul is closely connected to fate, and the turns of fate almost always go counter to the expectations and often to the desires of the ego. Even the Jungian idea of Self, carefully defined as a blend of conscious understanding and unconscious influences, is still very personal and too human in contrast to the idea of soul. Soul is the font of who we are, and yet it is far beyond our capacity to devise and to control. We can cultivate, tend, enjoy, and participate in the things of the soul, but we can't outwit it or manage it or shape it to the designs of a willful ego.

Care of the soul is inspiring. I like to think that it was the theology of soul worked out so painstakingly and so concretely in Renaissance Italy that gave rise to the extraordinary art of that period. The act of entering into the mysteries of the soul, without sentimentality or pessimism, encourages life to blossom forth according to its own designs and with its own unpredictable beauty. Care of the soul is not solving the puzzle of life; quite the opposite, it is an appreciation of the paradoxical mysteries that blend light and darkness into the grandeur of what human life and culture can be.

In these pages we will consider important differences between care and cure. We will look at several common issues in everyday life that offer the opportunity for soul-making, once we stop thinking of them as problems to be solved. Then we will try to imagine spiritual life from the point of view of soul—a different perspective that offers an alternative to the usual transcendent ideal that we bring to religion and theology. Finally, we will consider how we could tend the soul by living artfully.

Psychology is incomplete if it doesn't include spirituality and art in a fully integrative way.

As you read this book, it might be a good idea to abandon any ideas you may have about living successfully and properly, and about understanding yourself. The human soul is not meant to be understood. Rather, you might take a more relaxed position and reflect on the way your life has taken shape. Some of the points of view here may be surprising, but surprise is another gift of Mercury. The twisting of a familiar theme into a new shape is sometimes more revealing and ultimately more significant than acquiring new knowledge and a new set of principles. Often when imagination twists the commonplace into a slightly new form, suddenly we see soul where formerly it was hidden.

Let us imagine care of the soul, then, as an application of poetics to everyday life. What we want to do here is to re-imagine those things we think we already understand. If Mercury is present with his wit and humor, there is a good chance that the soul—as elusive, the ancient poets said, as a butterfly—will make an appearance, and my writing and your reading will themselves be a way of caring for the soul.

# CARE OF THE SOUL

---

*I am certain of nothing
but the holiness of the
Heart's affections and the
truth of the Imagination.*
JOHN KEATS

# CHAPTER I

# Honoring Symptoms as a Voice of the Soul

Once a week people in the thousands show up for their regular appointment with a therapist. They bring problems they have talked about many times before, problems that cause them intense emotional pain and make their lives miserable. Depending on the kind of therapy employed, the problems will be analyzed, referred back to childhood and parents, or attributed to some key factor such as the failure to express anger, alcohol in the family, or childhood abuse. Whatever the approach, the aim will be health or happiness achieved by the removal of these central problems.

Care of the soul is a fundamentally different way of regarding daily life and the quest for happiness. The emphasis may not be on problems at all. One person might care for the soul by buying or renting a good piece of land, another by selecting an appropriate school or program of study, another by painting his house or his bedroom. Care of the soul is a continuous process that concerns itself not so much with "fixing" a central flaw as with attending to the small details of everyday life, as well as to major decisions and changes.

Care of the soul may not focus on the personality or on relationships at all, and therefore it is not psychological in the usual sense. Tending the things around us and becoming sensitive to the importance of home, daily schedule, and maybe even the clothes we wear, are ways of caring for the soul. When Marsilio Ficino wrote his self-help book, *The Book of Life*, five hundred years ago, he placed emphasis on carefully choosing colors, spices, oils, places to walk, countries to visit—all very concrete decisions of everyday life that day by day either support or disturb the soul. We think of the psyche, if we think about it at all, as a cousin to the brain and therefore something essentially internal. But ancient psychol-

ogists taught that our own souls are inseparable from the world's soul, and that both are
found in all the many things that make up nature and culture.

So, the first point to make about care of the
soul is that it is not primarily a method of
problem solving. Its goal is not to make life
problem-free, but to give ordinary life the
depth and value that come with soulfulness. In
a way it is much more of a challenge than psychotherapy because it has to do with cultivating a richly expressive and meaningful life at
home and in society. It is also a challenge because it requires imagination from each of us.
In therapy we lay our problems at the feet of a
professional who is supposedly trained to
solve them for us. In care of the soul, we ourselves have both the task and the pleasure of
organizing and shaping our lives for the good
of the soul.

## Getting to Know the Soul

Let us begin by looking at this
phrase I have been using, "care of the soul."
The word *care* implies a way of responding to
expressions of the soul that is not heroic and
muscular. Care is what a nurse does, and
"nurse" happens to be one of the early mean-

ings of the Greek word *therapeia,* or therapy. We'll see that care of the soul is in many ways a return to early notions of what therapy is. *Cura,* the Latin word used originally in "care of the soul," means several things: attention, devotion, husbandry, adorning the body, healing, managing, being anxious for, and worshiping the gods. It might be a good idea to keep all these meanings in mind as we try to see as concretely as possible how we might make the shift from psychotherapy as we know it today to care of the soul.

"Soul" is not a thing, but a quality or a dimension of experiencing life and ourselves. It has to do with depth, value, relatedness, heart, and personal substance. I do not use the word here as an object of religious belief or as something to do with immortality. When we say that someone or something has soul, we know what we mean, but it is difficult to specify exactly what that meaning is.

Care of the soul begins with observance of how the soul manifests itself and how it operates. We can't care for the soul unless we are familiar with its ways. Observance is a word from ritual and religion. It means to watch out for but also to keep and honor, as in the observance of a holiday. The *-serv-* in observance originally referred to tending sheep. Observing the soul, we keep an eye on its sheep, on whatever is wandering and grazing—the latest addiction, a striking dream, or a troubling mood.

This definition of caring for the soul is minimalist. It has to do with modest care and not miraculous cure. But my cautious definition has practical implications for the way we deal with ourselves and with one another. For example, if I see my responsibility to myself, to a friend, or to a patient in therapy as observing and respecting what the soul presents, I won't try to take things away in the name of health. It's remarkable how often people think they will be better off without the things that bother them. "I need to get rid of this tendency of mine," a person will say. "Help me get rid of these feelings of inferiority and my smoking and my bad marriage." If, as a therapist, I did what I was told, I'd be taking things away from people all day long. But I don't try to eradicate problems. I try not to imagine my role to be that of exterminator. Rather, I try to give what is problematical back to the person in a way that shows its necessity, even its value.

When people observe the ways in which the soul is manifesting itself, they are enriched rather than impoverished. They receive back what is theirs, the very thing they have assumed to be so horrible that it should be cut out and tossed away. When you regard the soul with an open mind, you begin to find the messages that lie within the illness, the corrections that can be found in remorse and other uncomfortable feelings, and the necessary changes requested by depression and anxiety.

Let me give some examples of how we might enrich rather than deprive ourselves in the name of emotional well-being.

A thirty-year-old woman comes to me for therapy and confesses, "I have a terrible time in relationships because I become too dependent. Help me be less dependent."

I am being asked to take some soul stuff away. I should go to my toolbox and take out a scalpel, extractor, and suction pump. Instead, on the principle of observance, and not inclined in any case to this kind of pilfering, I ask, "What is it you find difficult about dependence?"

"It makes me feel powerless. Besides, it isn't good to be too dependent. I should be my own person."

"How do you know when your dependency is too much?" I reply, still trying to speak for the soul's expression of dependency.

"When I don't feel good about myself."

"I wonder," I continue in the same direction, "if you could find a way to be dependent without feeling disempowered? After all, we all depend on each other every minute of the day."

And so the talk continues. The woman admits she has always simply assumed that independence is good and dependence bad. I notice from the conversation that despite all her enthusiasm for independence, she doesn't seem to enjoy much of it in her life. She is identified with the dependency and sees liberation on the other side. She has also unconsciously bought into the prevailing notion that independence is healthy and that we should correct the soul when it shows some desire for dependence.

This woman is asking me to help her get rid of the dependent face of her soul. But that would be a move against her soul. The fact that her dependency is making itself felt doesn't mean it should be bludgeoned or surgically removed; it may be asserting itself because it needs attention. Her heroic championing of independence might be a way of avoiding and repressing the strong need of something in her to be dependent. I try offering some words of dependence that don't have the connotations of wimpiness that seem to bother her.

"Don't you want to be attached to people, learn from them, get close, rely on friendship, get advice from someone you respect, be part of a community where people need each other, find intimacy with someone that is so delicious you can't live without it?"

"Of course," she says. "Is that dependence?"

"It sounds like it to me," I reply, "and like everything else, you can't have it without its shadows: its neediness, inferiority, submission and loss of control."

I had the feeling this woman, as seems often to be the case, was avoiding intimacy and friendship by focusing these qualities into a caricature of excessive dependency. At times we live these caricatures, thinking we are being masochistically dependent, when what we actually are doing is avoiding deep involvement with people, society, and life in general.

Observing what the soul is doing and hearing what it is saying is a way of "going with the symptom." The temptation is to compensate, to be drawn toward the opposite of what is presented. A person fully identified with dependency thinks that health and happiness lie in the achievement of independence. But that move into opposites is deceptive. Oddly, it keeps the person in the same problem, only from the opposite side. The wish for independence maintains the split. A homeopathic move, going with what is presented rather than against it, is to learn how to be dependent in a way that is satisfying and not so extreme as to split dependence off from independence.

Another way of disowning the soul is merely to dip your toes in the sea of fate. A man came to me depressed and completely dissatisfied with his job. He had been working in a manufacturing shop for ten years, and all that time he planned his escape. He was going to go to school and enter a profession that he liked. But while he planned and kept his mind continually on his escape, his work in the shop suffered. Years went by and he was always dissatisfied, hating his job and wishing for the promised land of his ambitions.

"Have you ever thought," I asked him one day, "of being where you are, of entering fully this job that you're putting your time and energy into?"

"It's not worth it," he said. "It's beneath me. A robot could do it better."

"But you do it every day," I observed. "And you do it badly, and you feel bad about yourself for doing it badly."

"You're saying," he said incredulously, "that I should go to this stupid job as if my heart were in it?"

"*You're* in it, aren't you?"

He came back in a week to say that something had changed in him as he began to take his "stupid" job more seriously. It seemed that by entering his fate and emotions he might begin to taste his life and possibly find a way *through* his experience and into his ambitions. The sheep of his work fantasies had been wandering everywhere but in the shop. He had been living an alienated and divided life.

Observance of the soul can be deceptively simple. You take back what has been disowned. You work with what is, rather than with what you wish were there. In his poem "Notes Toward a Supreme Fiction" the poet Wallace Stevens wrote, "Perhaps the truth depends on a walk around a lake." Therapy sometimes emphasizes change so strongly that people often neglect their own natures and are tantalized by images of some ideal normality and health that may always be out of reach. In "Reply to Papini," Stevens put the matter more broadly, in lines that James Hillman has taken as a motto for his psychology. "The way through the world is more difficult to find than the way beyond it."

Renaissance philosophers often said that it is the soul that makes us human. We can turn that idea round and note that it is when we are most human that we have greatest access to soul. And yet modern psychology, perhaps because of its links to medicine, is often seen as a way of being saved from the very messes that most deeply mark human life as human. We want to sidestep negative moods and emotion, bad life choices and unhealthy habits. But if our purpose is first to observe the soul as it is, then we may have to discard the salvational wish and find deeper respect for what is actually there. By trying to avoid human mistakes and failures, we move beyond the reach of soul.

Sometimes, of course, it can be difficult to honor the soul's dramatic ways of expressing itself. An intelligent and talented young woman once came to me with the complaint that she was having trouble with food. She was embarrassed to bring up this symptom that had been at the center of her life for three years. She would eat almost nothing for a few days, then she would gorge and throw up. The cycle was completely out of her control, and it seemed that it would never end.

How do we observe these rites of the soul that are painful and even life-threatening? Does it make sense to give a place to horrible symptoms and hopeless compulsions? Is there any necessity in these extreme states that are beyond all rational control? When I hear a story like this and see a person so distressed, I have to examine carefully my own capacity for observance. Am I repulsed? Do I feel a savior figure rising up in me who will do anything to save this woman from her torment? Or can I understand that even these extraordinary symptoms are the myths, rituals, and poetry of a life?

The basic intention in any caring, physical or psychological, is to alleviate suffering. But in relation to the symptom itself, observance means first of all listening and looking carefully at what is being revealed in the suffering. An intent to heal can get in the way of seeing. By doing less, more is accomplished. Observance is homeopathic in its workings rather than allopathic, in the paradoxical way that it befriends a problem rather than making an enemy of it. A Taoist tone colors this care without heroics. The *Tao Te Ching* says (ch. 64), "He brings men back to what they have lost. He helps the ten thousand things find their own nature, but refrains from action." This is a perfect description of one who cares for the soul.

It is not easy to observe closely, to take the time and to make the subtle moves that allow the soul to reveal itself further. You have to rely on every bit of learning, every scrap of sense, and all kinds of reading, in order to bring intelligence and imagination to the work. Yet at the same time, this action-through-nonaction has to be simple, flexible, and receptive. Intelligence and education bring you to the edge, where your mind and its purposes are empty. Many religious rites begin with washing of the hands or a sprinkling of water to symbolize the cleansing of intention and the washing away of thoughts and purposes. In our soul work we could use rites like these, anything that would cleanse our minds of their well-intentioned heroism.

The soul of this young woman was portraying its current myth through the imagery of food. Over several weeks we talked about the place of food in her life, in the past and in the present. She talked about her discomfort in the presence of her parents. She wanted to wander around the world. She hated the idea of being home, and yet she was forced for economic reasons to live with her parents. She also had memories of a brother touching her immodestly once, just for a second. She hadn't been abused, but she was extremely sensitive about her body. Our conversations led to the mixed feelings she had about being a woman.

Then one day she brought me a dream that I thought captured the mystery that was at the heart of her problem. A group of elderly women were preparing a feast outdoors. They were stewing a great variety of food in huge pots over fires. The dreamer was invited to join the cooking and become one of the women. She bristled at first—she didn't want to be identified with those old gray women in peasant black dresses—but finally joined them.

The dream presented this woman with what she was most afraid of: her primordial femininity. Although she enjoyed her long blond hair and her girlfriends, she profoundly hated having periods and living with the possibility of one day bearing a child. The dream, which I took as promising, assumed the form of a primitive initiation into a mystery closely related to her symptoms. And it seemed to present her with a solution: become acquainted with the ancient and profound roots of womanhood and discover finally how truly to nourish yourself.

Even though it took place in sleep, the dream was an effective ritual. Our role was not to interpret the various figures, but to appreciate the significance and importance of the rites. Why would this woman feel so anxious about a crowd of old women standing over great pots of stew? As we talked over her fears about the women and their actions, certain themes in the dreamer's life came to light, such as specific thoughts about her body that disturbed her, and particular women in her family she wanted nothing to do with. She talked about her father's affection for her and her mixed feelings about him. It wasn't so much that the dream had a particular *meaning* that explained her symptoms, but that it generated deeply felt thoughts and memories, all related to the food problems. The dream helped us to feel her drama more intensely and to imagine it more precisely.

To feel and imagine may not sound like much. But in care of the soul there is trust that nature heals, that much can be accomplished by not-doing. The assumption is that being follows imagination. If we can see the story we are in when we fall into our various compulsive behaviors and moods, then we might know how to move through them more freely and with less distress.

What the great sixteenth-century physician, Paracelsus, said about healing applies to care of the soul: "The physician is only the servant of nature, not her master. Therefore, it behooves medicine to follow the will of nature." In caring for the soul, we imagine that even as troublesome a symptom as bulimia has its own will and that "curing" in some way means following that will.

Observance has considerable power. If you observe Christmas, for instance, you will be affected by that special season precisely because of your observance. The mood and spirit of the time will touch your heart, and over time, regular observance may come to affect you deeply. Or if you are a pallbearer at a funeral, if you sprinkle dirt or holy water at the grave, your observance places you deep within the experience of burial and death. You may remember that moment vividly for years. You may dream about it for the rest of your life. Simple gestures, taking place on the surface of life, can be of central importance to the soul.

Modern interventional therapy sometimes tries to solve specific problems and can therefore be carried out on a short-term basis. But care of the soul never ends. The alchemists of the Middle Ages seem to have recognized this fact, since they taught their students that every ending is a beginning. All work on the soul takes the form of a circle, a *rotatio*. People in therapy often say to me, "Aren't you tired of hearing the same things over and over again?" "No," I respond. "I'm quite happy with the old stuff." I keep in mind the alchemical *circulatio*. The life of the soul, as the structure of dreams reveals, is a continual going over and over of the material of life.

In memory we never tire of reflecting on the same events. I spent many summers in my childhood on a farm with an uncle who told stories endlessly. This, I now see, was his method of working the raw material of his life, his way of turning his experience round and round in the rotation that stories provide. Out of that incessant storytelling I know he found added depths of meaning. Storytelling is an excellent way of caring for the soul. It helps us see the themes that circle in our lives, the deep themes that tell the myths we live. It would take only a slight shift in emphasis in therapy to focus on the storytelling itself rather than on its interpretation.

## Learning to Love the Soul

One of the crucial things I have learned from my apprenticeship to James Hillman, the founder of archetypal psychology, is to nurture my curiosity about the ways of the psyche. He claims that a psychologist ought to be a "naturalist of the psyche." The professional should always be "in the field," as Hillman himself is without respite. In this sense a psychologist is someone who, like a botanist, is unusually preoccupied with nature, human nature. If this is true in professional psychology, it is also true in the care of soul that any of us can cultivate. This kind of care begins in deep curiosity about the ways the psyche shows itself, in others and in oneself.

Freud's *The Interpretation of Dreams* is

largely this kind of psychologizing. He analyzes his own dreams and arrives at theory from his self-analysis. He writes as though he is intensely interested in the ways of his own soul. He tells stories and dreams, not unlike my uncle, whose stories also condensed into a theory about life. We could all be a Freud to our own experiences. Taking an interest in the soul is a way of loving it. The ultimate cure, as many ancient and modern psychologies of depth have asserted, comes from love and not from logic. Understanding doesn't take us very far in this work, but love, expressed in patient and careful attention, draws the soul in from its dispersion in problems and fascinations. It has often been noted that most, if not all, problems brought to therapists are issues of love. It makes sense then that the cure is also love.

Taking an interest in one's own soul requires a certain amount of space for reflection and appreciation. Ordinarily we are so identified with movements of the psyche that we can't stand back and take a good look at them. A little distance allows us to see the dynamics among the many elements that make up the life of the soul. By becoming interested in these phenomena, we begin to see our own complexity. Usually we feel that complexity as it hits us unawares from outside, in a multitude of problems and in confusion. If we knew the soul better, we might be ready for the conflicts of life. I often have the sense, when someone tells me anxiously about some knot they find themselves in, that what they perceive as an impossible and painful situation calling for professional intervention is simply the complexity of human life once again manifesting itself. Most of us bring to everyday life a somewhat naive psychological attitude in our expectations that our lives and relationships will be simple. Love of the soul asks for some appreciation for its complexity.

Often care of the soul means not taking sides when there is a conflict at a deep level. It may be necessary to stretch the heart wide enough to embrace contradiction and paradox.

A man in his fifties came to me once and told me with considerable embarrassment that he had fallen in love.

"I feel stupid," he said, "like an adolescent."

I hear this often, that love arouses the adolescent. Anyone familiar with the history of art and literature knows that from the Greeks on down love has been portrayed as an untamable teenager.

"Oh, you have something against this adolescent?"

"Am I ever going to grow up?" he asked in frustration.

"Maybe not," I said. "Maybe there are things in you that will never grow up, maybe they shouldn't grow up. Doesn't this sudden influx of adolescence make you feel young, energetic and full of life?"

"Yes," he said, "and also silly, immature, confused and crazy."

"But that's adolescence," I responded. "It sounds to me like the Old Man in you is berating the Youth. Why make being a grown-up the supreme value? Or, maybe I should ask, who in you is claiming that maturity is so important? It's that Old Man, isn't it?"

I wanted to speak for the figure who was being judged and attacked. This man had to find enough space in him to allow both the Old Man and the Youth to have a place, to speak to each other and over time, maybe over his entire lifetime, to work out some degree of reconciliation. It takes more than a lifetime to resolve such conflicts. In fact, the conflict itself is creative and perhaps should never be healed. By giving each figure its voice, we let the soul speak and show itself as it is, not as we wish it would be. By defending the adolescent, being careful not to take sides against the mature figure, I showed my interest in his soul, and the man had an opportunity to find a way to contain this archetypal conflict of youth and age, maturity and immaturity. In the course of such a debate the soul becomes more complex and spacious.


## A Taste for the Perverse

One effective "trick" in caring for the soul is to look with special attention and openness at what the individual rejects, and then to speak favorably for that rejected element. For the man I was just discussing, feeling adolescent was something he saw as a problem. I tried to see value in that "problem" without sharing the man's distaste. We all tend to divide experience into two parts, usually the good and the bad. But there may be all kinds of suspicious things going on in this splitting. We may simply have never considered the value in certain things that we reject. Or by branding certain experiences negative we may be protecting ourselves from some unknown fears. We are all filled with biases and ideas that have snuck into us without our knowing it. Much soul can be lost in such splitting, so that care of the soul can go a long way simply by recovering some of this material that has been cut off.

What I am talking about here is a version of Jung's theory of shadow. For Jung, there are two kinds of shadow: one consists of the possibilities in life that we reject because of certain choices we have made. The person we choose to be, for example, automatically creates a dark double—the person we choose not to be. This compensatory shadow varies from one person to the next. For some people sex and money are looming shadows, while for others they are simply part of life. Moral purity and responsible living can be shadow aspects to some. Jung also believed there is an absolute shadow, not relative to our life choices and habits. In other words, there is evil in the world and in the human heart. If we don't recognize this, we have a naive attitude that can get us into trouble. Jung thought the soul can benefit by coming to terms with both kinds of shadow, losing some of its naive innocence in the process.

It appears to me that as we open ourselves to see what our soul is made of and who we really are, we always find some material that is a profound challenge. My middle-aged man had to reevaluate his adolescent feelings of silliness. My bulimic young woman had to come to grips with her complicated relationship to her father and her feelings about her brother. To some extent, care of the soul asks us to open our hearts wider than they have ever been before, softening the judging and moralism that may have characterized our attitudes and behavior for years. Moralism is one of the most effective shields against the soul, protecting us from its intricacy. There is nothing more revealing, and maybe nothing more healing, than to reconsider our moralistic attitudes and find how much soul has been hidden behind its doors. People seem to be afraid that if they reflect on their moral principles they might lose their ethical sensitivity altogether. But that is a defensive approach to morality. As we deal with the soul's complexity, morality can deepen and drop its simplicity, becoming at the same time both more demanding and more flexible.

I would go even further. As we get to know the soul and fearlessly consider its oddities and the many different ways it shows itself among individuals, we may develop a taste for the perverse. We may come to appreciate its quirks and deviances. Indeed, we may eventually come to realize that individuality is born in the eccentricities and unexpected shadow tendencies of the soul, moreso than in normality and conformity. One who cares for the soul becomes someone at ease with idiosyncrasies and the unexpected. When I lecture on shadow to therapists-in-training, I sometimes ask them, "Where is the line of perversity drawn for you, where is the place where you come up against your own fear and repulsion?" Some people say that sexual abuse is that line, and I wonder how they can work professionally with abused or abusing patients. Others say it is violence of any kind. Others find sexual fantasy perverse. We might ask ourselves the same question. Where do I run up against a wall when I look into my own heart? What is the limit?

Care of the soul is interested in the not-so-normal, the way that soul makes itself felt most clearly in the unusual expressions of a life, even and maybe especially in the problematical ones. I recall once being visited late at night by a woman in her late fifties. Her husband had just left her after twenty-five years of marriage. She didn't think she could go on. No one in her family, she kept repeating, had ever been divorced. Why had this happened to her? I noticed that of all the possible thoughts that could preoccupy her at this difficult time, the worst was the thought that she wasn't like the rest of her family. Something serious must be wrong with her, she thought. In a dark way, her individuality was asserting itself in this ordeal. I imagined that this in fact might be the "purpose" of the event: to bring her around to a sharp sense of her own uniqueness.

It is no accident that the history of art is filled with grotesque images—bloody and twisted crucifixions, gracefully distorted bodies, and surrealistic landscapes. Sometimes deviation from the usual is a special revelation of truth. In alchemy this was referred to as the *opus contra naturam,* an effect contrary to nature. We might see the same kind of artful unnatural expression within our own lives. When normality explodes or breaks out into craziness or shadow, we might look closely, before running for cover and before attempting to restore familiar order, at the potential meaningfulness of the event. If we are going to be curious about the soul, we may need to explore its deviations, its perverse tendency to contradict expectations. And as a corollary, we might be suspicious of normality. A facade of normality can hide a wealth of deviance, and besides, it is fairly easy to recognize soullessness in the standardizing of experience.

## Care vs. Cure

A major difference between care and cure is that cure implies the end of trouble. If you are cured, you don't have to worry about whatever was bothering you any longer. But care has a sense of ongoing attention. There is no end. Conflicts may never be fully resolved. Your character will never change radically, although it may go through some interesting transformations. Awareness can change, of course, but problems may persist and never go away.

Our work in psychology would change remarkably if we thought about it as ongoing care rather than as the quest for a cure. We might take the time to watch and listen as gradually it reveals the deeper mysteries lying within daily turmoil. Problems and obstacles offer a chance for reflection that otherwise would be precluded by the swift routine of life. As we stop to consider what is happening to us and what we're made of, the soul ferments, to use an alchemical word. Change takes place, but not according to plan or as the result of intentional intervention. If you attend the soul closely enough, with an educated and steadfast imagination, changes take place without your being aware of them until they are all over and well in place. Care of the soul observes the paradox whereby a muscled, strong-willed pursuit of change can actually stand in the way of substantive transformation.

Ancient psychology, rooted in a very different ground from modern therapeutic thinking, held that the fate and character of each of us is born in mystery, that our individuality is so profound and so hidden that it takes more than a lifetime for identity to emerge. Renaissance doctors said that the essence of each person originates as a star in the heavens. How different this is from the modern view that a person is what he makes himself to be.

Care of the soul, looking back with special regard to ancient psychologies for insight and guidance, goes beyond the secular mythology of the self and recovers a sense of the sacredness of each individual life. This sacred quality is not just value—all lives are important. It is the unfathomable mystery that is the very seed and heart of each individual. Shallow therapeutic manipulations aimed at restoring normality or tuning a life according to standards reduces—shrinks—that profound mystery to the pale dimensions of a social common denominator referred to as the adjusted personality. Care of the soul sees another reality altogether. It appreciates the mystery of human suffering and does not offer the illusion of a problem-free life. It sees every fall into ignorance and confusion as an opportunity to discover that the beast residing at the center of the labyrinth is also an angel. The uniqueness of a person is made up of the insane and the twisted as much as it is of the rational and normal. To approach this paradoxical point of tension where adjustment and abnormality meet is to move closer to the realization of our mystery-filled, star-born nature.

Obviously, care of the soul requires a different language from that of therapy and academic psychology. Like alchemy, it is an art and therefore can only be expressed in poetic images. Mythology, the fine arts, religions of the world, and dreams provide this priceless imagery by which the soul's mysteries are simultaneously revealed and contained. For guidance we can also turn to many different experts, especially to poetic-minded soul searchers such as the ancient mythographers and tragedians, Renaissance doctors, Romantic poets, and our modern depth psychologists, who respect the mystery of human life and who resist the secularization of experience. It takes a broad vision to know that a piece of the sky and a chunk of the earth lie lodged in the heart of every human being, and that if we are going to care for that heart we will have to know the sky and earth as well as human behavior. This is exactly the advice of the Renaissance doctor Paracelsus: "If the physician understands things exactly and sees and recognizes all illnesses in the macrocosm outside man, and if he has a clear idea of man and his whole nature, then and only then is he a physician. Then he may approach the inside of man; then he may examine his urine, take his pulse, and understand where each thing belongs. This would not be possible without profound knowledge of the outer man, who is nothing other than heaven and earth."

The Greeks told the story of the minotaur, the bull-headed flesh-eating man who lived in the center of the labyrinth. He was a threatening beast, and yet his name was Asterion—Star. I often think of this paradox as I sit with someone with tears in her eyes, searching for some way to deal with a death, a divorce, or a depression. It is a beast, this thing that stirs in the core of her being, but it is also the star of her innermost nature. We have to care for this suffering with extreme reverence so that, in our fear and anger at the beast, we do not overlook the star.

# CARE OF
# THE SOUL
# IN EVERYDAY
# LIFE

---

*Nature and God—I neither knew*
*Yet Both so well knew me*
*They startled, like Executors*
*of My identity.*

EMILY DICKINSON

# The Myth of Family and Childhood

"Eternity is in love with the productions of time," says William Blake. The soul prospers in an environment that is concrete, particular, and vernacular. It feeds on the details of life, on its variety, its quirks, and its idiosyncrasies. Therefore, nothing is more suitable for care of the soul than family, because the experience of family includes so much of the particulars of life. In a family you live close to people that otherwise you might not even want to talk to. Over time you get to know them intimately. You learn their most minuscule, most private habits and character-istics. Family life is full of major and minor crises—the ups and downs of health, success and failure in career, marriage, and divorce—and all kinds of characters. It is tied to places and events and histories. With all of these felt details, life etches itself into memory and per-sonality. It's difficult to imagine anything more nourishing to the soul.

When things go wrong in society, we imme-diately inquire into the condition of family life. When we see society torn apart by crime, we cry, "If only we could return to the good old days when family was sacred." But were the good old days so good? Was the family ever free of violence? Many people who come to therapy today were raised in the so-called golden age of the family, and yet they tell stories of abuse, neglect, and terrifying mor-alistic demands and pressures. Looked at coldly, the family of any era is both good and bad, offering both support and threat. This is why adults are so often ambivalent about vis-iting their families and spending time with them: they want the emotional rewards of the sense of connection, but they also want dis-tance from painful memories and difficult re-lationships.

Today professionals are preoccupied with the "dysfunctional family." But to some extent all families are dysfunctional. No family is perfect, and most have serious problems. A family is a microcosm, reflecting the nature of the world, which runs on both virtue and evil. We may be tempted at times to imagine the family as full of innocence and good will, but actual family life resists such romanticism. Usually it presents the full range of human potential, including evil, hatred, violence, sexual confusion, and insanity. In other words, the dynamics of actual family life reveal the soul's complexity and unpredictability, and any attempts to place a veil of simplistic sentimentality over the family image will break down.

When I see those three letters "dys-" in "dysfunctional," I think of "Dis," the old Roman name for the mythological underworld. Soul enters life from below, through the cracks, finding an opening into life at the points where smooth functioning breaks down. We bring the Dis-functions of family into the therapy room as problems to be solved or as explanations for current difficulties because intuitively we know that the family is one of the chief abodes of soul. In psychology there is much talk about family, and "family therapy" has become a major form of counseling. By "getting to the root" of present problems in family background, we hope to understand what is going on, and in that understanding we hope to find a cure. But care of the soul doesn't require fixing the family or becoming free of it or interpreting its pathology. We may need simply to recover soul by reflecting deeply on the soul events that have taken place in the crucible of the family.

According to the Bible, Adam was formed out of the mud of the earth. His parentage, his "family," was earthy, moist, dirty, even slimy. Starting with Adam, at our very root, we are not fashioned out of light or fire; we are children of mud. Scholars say that "Adam" means red earth. Our own families recapitulate this mythic origin of our humanity by being close to the earth, ordinary, a veritable weed patch of human foibles. In studying the mythologies of the world, you always find evil characters and some sort of underworld; the same is true of the family. It always has its shadow, no matter how much we wish otherwise. Its functioning is always soiled by Dis. If we don't grasp this mystery, the soulfulness that family has to offer each of us will be spirited away in hygienic notions of what a family *should* be. The sentimental image of family that we present publicly is a defense against the pain of proclaiming the family for what it is—a sometimes comforting, sometimes devastating house of life and memory.

At a certain level, then, it doesn't matter

whether one's family has been largely happy, comforting, and supportive, or if there has been abuse and neglect. I'm not saying that these failures are not significant and painful or that they do not leave horrifying scars. At a deep level, however, family is most truly family in its complexity, including its failures and weaknesses. In my own family, the uncle who was my ideal source of wisdom and morality was also the one who drank excessively and who scandalized the rest by refusing to go to church. In my practice I've worked with many men and women whose families were intolerably violent and abusive, and yet all that pain has been redeemable, able to become the source of much wisdom and transformation. When we encounter the family from the point of view of the soul, accepting its shadows and its failure to meet our idealistic expectations, we are faced with mysteries that resist our moralism and sentimentality. We are taken down to the earth, where principle gives way to life in all its beauty and horror.

*Family* has many meanings, depending on the context. The sociologist thinks of it as a social group or construct. The psychologist imagines a fount from which personality flows. The politician talks about the family in an idealized way, using the idea of family to represent his traditional program and values. But we all know the family in its particulars. This is the nest in which soul is born, nurtured, and released into life. It has an elaborate history and ancestry and a network of unpredictable personalities—grandparents, uncles, aunts, cousins. Its stories tell of happy times and tragedies. It has moments of pride and skeletons in its closets. It has its professed values and its carefully constructed image, as well as its secret transgressions and follies.

It is remarkable how often the family is experienced on two levels: the façade of happiness and normality, and the behind-the-scenes reality of craziness and abuse. I have heard many stories over the years of families that are picture-book perfect on the surface—family camping, Sunday dinners, trips, gifts, and play. But beneath it all is the remote father, the hidden alcohol, the abuse of a sister, and midnight violence. Television presents this bifurcation with sit-coms of sweet and successful families followed by news reports of family savagery. Some people believe the images of normality and maintain the secret of *their* family's corruption, wishing they had been born elsewhere in a land of bliss. But recovery of soul begins when we can take to heart our own family fate and find in it the raw material, the alchemical *prima materia,* for our own soul work.

For this purpose, "family therapy" might take the form of simply telling stories of family life, free of any concern for cause and effect or sociological influence. These stories generate a grand local, personal mythology. The family is to the individual what the origins of human life are to the race. Its history provides a matrix of images by which a person is saturated all through adult life. What the Greek, Christian, Jewish, Islamic, Hindu, and African mythologies are to the society—its formative mythology—stories of the family, good and bad, are to the individual. When we talk about family, we are talking about the characters and themes that have woven together to form our identities, which are intricately textured. We might imagine family therapy more as a process of exploring the complexity of our sense of life than of making it simple and intelligible. Care of the soul is not about understanding, figuring out, and making better; rather, it resuscitates images of family life as an enrichment of identity.

To care for the soul of the family, it is necessary to shift from causal thinking to an appreciation for story and character, to allow grandparents and uncles to be transformed into figures of myth and to watch certain familiar family stories become canonical through repeated tellings. We are so affected by the scientific tone in education and in the media that without thinking we have become anthropologists and sociologists in our own families. Often I will ask a patient about the family, and the answer I get is pure social psychology. "My father drank, and as a child of an alcoholic I am prone to . . ." Instead of stories, one hears analysis. The family has been "etherized upon a table." Even worse is the social worker or psychologist who begins talking about a patient with a singsong list of social influences: "The subject is a male who was raised in Judeo-Christian family, with a narcissistic mother and a codependent father." The soul of the family evaporates in the thin air of this kind of reduction. It takes extreme diligence and concentration to think differently about the family: to appreciate its shadow as well as its virtue and simply to allow stories to be told without slipping into interpretations, analysis, and conclusions. Professionals think it is their job to understand and correct the family without allowing themselves to be introduced fully to its genius—its unique formative spirit.

If we were to observe the soul in the family

by honoring its stories and by not running away from its shadow, then we might not feel so inescapably determined by family influences. Strongly influenced by developmental psychology, we assume we are ineluctably who we are because of the family in which we grew up. What if we thought of the family less as the determining influence by which we are formed and more the raw material from which we can make a life? In therapy, when I hear a story of an abusing father or uncle, I usually ask for details about this person's life. Is there a story behind his violence? What were other members of the family doing? What stories do they tell and what secrets do they harbor?

A young man, David, once consulted me with the complaint that he just couldn't get along with his mother. I call him a young man because his "eternal youth" was his most noticeable characteristic. When I first met him he was twenty-eight years old but he looked about sixteen. He lived in an apartment by himself but spent the weekends "at home" with his mother. Yet, when he was home, he always felt his mother was prying into his affairs, telling him how to live, and trying to get him to clean up his room. "You're just like your father," she said to him regularly. She had been divorced for several years.

"*Are* you just like your father?" I asked.

He looked surprised. "My mother's the problem," he said, "not my father."

"Tell me about your father anyway," I said.

"He'll never settle down. I see him rarely, when he's passing through. He's always on the road, always with a new woman."

"Are you just like your father?"

"No, I don't even have one woman in my life."

"Not even one?"

"Well, my mother."

He went on to tell me something I hear from the majority of my patients.

"I don't want to be like my father."

We may have suffered the excesses of one or both of our parents, and so we make the resolution that *I* am not going to be that way. We make every effort to avoid this parental influence. But the avoidance of parental influence and identification is a sure way to become a carbon copy—the return of the repressed. Usually when we make every effort not to be like our mother or father, there is some particular quality that we want to avoid, having known it too well as a son or daughter. But repression tends to make a wide swath; it's not very precise in its work of ridding the personality of some unwanted quality. David tried not to be like his father. Not wanting to have many intimate relationships, he had none. Not wanting to wander around the country aimlessly, he couldn't move far from home. Not wanting to be like his father, he had little trace of fathering of any kind in his own life.

I talked to him about his father without making the broad criticisms and judgments that he made continually and which kept his affections toward his parents split. I encouraged stories about his father, and over time a complicated picture emerged of a man who had a childhood much like David's. We began to make sense of his father's wandering, for all its neuroticism. In life David made some efforts to meet with his father and talk to him about his experiences. Discussing it afterward, we discovered that his father was trying, too, to keep a distance from his son. Eventually, motivated in part, I think, by a new interest in his father's life, the son insisted on contact and conversation.

By not cutting himself off from his father, David could look at himself more directly. Whether he liked it or not, his father's spirit was in him. Out of this spirit he could make a life. He would no longer have to be impoverished by his negative efforts to remain untainted by the family myth. In general, when we try to escape the family's "dysfunctions," we fall into complicated, paradoxical tangles. The wish for escape might well be balanced by a relentless bondage to the family, the unconscious assumption, for example, that "home" is where mother is.

A renewed entry into the family, embracing what has previously been denied, often leads to an unexpected alchemy in which even the most difficult family relationships shift enough to make a significant difference. Heroic efforts to make families work according to some norm get in the way of this alchemy. It is usually best, when caring for the soul, to sit with what is there and let your own imagination move, instead of making empty wishes or attempting heroic changes. Although we talk about the family as though it were a simple literal reality, it is always what we *imagine* it to be. This imagination can deepen and change over a period of time and unleash some of the soul that has been bound up in resentment and rigidity. I am convinced that David's stories about his father and mother had an effect on his relationship with them. His new, deeper imagining allowed him to pass through his former fixed views so that he could reconnect with his mother and father in ways he had not known before. They were still the same people, but David found a way to be that was less self-protective and therefore more open to his parents.

When we tell stories about the family without judgment and without instant analysis, the literal persons turn into characters in a drama and isolated episodes reveal themselves as themes in a great saga. Family history is transformed into myth. Whether we know it or not, our ideas about the family are rooted in the ways we imagine the family. That personal family, which seems so concrete, is always an imaginal entity. Part of our alchemical work with soul is to extract myth from the hard details of family history and memory on the principle that increase of imagination is always an increase in soul.

With this principle in mind, I want to look at family members as imaginal figures and to offer some suggestions for finding the myths in the ordinary roles of family life. For each individual, the myth will be different, and yet certain characteristics are constant. Every family member evokes the archetypal family, the myth in everyday life. The imagination of father, mother and child is vast, and so I can only give some hints toward a way of developing a family imagination, including some references to literature and mythology that offer a path toward understanding the family more imaginally.

## Father

One of the most extraordinary mythic stories from our own collective past, a story as sacred as any in religious literature, is about a man trying to reclaim his fatherhood, a wife longing for her husband, and a son out in search of his lost father. At the beginning of Homer's *Odyssey*, Odysseus is sitting on the seashore in the midst of his unplanned travels following a long, difficult war, wishing to be home with his son, his father, and the mother of his children. In his longing and melancholy he asks a famous question: "Does any person know who his father is?" It's a question many men and women ask in various forms. If my father is dead, or if he was absent and cold, or if he was a tyrant, or if he abused me, or if he was wonderful but is not there for me now, then who is my father now? Where do I get those feelings of protection, authority, confidence, know-how, and wisdom that I need in order to live my life? How can I evoke a fatherly myth in a way that will give my life the governance it needs?

The story of Odysseus gives us many clues toward finding that elusive father. However, it does not begin, as one might expect, with the father in the throes of his adventures, but with the son, Telemachus, distraught at the havoc created in his house by suitors vying for his mother's affections. The story gives us first an image of "absent-father neurosis." Without the father there is chaos, conflict, and sadness. On the other hand, by starting with the unhappiness of Telemachus, the story teaches us that the experience of father includes his absence and the longing for his return. For at the very moment Telemachus is bewailing his situation, Odysseus is on another beach on the same sea, pining for the same conclusion. If we understand *The Odyssey* as one of the stories of the soul's fatherhood, then at that very moment when we feel the confusion of a fatherless life and wonder where he could be, the father has been evoked. As we wonder where he is, he is finding his way back.

During this time of separation, Homer tells us, Odysseus' wife, Penelope, is at home weaving a shroud for Odysseus' father, and every night she unravels what she has woven. This is the great mystery of the soul: whenever something is being accomplished, it is also in some way being undone. A thirty-year-old man I worked with, who had a conflict-ridden rela-

tionship with his father and who found it difficult to father his own life, told me a dream in
which his father was hugging him and asking
him to remain with him; the son said he had
too much to do and had to go away. Later in
the dream, his brother came and took all the
dreamer's belongings. In this dream, I felt
there was a relationship between signs of reconciliation with the father and the loss of belongings, a motif not far from the themes of
*The Odyssey*. Sometimes we may have to feel
absence and emptiness in order to evoke the
father.

In a similar way, there is something frustrat-
ing about the very idea of *The Odyssey*. Why
don't the gods look compassionately on this
broken family and allow Odysseus to make a
beeline home? What possible value is there in
this father taking ten years on the sea, telling
his stories and surviving his risky adventures,
before he can finally return home and restore
peace? The only answer I can think of is that
this long, dangerous, adventure-filled journey
is the making of the father. Odysseus' return to
his family is analogous to the Gnostic stories
of the soul descending through the planets to
earth, picking up along the way the qualities it
will need for human life. Who is my father? I
won't know until the soul has been on its odyssey and returns with its stories of love, sex,

death, risk, and afterlife. If I am feeling the absence of fatherhood in my life, I may have to give up the project of forcing fatherhood into my character and instead open myself to my own unplanned and uncontrolled odyssey.

In many traditional cultures a person becomes an adult by hearing the secret stories of the community that have been handed down over generations. Elders give instructions, teaching the elements of ritual and art. Black Elk describes this process in detail in his memoirs of growing up in the Oglala Sioux. Sometimes the neophyte has to endure ordeals designed to draw out the adult. The point is to stir the young person so deeply that he or she experiences a major transformation of character.

Odysseus goes through many ordeals, so much so that his story looks exactly like an initiation into fatherhood. He learns from the lotus-eaters not to live on a diet of flowers and from the Cyclops not to live without law and culture. He is initiated into love by the magical women Circe and Calypso. The centerpiece of his journey is a visit to the land of the dead. There he meets recently departed friends, his mother, the blind prophet Tiresias, and other great figures of his history. True fatherhood is evoked not by a flexing of muscle but by initiation into family and culture in a profound, transformative way. It may also require a visit to our own depths and a conversing with figures of memory both personal and cultural. Education in history and literature, when done with sufficient depth, can make good fathers.

If the father seems absent in families today, that may be because he is absent as a soul figure in the society at large. We have replaced secret wisdom with information. Information does not evoke fatherhood, and it does not effect initiation. If education would speak to the soul as well as the mind, then we might be making fatherhood through our learning. Far from visiting the land of the dead, all too often we want to forget the dead and the burden of their lives. Our highly detailed investigations of the murders of the Kennedys and Martin Luther King, Jr., focus on facts and on a solution to the cases, thereby deflecting attention away from the meaning of those assassinations. Yet, *The Odyssey* implies that if we don't visit the land of the dead with reverence and in a spirit of initiation, we will not have a sustaining fatherhood in our collective soul. Without that deep spirit of the father, we are left with father substitutes—people willing to play the part for their own gain, offering superficial tokens of fatherhood, but not the father's soul.

I am not saying simply that to evoke the father you have to have experienced life. Odysseus doesn't experience life. He is away from life. He spends his time flirting with a witch-like goddess, outwitting monsters, and journeying to the underworld. A genuine odyssey is not about piling up experiences. It is a deeply felt, risky, unpredictable tour of the soul. A father is one whose perspective and knowledge are rooted in the underworld and tied to the forefathers, those who have gone before and have created the culture that the father now takes into his hands. A father's wisdom and moral sensibility find their direction from voices that are not now in life. His initiators are both those literal fathers who have created culture and his own deepest reflections.

This fatherhood of the soul is a face of what Jung called *animus*, which can be the father-spirit in a man, woman, family, organization, nation, or place. A nation might venture out on an odyssey and in the process find a fathering principle that will give it authority and direction. The fact that Telemachus is on the same sea where his father is being initiated suggests that we, identified with the son who feels the absence of the father, have to enter that same uncharted sea of odyssey if we are to link up with the spirit that is becoming father.

We have to dare to experience the unknown, to open ourselves to unexpected influences on the soul. Later we'll see how Tristan, a son and lover, has to abandon himself to the sea in order to find love.

The trouble with some of our modern therapies and psychologies is that they aim at goals that are known—fantasies of normality or unquestioned values. One psychologist says that people need to be empowered—that is her definition of health. But there are also times when we may need to be weak and powerless, vulnerable and open to experience, as were Odysseus and Tristan, both of whom used their wits rather than their muscles. Another psychologist says people need to be capable of intimacy—relationship is the ultimate goal. But soul also requires solitude and individuality.

The goals stated by these therapists are monolithic and monarchical. By focusing on a single value, we close ourselves off to many other possibilities that may seem contrary to the chosen one. In this sense, the image of odyssey serves the many-faceted soul. It offers an openness to discovery and a trust in movements that are not intended or even expected. The sea is fate, the world one is born into. It is unique and individual, always uncharted, teeming with its own dangers, pleasures, and opportunities. One becomes a father to one's own life by becoming intimately acquainted with it and by daring to traverse its waters.

I'm talking here about a deep father figure that settles into the soul to provide a sense of authority, the feeling that you are the author of your own life, that you are the head of the household in your own affairs. *The Odyssey* adds an interesting motif to this process. While Odysseus is away from home engaged in his own education for fatherhood, he has a stand-in at home by the name of Mentor, who cares for the house and teaches Telemachus. The father figures in our lives can be of two kinds. They may be substitutes who symptomatically play the role of father for us but interfere with our own fathering odysseys. But some father figures are true mentors, furthering the deep process of fatherhood by understanding their limited role and by not usurping the father's role for themselves, even as they teach and guide. Some teachers don't seem to understand the need in their students to be on an odyssey and to be discovering their own fatherhood. They expect their students to be a copy of themselves and to profess the same values and information. Some business and political leaders see their role in society as promoting their own personal ideologies rather than serving as genuine mentors; they don't understand that the populace must make its own collective odyssey in order to evoke a soulful fatherhood for the society. It takes genuine wisdom to be a mentor, the pleasure of which comes from instilling fatherhood rather than embodying it.

As the Bible gives us an image of a father in the sky, *The Odyssey* tells us about the father who is on the sea. While this second father is "at sea" being fashioned and enlightened, we need mentors, father figures who keep the notion of father alive in us. I don't think it helps much to think of father figures as "projections" onto certain people of our own expectations of father. It would be better to think of these significant people as mentors or as representatives of the father who is always—eternally—on the deep sea creating his paternity. We need father figures badly, people who can keep us in touch with or stimulate within us that profound principle in the soul that provides guidance and wisdom. In this sense the "image" of our senators and presidents is as important to the society, if not more so, than their achievements. By image I do not mean the advertising picture they intend to present, but rather the deeper fantasy of leader, debater, counselor, and decision maker that can make everyone feel secure because of its paternal authenticity.

Without soulful fathers, our society is left with mere reason and ideology as guides. Then we suffer collective fatherlessness: not having a clear national direction; giving the spoils of a wealthy economy to a few; finding only rare examples of deep morality, law, and community; not seeking out odyssey because we prefer the solid ground of opinion and ideology. To set out on the sea is to risk security, yet that risky path may be the only way to the father.

Culturally we are also suffering from the breakdown of patriarchy. Feminist thought properly criticizes the oppression of women on the part of long-standing male domination, but that political patriarchy is not the patriarchy of the soul. *Patri-archy* means absolute, profound, archetypal fatherhood. We need a return of patriarchy in this deepest sense, because to vacillate between embracing symptomatic and oppressive fathering on one side and criticizing it on the other gets us nowhere. In that divisiveness we will never find the spirit of fatherhood that we need both as a society and in our individual lives as men and women.

Our myth tells us that we will enjoy a restoration of the father once we are separated from the battle of everyday life—the Trojan war of survival—and wander from island to island on the great sea of imagination. We will be making father all the while we are surrendering to the winds and weather brought by the gods as our education in the geography and citizenry of the soul. Care of the soul's fathering, therefore, requires that we sustain the experiences of absence, wandering, longing, melancholy, separation, chaos, and deep adventure. There is no shortcut to the father. In soul time it takes ten symbolic years to establish a solid sense of father—that is to say, odyssey takes place eternally. It has its endings and its rewards, but it is also always in progress. And in the soul, time periods overlap; in part we are always on the sea, always approaching a new island, always returning home hoping to be recognized as father after deeply felt transformative experiences.

*The Odyssey* teaches us that it is a challenge to evoke the deep father and not to be satisfied with substitutes and empty roles. There is no easy route to soul and no simple way of establishing fatherhood. And yet, without the mythic father's guidance and authority, we are left disoriented and out of control. In times of chaos, especially, we might intensify and expand our prayer, speaking it from the heart: "Our father, who art in heaven and who art on the sea, hallowed be thy name."

## Mother

The Greeks told another story about a mythic family, a story so highly revered that it was ritualized in the Eleusinian mysteries, the great sacrament in which men and women were initiated into the heart of religious experience. These mysteries focused on the story of a divine mother, Demeter, who loses her beloved daughter, Persephone. Their importance in the spiritual life of ancient Greece might convince us that motherhood, too, is a mystery of the soul, represented in the relations between a mother and child but signifying, too, something even more fundamental.

A myth may be read as referring to many different levels of experience at once. The story of this mother and daughter is lived out between actual mothers and daughters, but it is also at work in interactions between ourselves and other maternal figures—men and women, or sometimes even those institutions, such as schools or churches, that serve as mothers for us. And internally, the story describes tensions between dimensions of our own soul.

The story, as we find it told in the ancient "Homeric Hymn to Demeter," begins when Persephone, apart from her mother, was picking flowers—roses, crocuses, violets, irises, hyacinths, and narcissi. The earth grew the narcissus as an enchanting lure. It was wonderfully bright, the hymn tells us, and astonished anyone who saw it. It had a hundred heads and a fragrance that pleased the sky, the earth, and the sea.

Persephone was just reaching for the narcissus when the earth opened up and Hades appeared, grabbing her to himself against her will. As he forced her into his golden chariot, she screamed, but no one heard her except the sun and the moon. Zeus was away on business, and besides, the hymn says, he was in favor of the abduction. Finally, Demeter heard her daughter's grieving, and "a sharp pain seized her heart." Immediately, throwing off her headdress and abstaining from divine food and drink, she went off in search of her daughter.

Hades is the "Invisible One," lord of the underworld. His is the realm of essences, the eternal factors that, while they are very much part of life, are invisible. For the Greeks, the underworld was the proper home of the soul, and if we are to have depth and soul, we need some relationship to this underworld, or at least a sense of being partly at home there. Odysseus, as we have already seen, needed to acquaint himself with the underworld as part of his fatherhood. Orpheus also visited the underworld and discovered that it is difficult sometimes to return from it. Jesus, too, journeyed to the land of the dead in the time between his death and resurrection, and Dante began his mystical pilgrimage there. The image of "underworld" in these stories has a relation to actual death, but it also represents the invisible, mysterious, unfathomable depths of a person or a society.

The Persephone myth informs us that sometimes one discovers soul and the underworld against one's will. Certain attractive things in the world may act as lures, setting us up for a challenging fall into the depths of self. I once knew a man who owned a successful business and was providing his family with an exceptionally comfortable way of life. One day he decided to visit a local art gallery, something he had never done before. He was particularly fascinated by some photographs, and decided then and there to become a photographer. He sold his business and gave up his income. The photographs he saw that day were like the hundred-headed narcissus—profoundly alluring; on that visit the earth opened up and his imagination was seized. His wife played the part of Demeter, grieving the loss of a comfortable and familiar life, but for him the fascination for his art was so great that he allowed his former life to crumble.

Parents know how easy it is for their children to be attracted to people and activities that are dangerous and that threaten to lead their children into dark places. To the child, antisocial behavior can be fascinating, while to the parent such a thing could destroy all their efforts to give the child a sense of values and a decent path in life. We might understand the story of Persephone as the myth of every child, realizing that the child's susceptibility to dark people and places may be a dangerous but sometimes unavoidable way of soul-making.

I've also known several women who have experienced this myth as a transformation in their lives. They began as naive, Persephone-like girls, but then fell in with dark men, an underworld of drugs and criminality, and sexual experimentation they never would have considered before. One woman, I recall, had a series of dreams in which a faceless, threatening man was hiding in shadows at the bottom of staircases. She had been quite innocent, but over a period of two years she changed, becoming more complicated and more worldly. Her abduction was from within.

Whether the situation is one of an actual mother dealing with her children, or any person feeling a strong emotional pull into the depths, the consequent loss of innocence may be painful and disorienting. Patricia Berry describes this maternal grief as a Demeter form of depression. The goddess's loss of interest in clothes, cleanliness, and food mimic the daughter's withdrawal from ordinary life, and the mother's depression is both a sympathetic echo of her daughter's fate and anger at the gods who allowed this to happen.

Demeter and Persephone are two aspects of the one mythic abduction. Something in us leans toward depth, toying with narcissistic lures, while something else tries to keep us on track, in a world of familiar, wholesome values. Demeter's love of Persephone and her persistence in searching for her allow the daughter to find the land of soul without losing her life altogether. Demeter shows us the ultimate test of the mother: affirming her attachment and her own wishes for her child, while at the same time remaining loyal to her as she goes through a transformative experience. The story shows us how deep is the love demanded of any mother who protects her child whom she knows must be exposed to darkness, and how much is expected from each of us whose soul, tempted by dangerous lures, will need our own maternal attachment and caring.

All mothering, whether in a family or within an individual, is made up of both affectionate caring and bitter emotional pain. Christianity gives us the great image of the Virgin Mary who is both the comforting madonna and the *mater dolorosa,* the sorrowful mother. In both emotions, the mother is close to the child, allowing the child, even as she feels her pain and anger, to become an individual through exposure to experience and to fate.

It is tempting to try to live without an underworld, without soul, and without concern for the mysterious elements that touch on the spiritual and the religious. In the story, when Demeter finds out that Zeus has approved her daughter's abduction, she decides to go into the world as a mortal. She takes an ordinary job as a nanny in a household at Eleusis, a town near Athens.

This move toward normality and mundane human life is a defense, Patricia Berry says, against the pull of the underworld. It is found in the advice friends give when some visitor from hell has left a person depressed or disturbed. "Lose yourself in your work," they say. Even professional psychology sometimes recommends the strategy of becoming absorbed in the details of ordinary life in order not to be lured by "crazy" fantasies. From the Demeter point of view, the abduction into depth is an outrageous violation. But we know, from the complicity of Zeus, that it is also a necessity. If Zeus approves, then whatever is happening is truly the will of God. It is in the nature of things to be drawn to the very experiences that will spoil our innocence, transform our lives, and give us necessary complexity and depth.

An infant boy, Demophoön, is put in Demeter's charge, and she cares for him, anointing him with ambrosia, breathing on him, and holding him—strong images of intimate caring for human life on the part of divinity. At night she places him in a fire in order to make him immortal, until his mother sees what is happening and screams out in terror. Demeter becomes very angry at the mortal's failure to understand. "You don't know when fate is bringing you something good or something bad," she shouts—a basic theme in this story in which Zeus and Hades, the Lord of Life and the Lord of Death, are at work. This is good advice from the mother of mothers: understand that sometimes things that look dangerous from a mortal point of view may be beneficial from a greater perspective.

In her brief term as a mortal nurse, Demeter gives us more lessons in mothering, showing us that motherhood is about nurturing not only in human ways but also in divine ways. Holding the child in fire is a way of burning away the human elements in order to establish immortality. We don't have to take "immortality" to mean literal life after death, but rather the soul's ever-present depth. Good Demeter mothering keeps a child in the heat and passion of life which immortalize and establish soulfulness. Mothering involves not only physical survival and achievement—Demeter's grain and fruit—it is also concerned with guiding a child to his or her unknown depths and the mystery of fate.

Often in my practice I encounter women and men who are identified with the mother. Whenever we identify too closely with an archetypal figure, we become tangled in distortion, exaggeration, and compulsion. Some people lose all their intelligence and control in the presence of a needy person. Some people say they married because their partner needed them so badly. Women may be drawn to wounded and sensitive men, boys not ripened by life; men may be drawn to fragile women who seem to need protection and guidance of a maternal kind. These problems of a "mother complex" require a deeper sense of what mother is, and the knowledge that often we can best give maternal care to another, not by being mother ourselves, but by finding ways to stir the maternal impulse in the other.

The myth of Demeter and Persephone

teaches us that mothering is not a simple matter of taking care of the immediate needs of another; it is a recognition that each individual has a special character and fate—qualities of soul—that must be safeguarded even at the risk of losing ordinary assurances of safety and normality. Burning the child in the fire of fate and experience goes against the natural desire for protection. The myth shows us that there is a difference between human mothering and divine mothering. The latter has a broader perspective and is a deep form of the maternal impulse.

In the myth, Demeter then shows her divinity and asks that a temple be built in her honor; we go from Demeter as mortal nanny to Demeter as revered goddess. Each of us might be encouraged to build such a temple to the mother, so that the mothering that goes on in life, on our behalf and from our own actions, is an evocation of the Great Mother, a mothering that is greater in scope than any human maternal care could ever be. In practical terms, whenever we sense that we are overdoing it as mothers, or being too sensitive to the needs of others, then it may be time to honor a greater mother, to evoke the spirit of Demeter rather than to take that role upon ourselves.

It is precisely at this point in the story—at

the end of her role as mortal nursemaid—that Demeter refuses to allow the fields to bear fruit and threatens the extinction of the human race. In ordinary life, when we are being initiated into the mysteries of Demeter—becoming an individual by being seized from deep within—there may be a loss of meaning and fruitfulness in the external world. Ordinarily, Demeter is Mother Nature giving us food and the materials for clothing; she is the goddess of survival needs and of the pleasures of the natural world. But when we find ourselves captured by this myth, these outer benefits may diminish, while inner, underworld activities take precedence.

At this point, because Demeter's suffering is painful to everyone, Zeus is compelled to seek out arbitration, so that there might be some compromise between the legitimate claims of Hades and Demeter's fierce desire to have her daughter back in life. He calls upon Iris, the rainbow, to ask Demeter to return to her place among the gods, but Iris's attempt at persuasion is unsuccessful. Next he sends each of the gods, one by one, but none is able to convince Demeter to let the earth be fruitful. Finally, he dispatches Hermes, the consummate go-between and arbiter, to ask Hades for help.

Hades "smiled grimly and did not disobey the commands of King Zeus." He tells Persephone to return to her mother, but first he secretly puts a pomegranate seed in her mouth, ensuring that she will never be completely free of his realm. She will spend one-third of her time with him, and the rest with her mother.

A student once pointed out to me that these are the proportions of sleeping and waking. Internal images and emotions of the night can be different in quality from those of the day; they may be particularly vivid and disturbing. We get a glimpse sometimes in our pleasurable night dreams of the lovely hundred-headed narcissus, which has a beauty beyond what is natural; but we may also feel the terrors of the dark underground of Hades. At least a third of life, too, seems to belong to the lord of death, as we feel the pain of lost relationships, fading hopes, and failed endeavors.

A way to reconcile these intimations of death with vibrant Demeter life is to turn to Hermes—to "hermeneutics," the art of reading our experiences for their poetry. This Hermes point of view can perceive how our experiences of depth and darkness may be reconciled with ordinary life. According to the myth, Hermes can restore the relationship between the mother-soul, who wants life to thrive no matter what, and the daughter-soul, who has an inclination away from life toward the unknown. With the help of Hermes, we can "see through" our self-destructiveness and depression, our flirtations with danger and our addictions, and ask what they might be accomplishing in our lives and what they are expressing.

A common problem with mothers is that they may be so concerned with the welfare of their children, or so completely taken up by the role of mother, that they find it difficult to allow their children to become individuals, different from themselves. I also often hear from women that they don't want to be like their mothers, and from men that they don't want to be dominated by their mothers. If we could take these problems out of the personal realm, we might see the myth of Demeter-Persephone at work. We all need to find a way to become individuals, by finding our own depths and even our own darkness, without cutting ourselves off from the maternal guidance within ourselves that keeps us in life and in community.

The Eleusinian mystery is fundamental because it concerns our very survival, both physical and psychological. We become persons through dangerous experiences of darkness; we can survive these difficult initiations. Any real initiation is always a movement from death to new life. The Eleusinian mystery involves our resurrection—like Persephone, like the appearance of fruit and grain in season—from soul-making depth into continuous, bountiful life. Like Odysseus' wife Penelope weaving a shroud the whole time of the odyssey. Demeter's pain, neurotic activities, and rage accompany, and therefore serve, the soul's visit to the underworld.

Persephone was known as the queen of the underworld and was pictured in art seated on her throne next to Hades. She has an eternal place of honor there, even as she returns to her mother and tells her, as any daughter would, all the details of her abduction. The soul needs to establish itself in the deathly realm, as well as in life.

Most of us can probably tell stories of three or four Persephone experiences, and as we tell the stories, we probably include the theme of resurrection. "I got through this period in my life, and now I'm the better for it." What got us through these encounters with Hades was the profound maternal feeling in us for life, continuity, and fruitfulness. Such a deep-seated love of life and its possibility is the gift of Demeter, which paradoxically becomes more intense and more solidly established in those episodes when it is severely threatened. We could do what the celebrants at Eleusis did in their great celebrations of Demeter: hold a shoot of grain in our hands and recall that life continues to be fruitful in a world that is ever being penetrated by all forms of death.

The story also serves as a meditation on death itself. Hades may pull us under by means of an experience of death, either a close call for ourselves, or the death of someone close. It takes a profound maternal affirmation of life to allow such deaths to affect us, to acquaint us with the mysteries of the underworld, and then to send us back into life, never to be the same again. When we allow experiences of death to touch us and take us down, we come back with seeds of the pomegranate in us, that fruit that looks sunny and whole on the outside, and yet has a highly articulated interior and is filled with dark seeds that recall the underworld.

The wise mother knows that her child can become a person only by living this mystery that was dramatized at Eleusis many centuries ago. We can't hide all the lures that lead us into dissolution. We try in vain to keep our children away from the contamination of death, as we learn from the story of Buddha's parents, who tried to protect him from all human suffering; but full mothering demands that the child be allowed to take the risk. A profound notion of motherhood embraces the great capacity of Demeter to love her daughter and still honor other gods, who have their own designs and requirements.

In the end, Demeter brings back the richness and fullness of nature, and the singer of her hymn reminds us that Hades is also known as Pluto, the god of wealth. Both Demeter and Pluto enrich life, though their harmony most frequently appears as a riddle. The hymn ends with a prayer that is a petition to the most profound mother of all:

Lady, who bears such great gifts,
who brings the seasons,
sovereign, Deo,
you and your very beautiful daughter, Persephone,
be kind, and, in exchange for my poem,
give me the kind of life my heart wants.

## Child

At the beginning of midnight Mass in the Roman Catholic church the choir chants, "*Puer natus est nobis*." "A child is born to us." Christmas is the celebration of Jesus as infant and divinity entering the human arena. This motif of the divine child is common to many religions, suggesting not only the childhood of the God, but also the divinity of childhood. Just as the mythic mother is a foundational principle of all life, so the divine child is an aspect of all experience. Jung, inspired by mythological stories of heroes' childhoods, described the child of the soul, the archetypal child, as everything that is abandoned, exposed, vulnerable, and yet divinely powerful. Once again we find the richness of paradox, a Janus-faced archetype of both power and weakness in play at the same moment.

Mythology from many cultures tells of the special child, abandoned by its parents, raised in the wild or by lowly foster parents. There is, in fact, an aspect of the child that is utterly exposed to fate, time, and conditions—not protected by being in a more personal context. Yet, this exposure is what allows the child to become someone new and powerful. Our own exposure to life is both a threat and an opportunity. In those moments when we feel particularly vulnerable, that child might appear as both defenseless and ready to be prepared for a special role in life.

Some modern psychologies see the "child within" as a figure of creativity and spontaneity. But Jung's child is more complex. We approach the power of this child not by fleeing its vulnerability, but by claiming it. There is a special power associated with the very ignorance and incapacity of the child figure. Children often appear in dreams wandering down a city street, abandoned, not knowing where to go or how to get help. This is a condition of the soul's childhood. We may be tempted, upon awakening from such a dream, to resolve never to be so lost and disoriented. But if we are going to acknowledge the child and care for this figure, too, without trying to "improve" upon it, then we have to find a place for wandering, dislocation, and helplessness. These, too, are the child.

In an early essay on the child, Hillman makes the important point that we shy away from the inferiority of this child and try to change it with education, baptism, and growth. He speaks against making a creed out of growth. Sometimes we may need to stop growing. We may need to backstep and regress. Growth, so often these days assumed automatically to be a goal in psychology and in life in general, can become a sentimental value that overlooks the necessity of such things as stagnancy and slippage. The child is not honored if we always expect him to grow up, because a child is not grown up.

Every day we use phrases that subtly speak against the child. "I'm being very immature," a person will say self-critically about the expression of some primitive feeling. If you can make that statement without its being a criticism of the child, simply as a matter of fact, then it may be an accurate description of the myth that is being lived at the moment. I am being immature. Immaturity is part of my nature. But often such a statement means, I feel uncomfortable with this sudden, unwanted feeling of immaturity. I want to grow out of it.

Or we might say, "This is an old problem, going back to childhood." Again, we think of childhood as something to grow out of. It is the cause of all present trouble. If only it had been different! But this rejection of the child is another way to reject oneself and certainly not to care for the soul. That child who is eternally present in our thoughts and dreams may be full of weakness and faults, but that is who we are. We are who we are as much because of our gaps and failures as because of our strengths. Besides, the thought that adult problems go back to childhood keeps us in touch with that divinely powerful child and its fertile inferiority. Remember, soul appears most easily in those places where we feel most inferior.

Sometimes you hear adults in their thirties and forties say lightheartedly, "I still don't know what I'm going to be when I grow up." No matter how lightly this common sentiment is stated, the feeling is full of inferiority. What's wrong with me? I should be a success by now. I should be making plenty of money. I should be settled. But in spite of these wishes, the sense of the child who is not yet ready for success and settling is strong. This recognition can be a soulful moment. It bears a melancholic tone that is a signal of soul reflecting on its fate and wondering about its future. It is a potential opening to imagination, and to some extent this is the power of the child. The child's smallness and inadequacy is the "open sesame" to a future and to the unfolding of potentiality.

The child's unknowing is also fertile. In the Gospel, the child Jesus is separated from his parents on a trip to Jerusalem, and he is found discussing points of theology with the rabbis in the temple. Is this a miracle story, or is it a reminder of the special intelligence of the child, so unformed and yet, as Jung says, so wise? Nicholas of Cusa, the great fifteenth-century theologian who wrote a book about the importance of "educated ignorance," says we have to find ways to unlearn those things that screen us from the perception of profound truth. We have to *achieve* the child's unknowing because we have been made so smart. Zen also recommends not losing the "beginner's mind," so important for immediacy in experience.

These are child qualities that never grow up, that we never grow out of. Because the presence of the soul child with its ignorance and clumsiness generates such discomfort, it is tempting to deny the child or try to cover it up or force it to disappear. But such forms of repression only make the child more difficult to deal with. The more we try to cover up our ignorance, the more it is displayed. The more we try to act cool and suave, the more obvious our inexperience. The more adult we try to be, the more childishness we betray.

I suspect, further, that if we could come to appreciate the archetypal child whom we feel within ourselves, we might have a more open and appreciative relationship to actual children. For example, an eternal question about children is, how should we educate them? Politicians and educators consider more school days in a year, more science and math, the use of computers and other technology in the classroom, more exams and tests, more certifications for teachers, and less money for art. All of these responses come from the place where we want to make the child into the best adult possible, not in the ancient Greek sense of virtuous and wise, but in the sense of one who is an efficient part of the machinery of society. But on all these counts, soul is neglected. We want to prepare the ego for the struggle of survival, but we overlook the needs of the soul.

*Education* means "to lead out." We seem to understand this as leading away from childhood, but maybe we could think of it as eliciting the wisdom and the talents of childhood itself. As A. S. Neal, founder of the Summerhill School, taught many years ago, we can trust that the child already has talents and intelligence. We believe that the child intellectually is a *tabula rasa,* a blank blackboard, but maybe the child knows more than we suspect. Child wisdom is different from adult wisdom, but it has its place.

Any move against the archetypal child is a move against soul, because this child is a face of the soul, and whatever aspect of the soul we neglect, becomes a source of suffering. We are a society that finds it difficult to discover the exuberant joy and spontaneity of childhood; instead, we spend great sums of money on electronic entertainment centers that don't speak to the soul's need for childlike direct pleasure. The United States ranks low on the list of how well nations take care of their children. For all our sentimental advocacy of children, we don't make genuine efforts on behalf of children. In our country child abuse is rampant, yet it is still largely covered up and denied. This tragic situation is both a symptom and a cause of our failure to appreciate the archetypal child. To embrace the child may threaten the adult who values information above wonder, entertainment above play, and intelligence above ignorance. If we were really to care for the child, we would have to face our own lower natures—our indomitable emotions, our insane desires, and the vast range of our incapacity.

In his memoirs Jung makes a remarkable statement about the child. Childhood, he says, "sketches a more complete picture of the self, of the whole man in his pure individuality, than adulthood." He goes on to say that a child will arouse primitive longings in an adult for unfulfilled desires that have been lost in adaptation to civilization. Certainly the widespread physical abuse and sexual exploitation of children has to do with the difficult relationship we have to the archetypal child. We have been seduced into the myth of progress, so that at the social level we assume that we are more intelligent and more developed than our ancestors, and at the personal level we assume that adults are more intelligent than children. This developmental fantasy runs deep, affecting many of our values. We live in a hierarchical world in which we defend ourselves from our primitive nature by looking down on less developed cultures, and from our eternal infancy and childhood by insisting on a graded, necessary elevation through learning and technological sophistication out of the child into the adult. This is not a true initiation that values both the previous form of existence and the newly attained one; it is a defense against the humiliating reality of the child, a humility that embarrasses the Promethean longing for adult control of life but nevertheless is full of soul. We are not caring for the soul when we fabricate ways of denying its inferior stations, childhood prominent among them. We care for the soul by acknowledging the place of eternal childhood, seeing its disadvantages to be virtuous and its inadequacies to be the conduits of soulful sensitivity.

# CHAPTER 3

# Self-love and Its Myth: Narcissus and Narcissism

Mainstream psychology puts a great deal of faith in a strong ego. Ego development and positive self-concept are considered important ingredients of a mature personality. Yet narcissism, the habit of focusing attention on oneself rather than the world of objects and of others, is considered a disorder. On the other hand, Jungian psychology, with its emphasis on the unconscious, and archetypal psychology, with its high regard for the non-ego personalities of the psyche, give the impression that the ego is a sinner, literalizing all over the place and generally making a mess. Even in the analysis of dreams, it is tempting to see the ego as always making a mistake. Add religion's longstanding warnings against selfishness and self-love, in which pride is considered one of the cardinal sins, and it begins to look as though there is a moral conspiracy against the ego.

The one-sidedness and moralism of the various attacks on narcissism suggest that there may be some soul lying around in this rejected pile of ego and self-love: anything that bad must have some value in it. Could it be that our righteous rejections of narcissism and love of self cover over a mystery about the nature of the soul's loves? Is our negative branding of narcissism a defense against a demanding call of the soul to be loved?

The problem is not just theoretical. I'm often surprised in my therapeutic work when an otherwise mature and discerning adult who is faced with some tough choice collapses everything into the statement "I can't be selfish." When I explore this weighty moral imperative with the person further, I usually find that it is tied to a religious upbringing. "I was taught never to be selfish," she will say with finality. I notice, however, that while this person insists on her selflessness, she seems in fact to be quite preoccupied with herself. In pursuit of the virtue of selflessness, attention to self can go underground and become an unconscious and corrosive attachment to pet theories and values. Now when I hear someone say, "I don't want to be selfish," I prepare myself for a difficult struggle with the ego.

Our common intolerance for narcissism in another is an indication that there is sand in that particular oyster; our reaction is a signal that this area may hold something of importance. In this sense, narcissism is a shadow quality. Jung explains that when we meet something of the shadow in another, we often feel repulsed, but that is because we are confronting something in ourselves that we find objectionable, something with which we ourselves struggle, and something that contains qualities valuable to the soul. The negative image we have of narcissism may indicate that self-preoccupation contains something we need so badly that it is surrounded with negative connotations. Our irritated moralism keeps it at bay, but also signals us that soul is present.

How, then, do we preserve the symptom of narcissism, assuming that there is a gold nugget in that clump of dirt? How do we penetrate through the superficial sludge to the deeper necessity? The answer, as we are beginning to recognize by now, is to bring the wisdom of the imagination into play. In the case of narcissism, the path is clearly laid out: we can study the myth of Narcissus, after whom the disorder is named.

## Narcissus

The ancient story of Narcissus, as told in the *Metamorphoses* of the Roman writer Ovid, is not just a simple story of a boy falling in love with himself. It has many subtle, telling details. Ovid tells us, for instance, that Narcissus was the son of a river god and a nymph. In mythology, parentage can often be taken as holding poetic truths. Apparently there is something essentially liquid or watery about Narcissus, and by extension, about our own narcissism. When we are narcissistic, we are not on solid ground (earth) or thinking clearly (air) or caught up in passion (fire). Somehow, if we follow the myth, we are dreamlike, fluid, not clearly formed, more immersed in a stream of fantasy than secure in a firm identity.

Another detail that appears at the opening of the story is the prophecy of Tiresias, the renowned seer: "He will live to a ripe old age," he pronounces about Narcissus, "provided he never comes to know himself." This is a strange foretelling: it indicates that the story is about knowing oneself as well as loving oneself and that self-knowledge will lead to death. This aspect of the myth gives the impression that we are in the realm of mystery rather than of a simple syndrome.

The next we hear of him, Narcissus is sixteen and so lovely that many young people are attracted to him; but he is filled with a "hard pride," Ovid says, and no one can truly get through to him. One nymph who falls in love with him, Echo, has her own peculiar qualities: she can only speak words and phrases she has just heard from someone else. One day Narcissus loses sight of his friends and cries out, "Is anyone here?"

"Here," Echo answers.

"Let's meet here," Narcissus says.

"Meet here," Echo responds. But when she approaches him, Narcissus backs away.

"I would die before I would give my power to you," he says.

"I would give my power to you," she says in her own way. In her grief, feeling rejected and frustrated, Echo then loses her body and becomes a mere voice.

In this early episode we see Narcissus before he has attained self-knowledge. He presents an image of narcissism that has not yet found its mystery. Here we see the symptom: a self-absorption and containment that allows no connections of the heart. It is hard as a rock and repels all approaches of love. Obsessive, but not genuine, self-love leaves no room for intimacy with another. The echoing aspect of narcissism—the feeling that everything in the world is only a reflection of oneself—doesn't want to give away power. To respond to another or to an object in the outside world would endanger the fragile sense of power which that tight, defensive insistence on oneself maintains. Like all symptomatic behavior, narcissism reveals, in the very things it insists on, exactly what it lacks. The narcissistic person asks over and over, "Am I doing all right?" The message is, "No matter what I do or how much I try to force it, I can't get to the place where I feel that I'm doing okay." In other words, the narcissist's *display* of self-love is in itself a sign that he can't find a way adequately to love himself.

In Jungian language we could recognize the *puer* or boyish side of the psyche in Narcissus—distant, cold, self-contained. Echo is the anima, the soul in desperate need of attachment to the boyish beauty. But in the presence of Narcissus the soul shrivels into an echoing voice. Narcissism has no soul. In narcissism we take away the soul's substance, its weight and importance, and reduce it to an echo of our own thoughts. There is no such thing as the soul. We say. It is only the brain going through its electrical and chemical changes. Or it is only behavior. Or it is only memory and conditioning. In our social narcissism, we also dismiss the soul as irrelevant. We can prepare a city or national budget, but leave the needs of the soul untended. Narcissism will not give its power to anything as nymphlike as the soul.

But fortunately, the story goes on. One of the young people scorned by Narcissus offers a curse: "May he fall in love and not have what he loves." This is a curse we might well utter under our breath when we feel that cold haughtiness of narcissism around us. A frustrated lover says, "I hope one day you find out what it's like to love someone and not have it returned." We sense the chill of soullessness and utter a curse, which, like the prophecy of Tiresias in the story, is actually a blessing in disguise. If the curse works, the person might be changed.

In myth, curses are sometimes fulfilled dramatically. In this case the goddess Nemesis hears the prayer and decides to answer it; this leads us to the next phase of the story, which at first glance looks as though it concerns punishment for pride. Narcissus is about to have a transforming, life-threatening, psychotic episode at a pool of water. The intervention of a god, however, may signal a breaking up of symptomatic behavior, the neurosis beginning to dissolve in painful disorientation. The divine breaking up of narcissism may be expected to center on self-knowledge and self-love. Identity may become even more confused and fluid.

As the story continues, the young man approaches a pool of water, so still and smooth that it has never been disturbed by either human or animal. It is surrounded by a cool, dark grove of trees. As Narcissus puts his head to the water to get a drink, he sees his image in the water and his attention is frozen. Ovid describes Narcissus as fascinated by this visage that looks as though it were carved from marble, and especially by the ivory neck. (Notice the imagery of hardness, a key quality in narcissism.) Like the young people who desired him before, Narcissus feels a great yearning to possess this form. He reaches into the water, but he can't get hold of it. "What you are looking for," says Ovid, "is nowhere. Turn your head away and what you love will be lost."

Here we see the beginning of the symptom's fulfillment. Narcissism, that absorption in oneself that is soulless and loveless, turns gradually into a deeper version of itself. It becomes a true stillness, a wonder about oneself, a meditation on one's nature. For the first time the narcissist reflects—a major image in the story—on himself. Formerly, his preoccupation with himself was empty, but now it stirs wonder. In symptomatic narcissism there is no reflection and no wonder. But now, as it undergoes transformation into a deeper version of itself, the narcissism takes on more substance. The narcissist may love to see himself in an actual mirror, but only at a moment of transformation into soul does he enjoy a deeper, inner reflection. Like Narcissus, he needs an image of himself for his meditation, something far more effective and soulful than the literal mirror image used for more shallow acts of self-approval.

The image in which narcissism is fulfilled is not a literal one. It is not the image one sees in a mirror, not the "image," as they would say on Madison Avenue, that you want to project, not the self-concept, not the way you see yourself. The image Narcissus sees is a new one, something he had never seen before, something "other," and he is mesmerized by it, charmed. Ovid says, "the image you seek is nowhere." It cannot be found intentionally. One comes upon it unexpectedly in a pool in a woods where the sun doesn't shine brightly and where human touch is absent. What the narcissist does not understand is that the self-acceptance he craves can't be forced or manufactured. It has to be discovered, in a place more introverted than the usual haunts of the narcissist. There has to be some inner questioning, and maybe even confusion. He may have to come to the point where he asks, "What's going on here?"

It's particularly suggestive that Narcissus finds this new view of himself in water. In this element that is his special essence, his birthright, he finds something of himself. I don't want to treat this narcissus water as a symbol and say it is the unconscious or mother's womb or something else. It would be better to reflect directly from the image: Is there something in me that is like this pool? Do I have depth? Do my feelings and thoughts pool somewhere so off the beaten path that it is utterly still and untouched? Is there someplace wet in me, not the place of dry intellectualism but rather of moist feeling and green, fertile, shady imagination, far from human influence? Do I find myself in rare moments caught in a place of reflection where I have to take a break for reverie and wonder and there catch a glimpse of some unfamiliar face that is mine? If so, then the myth of Narcissus, the cure for narcissism, may be stirring in me.

The story then tells how Narcissus feels the longing to be united with the image he has found. Now like the lovers he spurned, he pines and suffers. One wonders if he will become in his grief like Echo and lose his body. But there is no doubt about the intensity of his emotional suffering. He talks to the trees, saying, "Has anyone ever had as much longing as I have?" Talking to nature shows that his grief is giving him a new connection to the soul. When soul is present, nature is alive.

I suspect that this is a very concrete part of curing narcissism—talking to the trees. By engaging the so-called "inanimate" world in dialogue, we are acknowledging its soul. Not all consciousness is human. That in itself is a narcissistic belief. Whenever a psychologist says that we are projecting personality in the world when we talk to it, that psychologist is speaking narcissistically, as though personality and soul belong only to the human subject. But if all we are doing in imagination is bumping into ourselves as in a house of mirrors, then there is no soul, only "me" and "me-products"—projections. Then our longings are not articulated but only acted out in endless, fruitless satisfying of desire.

James Hillman has written about longing as an important activity of the soul, especially the young soul, *puer*. That which is young in us pines and yearns. It feels separation keenly and painfully desires attachment. So, the myth suggests that we are on our way toward healing narcissism when we feel an overwhelming desire to be the person we newly imagine ourselves to be. Nations, as well as individuals, can go through this initiation. America has a great longing to *be* the New World of opportunity and a moral beacon for the world. It longs to fulfill these narcissistic images of itself. At the same time it is painful to realize the distance between the reality and that image. America's narcissism is strong. It is paraded before the world. If we were to put the nation on the couch, we might discover that narcissism is its most obvious symptom. And yet that narcissism holds the promise that this all-important myth can find its way into life. In other words, America's narcissism is its unrefined *puer* spirit of genuine new vision. The trick is to find a way to that water of transformation where hard self-absorption turns into loving dialogue with the world.

But the way through a symptom is never easy. Narcissus lies at the edge of the pool tormented by the realization that this boy in the water is separated from him by the thinnest membrane. The face is so close and yet impossible to reach. He is in the midst of these thoughts when a realization strikes him suddenly. "It's me!" he says in profound surprise. Up to this point he did not know that the face he loved so much was his own.

This is a key point in the story. Narcissus falls in love with a person in a watery mirror who he thinks is someone else, even though it is himself. Narcissism gets stuck on certain familiar images of self. We love the surface image we identify as ourselves, but Narcissus discovers by accident that there are other images just as lovable. They are in the pool, at the very source of identity. The cure for narcissism, certainly a way of caring for the soul, is to be open to these other images. Narcissism, like the neurotic Narcissus, is hard and impenetrable. But Narcissus at the pool recovers his natural moisture. As with the flower, he has become flexible, beautiful, planted.

A subtle point: Narcissus becomes able to love himself only when he learns to love that self as an object. He now has a view of himself as someone else. This is not ego loving ego; this is ego loving the soul, loving a face the soul presents. We might say that the cure for narcissism is to move from love of self, which always has a hint of narcissism in it, to love of one's deep soul. Or, to put it another way, narcissism breaking up invites us to expand the boundaries of who we think we are. Discovering that the face in the pool is his own, Narcissus exclaims, "What I long for I have." Love of a new image of self leads to new knowledge about oneself and one's potential.

Then, in another subtle development in a story filled with significant details, Narcissus begins to entertain thoughts of death. "Now grief is sapping my strength," he says, "and only a brief space of life remains for me. I am cut off in life's prime." We are led to a mystery that is embedded in all initiations and in every rite of passage: the end of a previous form of existence is felt as a real death.

Images of dying may attend movements in our own narcissism: that hard-shelled boy has to surrender his existence. The only way through our narcissism is to feel the mortal wound, an end to the I-project we have set up and maintained with such attention. Narcissism is not going to be cured by literal fulfillment of the grandiose expectations for oneself entertained in fantasy. That has to fail so that an "other" may appear.

The Narcissus myth can be lived in many ways. Sometimes the pool may appear in another person. In that person I might recognize an image I could love and be. But such chance encounters with an image that is at once both me and not-me are dangerous. Life may never again be the same. The "I" I have been may quickly deteriorate and succumb to the process of self-transformation. Narcissism is like a carrot leading us through life from one desirable "self" to another.

In therapy sometimes the moment arrives when the patient says, "I think I'd like to be a therapist." You can hear a narcissistic tone in the statement, but maybe it is more Narcissus speaking. This person's imagination has taken a turn, maybe has found a pool, seen an image—the Therapist—reflected in that pool, likes it if not loves it, and speaks for the myth. As a therapist myself I would nurture that statement precisely as a myth. I would try not to confuse Narcissus with narcissism, especially if I might be annoyed by the latter. Such a moment could be crucial. It could be the beginning of a new branch of life and is not something to be taken lightly.

Ovid next shifts his imagery to the element fire. First Narcissus strikes his chest in grief, and his skin "takes on a delicate glow," like the flush of an apple. But then, like wax melting in the presence of a gentle heat, like frost melting in the morning sun, Narcissus is consumed by the hidden fire of love. Love's fire chases the chill that had been characteristic of the old Narcissus. Theological commentaries on this tale used it as moral evidence against self-love, but in fact the story shows that love is the transforming factor. Warming love creates soul.

Narcissus lays his head on the grass by the pool, and then he quietly disappears into the underworld, where he continues to gaze at the image in the waters of the river Styx. Our images, especially those that appear in life and play important roles in episodes of transformation, stay with us forever. Once we have entertained an image, it is always potentially present to our gaze. You visit the Uffizi Gallery and see Botticelli's "Primavera," and then for a lifetime you dream of it or you talk about it frequently as a measure of beauty. Unexpectedly it presents itself in a moment of thought or in a discussion, reminding you of its eternal presence. This fragment of the myth suggests that we might continually make soul out of our narcissism by preserving and tending to the images that have come to us throughout our lives. This is the basis of art therapy or journal-keeping: making a home for certain images that have been transforming. Certain photographs or old letters might be related to the pool of water. Culturally, of course, we are constantly invited into the depths of ourselves by the plays, paintings, sculptures, and buildings of past centuries. Art can be a cure for narcissism. The words "curator" and "curé" are essentially the same. By being the curator of our images, we care for our souls.

The story in Ovid ends with a colorful detail. His companions look for his body but cannot find it. In its place they find a flower with a yellow center and white petals. Here we see the hard, rigid marble narcissism transformed into the soft, flexible textures of a daffodil, the narcissus. A Renaissance magus would probably suggest that in moments of narcissism we should place some fresh daffodils around the house, to remind us of the mystery we're in. The story begins with rigid self-containment and ends with the flowering of a personality. Care of the soul requires us to see the myth in the symptom, to know that there is a flower waiting to break through the hard surface of narcissism. Knowing the mythology, we are able to embrace the symptom, glimpsing something of the mysterious rule by which a disease of the psyche can be its own cure.

## Narcissism and Polytheism

The story of Narcissus makes it clear that one of the dangers of narcissism is its inflexibility and rigidity. Suppleness is an extremely important quality of soul. In Greek mythology, the flexibility of the gods and goddesses is one of their primary traits. They may fight each other, but they recognize each other's validity. Each of the gods and goddesses has a particular way of sustaining the polytheism of their arrangement.

Polytheism understood as a psychological model rather than a religious belief is easily misunderstood. Stated simply, it means that psychologically we have many different claims made on us from a deep place. It is not possible, nor is it desirable, to get all of these impulses together under a single focus. Rather than strive for unity of personality, the idea of polytheism suggests living within multiplicity. Some, without investigating the idea deeply enough, have assumed that this means that morally anything goes, that there is no code of ethics, and that whatever happens happens; but *poly* means "several," not "any." In a polytheistic morality we allow ourselves to experience the tensions that arise from different moral claims.

Psychological polytheism is more a matter of quality than quantity. When you find tolerance in yourself for the competing demands of the soul, life becomes more complicated, but also more interesting. An example might be the contradictory needs of solitude and social life. In most of us there is both a spirit of community and a spirit of solitariness. Sometimes they seem to war against each other. Sometimes other people complain about our loyalty to one or the other. But both can be woven into a life, not only logistically, but deeply. In fact, the deeper one takes the complicated, competing demands, the more subtle each becomes. One can find some country in the city, and community and sophistication in the country. The polytheistic life can be difficult to bring off, but it keeps life interesting and in motion. Furthermore, the soul is fostered in the tangles of polytheism just as it is in the many turns of the labyrinth.

The most rewarding quality of polytheism is the intimacy it can make possible with one's own heart. When we try to keep life in order with a monotheistic attitude—do the right thing, keep up the traditions, and be sure that life makes sense—our moralism against ourselves can keep certain parts of our nature at a distance and little known. A man who had never gone camping in his life was sure he would hate it, but then he fell in love with a woman who loved to sleep under the stars. On their first night outside he looked up at the brilliant sky and confessed that he never knew he could appreciate such a lovely, simple act. He didn't know he had it in him, he said, in a statement that intimates a small opening into polytheism.

An attitude of polytheism permits a degree of acceptance of human nature and of one's own nature that is otherwise blocked by single-mindedness. A neurotic narcissism won't allow the time needed to stop, reflect, and see the many emotions, memories, wishes, fantasies, desires, and fears that make up the materials of the soul. As a result, the narcissistic person becomes fixed on a single idea of who he is, and other possibilities are automatically rejected. We can read the myth, especially the discovery of the "other" face in the pool, as a lesson in polytheism.

We can see narcissism, then, as an opportunity rather than as a problem: not a personality defect, but the soul trying to find its otherness. Narcissism is less a simple focus on ego and more a manifestation of the need for a paradoxical sense of self, one that includes both the ego and the non-ego.

This approach to narcissism suggests, I think, that it is wrong to be negative toward the ego and even egotism. The ego needs to be loved, requires attention, and wants exposure. That is part of its nature. Every figure of the psyche has needs that seem distasteful, even outrageous. Popular psychology tends to romanticize the child figure. People go to workshops to "discover the child within," but do they go to these events to reawaken the child who cries, is needy, pouts, spills everything in sight, and dirties his pants? Yet all of this is the child, too. The ego, that whole construct we so easily name "I," also has its less than appealing needs. If we are going to recognize the many people we are, the multiple figures of our soul, then I would think we have to find a place for that personality we call on more than any other—the "I."

Narcissism is not about giving this "I" too much attention. If we can be instructed by the myth, narcissism is the unlucky situation in which we have yet to discover that we have a pool in us where a deeper sense of "I," another ego, may appear for our attention and affection. The narcissistic person simply does not know how profound and interesting his nature is. In his narcissism he is condemned to carry the weight of life's responsibilities on his own shoulders. But once he discovers that there are other figures who surround the "I" personality, he can let them do some of the work of life. Narcissism may look like an indulgent pleasure, but beneath the façade of satisfaction lies an oppressive burden. The narcissistic person tries very hard to be loved, but he never succeeds because he doesn't realize yet that he has to love himself as other before he himself can be loved.

## The Flowering of Life

Some years ago, when I was teaching psychology at a state university, a bright, interesting young man came into one of my classes. He seemed quite mature: he was dedicated to social issues and he liked to discuss ideas. He even read serious books on his own, something rather unusual in this school. But I could also sense early Narcissus in him, a way he had of drawing people around him and yet keeping a distance. Echo was there, too. He had a habit of repeating many ideas he had heard from several sources as though they were his own—one of the telltale signs of narcissism. But I didn't realize how much he was fated toward the myth until one day he asked to have a private talk with me.

He sat across from me looking uncharacteristically serious.

"What's up?" I asked.

"I have to tell somebody," he said with fire in his eyes, "what has happened to me."

"Go on," I said.

"I have discovered something about myself."

"Yes."

"I'm Jesus Christ."

"Oh," I said. I wasn't prepared for such a stark expression of his self-esteem.

"I have a mission to save the world," he went on. "I know I can perform miracles, and in case you get me wrong, I don't mean I am a Christian or a follower of Jesus or Christlike. I am Jesus himself come back to earth. I know it sounds crazy, but it's true."

I believe this young man did indeed have a strong calling in his life. He had talent, conviction, idealism, and energy. But certainly if his symptomatic narcissism never deepened, he would be in trouble. He would never be able to accomplish anything in the world, and at best he might be condemned to a life of frustrated idealism. I once told this story to a colleague who works in a state hospital. His response was, "Oh, we have quite a number of Jesuses on our ward." But I thought my student's potential for real life was as great as his narcissistic fantasies were absurd. For him, care of the soul would mean tending these fantasies, nurturing them until they coalesced into power and effectiveness. Rather than judge this man's fantasies as plain pathology, I wanted to see them as an invitation to a committed, highly motivated life. Rather than ask, where did these outrageous thoughts come from, I asked myself, how can this young man fulfill his dreams? I don't mean to dismiss the danger and the craziness in the identification with Jesus. It could also lead to a bizarre Jim Jones career. But if narcissism is treated carefully and positively, it can find its flowering in ordinary life.

Some psychologists argue that the soaring, idealistic *puer* cries out for grounding. He needs to experience life and tether his fanciful thoughts to a humbler life. He needs to be pulled down to where the rest of us live. But I have doubts about such a compensatory move into an opposite attitude. It could maintain the split and completely confuse the individual so caught up in flights of fantasy. We could take a more homeopathic approach, accepting what is given in the symptom while at the same time deepening it.

In the myth, Narcissus's own nature flowers, literally. He doesn't become a mature adult full of remorse for his adolescent foolishness. In fact, the motif of the boy in the underworld eternally meditating on his image suggests that narcissism is healed when it is invited into the very essence of the personality and when that youthful spirit becomes lodged eternally in the soul. In general, behavior is symptomatic when it is not brought home and honored as a legitimate part of our nature. My young student may have needed years of reflection before his narcissism could transform into a deep myth informing his life. But where would we be as individuals or as a society without outrageous youthful idealism and extravagant identifications with Jesus or Mozart or Martin Luther King, Jr.? Idealism, winged with narcissism, does not need forced grounding; it requires acceptance and meditation and close embrace, so that it can turn naturally from hard ivory expectations to soft, beautiful, earthly life.

Often we are blocked from seeing a possible positive outcome in narcissism because it generates such strong shadow feelings. It goes against one of the professed virtues of American culture: humility. We are supposed to be humble and unassuming. Narcissism is the shadow of that humility, and so we try to pull it down to an acceptable level. But narcissism, even at a social level, suggests that what we need is not humility, especially the false kind that arises from the repression of ambition, but great dreams, high ideals, and pleasure in our own talent and abilities.

The problem in narcissism is not the high ideals and ambitions, it's the difficulty one encounters when trying to give them body. The narcissist finds resistance to his myth both within himself and in the people around him.

Friends and colleagues are put off by the tone of narcissism. Their reaction, their "counter-transference" to this myth, is frequently parental and moralistic in tone. "That young man needs to experience life and get off his high horse." Or "When is she going to grow up?" But the solution to narcissism is not "growing up." On the contrary, the solution to narcissism is to give the myth as much realization as possible, to the point where a tiny bud appears indicating the flowering of personality through its narcissism.

## Self-love

Narcissism is a condition in which a person does *not* love himself. This failure in love comes through as its opposite because the person tries so hard to find self-acceptance. The complex reveals itself in the all-too-obvious effort and exaggeration. It's clear to all around that narcissism's love is shallow. We know instinctively that someone who talks about himself all the time must not have a very strong sense of self. To the individual caught up in this myth, the failure to find self-love is felt as a kind of masochism, and, whenever masochism comes into play, a sadistic element is not far behind. The two attitudes are polar elements in a split power archetype.

The narcissist is clearly sadistic in his rejection of others and in his feelings of superiority. Masochism, on the other hand, appears with particular clarity in what I call "negative narcissism." Some people think they avoid narcissism by constantly judging and berating themselves. Even though this may look like the opposite of self-love, it is still narcissism: a focus, albeit negative, not on life and objects, but on self. The masochism may appear as a habit of self-criticism.

One time an artist was talking to me about her painting. She showed me samples of her work, and it seemed to me that she was very talented and could well devote her life to art. But as we talked, I noticed that something in her attitude toward herself and her work interfered.

"I particularly like the realism without perspective in your recent paintings," I said.

"Oh, I don't know," she said. "I think it just shows that I haven't studied enough. You know, I always wanted to go to art school, but my family could never afford to send me."

"How do you manage to make those colors look so harmonious and yet filled with contrast, all at the same time?" I asked, truly taken by her style.

"I'm not really trained in these things," she went on, with her concern about her background and pedigree.

Putting oneself down is narcissism in reverse. It robs the soul of its attachment to the world. This woman not only couldn't talk to trees—in the myth talking to trees was a sign that Narcissus was getting somewhere—she couldn't talk about her paintings. Her "self" got in the way. She wasn't attached to her work because of her overriding concern with her image. I suspect that if she had an image of herself as an artist, and loved it, she would be able to forget about her inferior feelings about herself and concentrate on her work. Soul always includes an element of attachment, but narcissism, as we have seen from the myth, is the failure to make oneself available for attachment. In our narcissism, we are as if made of ivory—beautiful, but also cold and hard.

Even though they are opposites, many people seem to have difficulty distinguishing narcissism from a proper and necessary love of self. Therefore, the person confused about being too hungry for praise holds back from the pleasure of achievement. He makes little of an obvious success or has difficulty accepting compliments and praise, thinking that in this way he will avoid the dreaded narcissism. False humility denies the ego the attention it craves, but the denial itself is narcissistic, since it is a negative focus on ego rather than on the pleasurable possibilities of life.

The healing of narcissism, the fulfillment of its symptomatic hunger, is achieved by giving the ego what it needs—pleasure in accomplishment, acceptance, and some degree of recognition. Masochistic refusal of the ego's desire is no way to care for the soul. On the contrary, it is an ascetic bargain that buys a false sense of virtue at the cost of the soul's need. Motivated by thoughts of purity and self-control, a person can deny the ego all kinds of comforts, and yet narcissism may abound. Spiritual programs are filled with concerns for individual progress, acceptance by authorities, and the wish for sainthood or some other high position. An alternative approach is to hear the soul's complaint and give it love and attention where it most needs it, even where we are most suspicious.

The secret in healing narcissism is not to heal it at all, but to listen to it. Narcissism is a signal that the soul is not being loved sufficiently. The greater the narcissism, the less love is being given. This myth is extraordinarily subtle. Narcissus falls in love with his image, but he doesn't know it is he that is loved. He discovers by his own experience that he is lovable. Further, he loves himself as an object. In our age of personalism and subjectivity it is considered a sin to make a person into an object. Yet that is the only way to see ourselves objectively. We can examine the stuff of our lives and personalities as material separate from the "I." I am stuff. I am made up of things and qualities, and in loving these things I love myself.

One of the advantages of turning to alchemy, as Jung did, for insight into the soul is the view it offers of the self as made up of materials and their processes and qualities: salt, sulphur, iron, water; cold, warm; dry, moist; cooking, simmering, stewing, boiling. We use some of these words in everyday speech to describe the condition of the soul. When we recognize the objective nature of the soul, so that we may love it without becoming caught in solipsistic self-absorption, we can love ourselves as Narcissus did, as Other. Even the ego can be experienced this way. We know our habits, our weaknesses, our strengths, our quirks. Looking at them with interest and love does not have to be narcissistic. In fact, an awareness of the qualities of soul—the distance Narcissus feels from his love object—may help transform narcissism into genuine love of self.

Narcissism, by the way, is not always the condition of a person. Our buildings, a piece of art, a city's design, a highway, a movie, a law—all these can have a tinge or even a grand streak of narcissism in them. A narcissistic object is a thing that shows that it does not love itself. It's an odd thing to say, but a building may go overboard flaunting itself when its essential form is sufficient and lovable in itself. To me, for example, the Empire State Building stands tall and self-assured, but many buildings in our cities insist too much on their individuality. They seem to want to stand apart. It is as if they feel inferior in the community of other buildings, and so they have to exaggerate themselves to be noticed. The Empire State Building loses no stature because buildings near it are taller and newer. It seems secure in its self-love.

The myth also teaches us something else: that narcissism is a piece in a larger scheme of transformation. In the story, the scene shifts from woods to underworld, the character from human to flower, that is, from person to object. I see in this a movement away from human subjectivity and into nature. Narcissism heals itself away from loneliness into creation: in our narcissism we wound nature and make things that cannot be loved, but when our narcissism is transformed, the result is the love of self that engenders a sense of union with all of nature and things. You might say that we then have a shared narcissism, a mutual self-love, a kind of mystical consanguinity among all creatures. Not shying away from mysticism, we might say that symptomatic narcissism can only be healed when it becomes a genuine religious virtue. All human symptoms and problems, when they are taken to their depth and realized in a soulful way, find their ultimate solution in a religious sensibility.

Rainer Maria Rilke was the poet of this philosophy of transforming the everyday into the sacred, the visible into the invisible. In a famous letter of 1925 he writes, "Our task is to stamp this provisional, perishing earth into ourselves so deeply, so painfully and passionately, that its being may rise again, 'invisibly,' in us." This reminds me of Narcissus becoming the flower: nature manifests itself through our human lives, and our personalities flower as acts of creation. In his *Sonnets to Orpheus* Rilke again refers plainly to Narcissus:

> Though the reflection in the pool
> Often swims before our eyes:
> Know the image.
>
> Only in the dual realm
> do voices become
> eternal and mild.

The narcissist can be hard and cruel, even as he or she suffers harsh self-criticism. But when the "dual realm" is discovered and Narcissus lies at the pool in touch with his otherness, then the lasting, eternal, unperturbed depths provide grounding and confidence. They also take the sharp edge off narcissism's sadism, for there is mildness in the waters of self-discovery. As Narcissus we are no longer marblelike in our attempts at self-preservation; rather, we become more like the flower whose roots are deep and whose indulgent beauty is grounded, enjoying the honest humility of nature.

The trouble is that all too often our symptoms go unworked. Metamorphosis doesn't happen without our artful participation. This is the teaching of the Renaissance magicians like Ficino and Pico della Mirandola, who wrote that we need to be the artists and poets of our own lives. Symptoms are transformed by imagination. If I hear a bit of narcissism shoot out of my mouth, I can take the clue and look for those places where I am not loving and tending my soul. The circumstances, the timing, and the particular language of my narcissism tells me exactly where to look and what to do. Oddly, I can be thankful for my narcissism, if I recognize it as such and hear within it the rumblings of myth. It contains the seeds of self-acceptance and a loving attachment to the broad world.

CHAPTER 4

# Love's Initiations

Love is a kind of madness, Plato said, a divine madness. Today we talk about love as though it were primarily an aspect of relationship and also, to a great degree, as if it were something within our control. We're concerned about how to do it right, how to make it successful, how to overcome its problems, and how to survive its failures. Many of the problems people bring to therapy involve the high expectations and the rock-bottom experiences of love. It is clear that love is never simple, that it brings with it struggles of the past and hopes for the future, and that it is loaded with material that may be remotely—if at all—connected to the person who is the apparent object of love.

We sometimes talk about love lightly, not acknowledging how powerful and lasting it can be. We always expect love to be healing and whole, and then are astonished to find that it can create hollow gaps and empty failures. Going through a divorce is often a long and painful process that never truly ends. Often we never know completely if we've done the right thing, and even if we enjoy some peace of mind about the decision, memory and attachment continue to persist, if only in dreams. People are also tortured emotionally about love that was never expressed. A woman cries whenever she thinks of her father going into surgery the last time she saw him. She felt a strong urge within herself to tell him that she loved him, even though their relationship had been strained all her life, but she held back, and then it was too late. Her remorse is bitter and persistent. In his *Symposium,* his great book on the nature of love, Plato called love the child of fullness and emptiness. Each of these aspects somehow accompanies the other.

Our love of love and our high expectations that it will somehow make life complete seem to be an integral part of the experience. Love seems to promise that life's gaping wounds will close up and heal. It makes little difference that in the past love has shown itself to be painful and disturbing. There is something self-renewing in love. Like the goddesses of Greece, it is able to renew its virginity in a bath of forgetfulness.

I suppose we do learn some things about love each time we experience it. In the failure of a relationship we resolve never to make the same mistakes again. We get toughened to some extent and perhaps become a little wiser. But love itself is eternally young and always manifests some of the folly of youth. So, maybe it is better not to become too jaded by love's suffering and dead ends, but rather to appreciate that emptiness is part of love's her-itage and therefore its very nature. It isn't necessary to make strong efforts to avoid past mistakes or to learn how to be clever about love. The advance we make after we have been devastated by love may be to be able simply to enter it freely once again, in spite of our suspicions, to draw ever closer to the darkness and hollowness that are mysteriously necessary in love.

It may be useful to consider love less as an aspect of relationship and more as an event of the soul. This is the point of view taken in ancient handbooks. There is no talk about making relationships work, although there is celebration of friendship and intimacy. The emphasis is on what love does to the soul.

Does it bring broader vision? Does it initiate the soul in some way? Does it carry the lover away from earth to an awareness of divine things?

Ficino says, "What is human love? What is its purpose? It is the desire for union with a beautiful object in order to make eternity available to mortal life." It is a fundamental teaching of the Neoplatonists that earthly pleasures are an invitation to eternal delights. Ficino says that these things of ordinary life that enchant us toward eternity are "magical decoys." In other words, what appears to be a fully earthly relationship between two human individuals is at the same time a path toward far deeper experiences of the soul. Love confuses its victims because its work in the soul does not always coincide in every detail with the apparent tempos and requirements of relationship. The early Romantic German poet Novalis put it quite simply: love, he says, was not made for this world.

Freud offers one way of turning our focus in love away from the contingencies of life and toward the soul. He says that love always involves a transference to the present relationship of early family patterns. Father, mother, brother, and sister are always implicated in love as invisible but influential presences. Freud turns our attention toward deeper fantasies that wake into action when love stirs. Of course, we can read Freud reductionistically as saying that the present love is only an old love resurrected. Or we can be invited by Freud to consider how love makes the soul fertile with memories and images.

We can understand Freud to be reminding us that love ushers in a whole community of people. I recall a dream I had about fifteen years ago. I was in a large bedroom with a beautiful woman whom I didn't know from life. I wanted to turn off the bright lights, which were a distraction. I found a long light switch on the wall with about twenty buttons on it. As I pressed one, some lights would go out and others would go on. I pushed and pushed those buttons, but I couldn't achieve the darkness I wanted. Finally I gave up, and then crowds of people began to come into the bedroom. It was hopeless. I couldn't have the darkness or the privacy I craved.

There is something about being in love that wishes for blindness, pure absorption and freedom from complexity. In that dream I didn't want all the other figures of the soul to have any part in this opportunity for plain, unadulterated love. Nor did I want any light. I wanted pure unconsciousness, absolute darkness. In fact, as love between people becomes more complex, it feels like a sacrifice to entertain thoughts about each other and about what is going on. It isn't easy to allow the soul to enter with its history and its other complexities.

I once worked with a woman who was about to be married. During that time she had a series of disturbing dreams in which her brother kept interfering with her wedding. He was in love with her, and he was determined to destroy this marriage that would end his intimacy with his sister. The woman told me she also had waking images about loving her brother and wishing she could marry both him and her fiancé. What was particularly interesting about the intensity of her feelings was that in life she had no brother. He was a strong, active, interfering figure of her soul. Apparently he was giving her the opportunity to reflect and question. In Jungian terms, he acted as a valuable animus figure, offering criticism and pause. He was also a representative of the soul, reminding her that human love is not as simple as it appears. In his essay on marriage, Jung says that love always involves four persons: the person, the lover, the anima and the animus. But these dreams suggest that many more are involved and may be present on the wedding night.

A general principle we can take from Freud is that love sparks imagination into extraordinary activity. Being "in love" is like being "in imagination." The literal concerns of everyday life, yesterday such a preoccupation, now practically disappear in the rush of love's daydreams. Concrete reality recedes as the imaginal world settles in. Thus, the "divine madness" of love is akin to the mania of paranoia and other dissociations.

Does this mean that we need to be cured of this madness? Robert Burton in his massive self-help book of the seventeenth century, *The Anatomy of Melancholy*, says there is only one cure for the melancholic sickness of love: enter into it with abandon. Some authors today argue that romantic love is such an illusion that we need to distrust it and keep our wits about us so that we are not led astray. But warnings like this betray a distrust of the soul. We may need to be cured by love of our attachment to life without fantasy. Maybe one function of love is to cure us of an anemic imagination, a life emptied of romantic attachment and abandoned to reason.

Love releases us into the realm of divine imagination, where the soul is expanded and reminded of its unearthly cravings and needs. We think that when a lover inflates his loved one he is failing to acknowledge her flaws—"Love is blind." But it may be the other way around. Love allows a person to see the true angelic nature of another person, the halo, the aureole of divinity. Certainly from the perspective of ordinary life this is madness and illusion. But if we let loose our hold on our philosophies and psychologies of enlightenment and reason, we might learn to appreciate the perspective of eternity that enters life as madness, Plato's divine frenzy.

Love brings consciousness closer to the dream state. In that sense, it may reveal more than it distorts, as a dream reveals—poetically, suggestively, and, admittedly, obscurely. If we were to appreciate truly the Platonic theory of love, we might also learn to see other forms of madness, such as paranoia and addiction, as evidence of the soul's reaching toward its proper yearnings. Platonic love is not love without sex. It is love that finds in the body and in human relationship a route toward eternity. In his book on love, *Convivium*—his answer to Plato's *Symposium*—Ficino, who is credited with coining the phrase "Platonic love," says concisely, "The soul is partly in eternity and partly in time." Love straddles these two dimensions, opening a way to live in both simultaneously. But incursions of eternity into life are usually unsettling, for they disturb our plans and shake the tranquillity we have achieved with earthly reason.

# Tristan and Isolde

In order to appreciate the *mystery* of love, we have to give up the idea that love is a psychological problem and that with enough reading and guidance we can finally do it right, without illusion and folly. We do not care for the soul by shrinking it down to reasonable size. Our era's preoccupation with mental hygiene encourages us to think of all forms of mania as disease. But Plato's divine madness is not pathological in our hygienic sense, but more an opening into eternity. It is a relief from the stringent limits of pragmatic, sanitized life. It is a door that opens out from human reason into divine mystery.

The great love stories in our Western tradition help us meditate on the eternal dimensions of love. Many of these stories have such depth of mystery and grandeur of expression that they are considered almost canonically sacred. They are properly bound in red leather, marked with ribbon, and read with some ceremony. Showing the many sides of love, they include the Passion of Jesus ("passion" has rich multiple meanings), the Creation in Genesis, the Homecoming of Odysseus, the Melancholy of Hamlet, and the Star-crossed Fate of Tristan and Isolde.

The last is particularly poignant and relevant

to our theme. It is a story about love's sadness. The lover's name, Tristan, means sad—*triste*. He received his unusual name when he was born, because his father was mortally wounded in battle and his mother died in childbirth. Like many heroes of legend and mythology, he was raised by a second set of parents; in fact, his mother's brother, King Mark, later adopted him as his son, so all told he had three fathers. We can see this multiple parentage as a sign of special fate, a soul exposed in an unusual way to the vagaries of life.

At first Tristan is a son and a typical young man. He is an example of what Jungian psychology calls *puer*. He is charming, daring, and inventive, and he is ever on the edge of pathos and tragedy. He is gifted, yet he is extraordinarily vulnerable. Gottfried von Strassburg, author of one of the classic versions of the story, describes Tristan as talented in music, languages, rituals of the hunt, games, and conversation. Whenever he traveled to new lands, he quickly learned the local language, made up convincing tall stories of his adventures, sang enchanting songs, and won the hearts of the people. The tale of Tristan and Isolde, therefore, is about love entering the tragic side of life from this glowing *puer* place: our boyish spirit, relying on its own naïveté and talent, falls into complicated, entangling, overwhelming love.

A telling leitmotif in the story of Tristan is the image of water. His adventures begin when he is playing chess with visiting Norwegian sailors on a ship in the harbor. They abduct him and sail off with him. A storm rises, and to appease the storm gods they send him off alone in a skiff. He arrives in Ireland and meets the queen and her daughter Isolde. He lies to them about who he really is, changing his name to Tantris. He doesn't want them to know that one of the enemies he once killed was Isolde's uncle. But while he is sitting in a bathtub, Isolde discovers his identity and solves the riddle of his name. The scene is a kind of baptism, a christening of the love of the two young people. Finally, on another occasion, equipped only with his harp, Tristan sails to Ireland in a small boat, without oar or rudder, a scene Joseph Campbell describes as a trusting to fate while armed with the music of the spheres.

Tristan is the epitome of talent and cleverness, whose identity is revealed most clearly when he is adrift or in water, always newly born, eternally young, free of the limitations of pragmatic life. Sometimes when I hear a man or woman tell a dream of floating in a lake or sitting in a bathtub I think of Tristan. He is not a swimmer; he is always contained in a vessel in the water, but he is also always drifting, having no ordinary practical means of control and safety. His technology in the water is aesthetic and spiritual. He is extremely vulnerable as he drifts toward his fate, yet he enjoys the confidence of his own abilities and his aesthetic contact with the laws of life. He is fluid but not wet.

This buoyant frame of mind falls heavily into love. Unknowingly, Tristan and Isolde drink a love potion the queen has made for Tristan's Uncle Mark, and the second half of their story concerns their dangerous attempts to be illicit lovers in a threatening, castigating world. Their love is too strong to be undone by obligation or social propriety, yet it can never be secure and protected. It ends unfulfilled in the tragic death of the lovers. Like an ever-present shadow, sadness accompanies every thrill and success the two young people squeeze from fate.

If we can avoid the temptation to take this story literally and find a moral in it, concluding that illicit love gets its just punishments or that romantic love is immature and doomed to disaster, we can find some hints of how to care for the soul in times of love.

Taking a hygienic approach to the psyche,

we want to live and love successfully. Deviations from these hygienic expectations are characterized as disorders. There is little room for sadness. Today Tristan would have to be called Depresso, because we have clinicalized the soul's sad longings as depression, for which we seek chemical cures. But this medieval tale profoundly satisfies our need to be positively in touch with the unavoidable tendency of the soul to get itself into love trouble. The story honors love's pathos, and, like a homeopathic remedy, it plucks the familiar strains of sadness we know from experience. Its catharsis is achieved not by moralizing against love's range of emotion, but by giving us strong images of the very sadness that completes love's saturation of the soul. It also helps us see the close relationship between our *puer* spirituality and its cure in tragic love.

Care of the soul means respecting its emotions and fantasies, however objectionable. Reading the story of Tristan and Isolde, we are caught in the vise between affirmation of their intense love and repugnance in the face of their deceptions. Georges Bataille, the extraordinary French writer who has long spoken for the dark passages in the soul's journey, says that every love involves a transgression. Soul is to be found in the vicinity of taboo. In stories, movies, biographies, and news accounts we are fascinated by the many illicit conjunctions and tragic deceptions of love.

One of the difficulties in care of the soul is to recognize the necessity of pathos and tragedy. If we view love only from a high moralistic or hygienic peak, we will overlook its soul settling in the valleys. When we reflect on the tragedies of our own loves, when we slowly find our way through their miseries, we are being initiated into the mysterious ways of the soul. Love is the means of entry and our guide. Love keeps us on the labyrinthine path. If we can honor love as it presents itself, taking shapes and directions we would never have predicted or desired, then we are on the way toward discovering the lower levels of soul, where meaning and value reveal themselves slowly and paradoxically. There we become like Tristan, sailing trustingly toward fate, while plucking the strings of our own resources. Tristan is a religious figure, a monk on the spiritual path to love. Consistently he displays his attitude of complete trust. He is always in baptism, always being named, always in touch with the waters of his origination and sustenance. Being so close to himself, he finds the completion of his spirited nature in the impossibilities of love. Wit and impossibility meet continually as his fate unfolds, a pattern that may take form in the loves of any of us.

If we see Tristan as a figure of our sadness in love, and not as a literal representative of its absolute failure, then we have an image that respects love's dark depths as well as its brilliant heights. When love's sadness visits us, that is Tristan floating on his skiff, trusting and yet moving ever closer to the tragic side of life that redeems his light spirit. It isn't necessary to take a pill or search out a therapeutic strategy to dismiss the feeling, because to dismiss that feeling is to banish an important soul visitor. The soul apparently needs amorous sadness. It is a form of consciousness that brings its own unique wisdom.

## Failure, Loss, and Separation

When we read the tale of Tristan and Isolde as myth, we are guided toward reflecting on failure and complexity as part of love, not as something foreign to it. We are also led to a less literal view of separation and loss. The thought of separating enters the minds of many people living a pact of love. But the thought is not the same as literal action. The idea of separation might suggest many things about the love, but the act means only one thing: the destruction of the relationship in its current form.

As we care for the soul, we give its fantasies validity and weight without reducing them all to action. Of course, we have to act sometimes, but perhaps not as often or as quickly. Or our actions might be seen with more imagination than we customarily give them. What does it mean, for instance, when an otherwise perfectly healthy relationship between two people is suddenly invaded by thoughts of separation? Does it mean the end of the relationship, or does it suggest something deeper?

A sensitive, thoughtful, well-meaning woman, Marianne, once came to me with one idea in mind. "I need to separate from my husband," she said with pain on her face, "and I don't know if I can do it."

"What's going on?" I asked.

"He's a wonderful person," she said. "I love him, and I respect him. But I have an overwhelming need to get away from him. We argue a lot, and our sex life has hit rock bottom. We have three children, and he's a great father. But my need to separate is stronger than my concern for my kids."

I noticed that she used the word "separation" over and over. We talked about her thoughts and expectations. She felt devastated by the idea of leaving her marriage, but the need was so strong she knew she couldn't be persuaded out of it. I decided to focus on the precise image her soul was presenting—separation.

Jung talks about separation as an activity of the soul in his studies on medieval alchemy. *Separatio* was an operation the alchemists considered essential to the process of turning ordinary materials into gold. Jung understood the obscure imagery psychologically: to him *separatio* was a breaking into parts of materials in the psyche that needed differentiation. They were perhaps too tightly packed and couldn't be known for what they were individually. Paracelsus understood *separatio* as the primary activity in creation, both in the creation of the world and in every human creative act. These antique notions were in the back of my mind when I listened to Marianne refer to her desire to separate.

The most obvious cause of the need for separation in a marriage like Marianne's is the lack of differentiation of the two individuals. When two people fall in love, come together, and make a household, their deep fantasies sometimes mesh, and then each lives out his or her own myth through the other. In such a situation, it can be difficult to feel one's own individuality. As we talked, it became clear that Marianne had other stories about strong identifications from which she had attempted freeing herself. Her parents, for instance, were overbearing for her and wouldn't let her live her own life. She also had a sister who she felt interfered too much with her life.

She talked about the desire she had had at the beginning of her marriage to create her own family, separate from her parents and be free of their influence. But again and again, through their financial support, her parents found their way into the center of her family. She also seemed unconscious of the extent to which she didn't allow her husband his own individuality, but rather acted toward him the way her parents did toward her. All in all, it appeared to me that she needed many kinds of separation in many parts of her life, and especially, of course, in her way of being with others. As for her own psyche, she seemed to crave a release of her spirit from the imprisonment she had felt for many years.

One day Marianne came to tell me that she had decided to move out. She was going to make the separation real, she said. We had been talking for some time about various levels of meaning in her desire for separation, and she told me she was taking those thoughts with her, but she felt intuitively that she had to do more than talk about it. Her decision made sense to me, too. A deepening of consciousness sometimes requires a strong move in life. Living on her own could be a way of getting to know more precisely what it was her soul was seeking.

She moved out, got a new job, and made new friends. She dated a few men and generally enjoyed her new freedom. She was surprised to discover that her husband adjusted well to the new arrangement, and for the first time in years she began to have some feelings of jealousy. She realized that one of her motives in separating, quite unconscious until then, was to punish her husband or at least show him how deep her anger was.

She tasted life outside the childhood pattern. Her parents, of course, objected strongly to the separation, but for her this was an added benefit. It pleased her to go against their values and approval. She had married young, and for the first time in her life she found out what it was like to be relatively single and independent, and she liked it. She saw and felt herself in new ways.

After three months of *separatio,* she decided to go back to her home and husband. Several years later she is thriving in that home and is no longer plagued with thoughts of leaving her relationship. Other themes, no less challenging but having little to do with marriage, have entered her life. In one sphere, at least, she is a "separated" person.

Marianne's story gives us an example of the

way that caring for the soul's messages can take us to unexpected places. Separation ideas seem to be opposed to love and marriage, but maybe they are a part of it, the underside, which can be accepted with imagination without destroying the love. Even divorce might be seen as one kind of fulfillment of love, the living out of its fullness. Love asks many things of us, including actions that seem to be utterly counter to feelings of attachment and loyalty. Yet these shadow qualities may ultimately bring the love to its proper, if mysterious and unpredictable, home.

## Love's Shadows

Unless we deal with the shadow of love, our experience of it will be incomplete. A sentimental philosophy of love, embracing only the romantic and the positive, fails at the first sign of shadow—thoughts of separation, the loss of faith and hope in the relationship, or unexpected changes in the partners' values. Such a partial view also presents impossible ideals and expectations. If love can't match these ideals, it is destroyed for being inadequate. I like to keep in mind that in the heritage of our literature and art, love is portrayed as a child, often with eyes blindfolded, or as an unruly adolescent. By nature love feels inadequate, but this inadequacy rounds out the wide range of love's emotions. Love finds its soul in its feelings of incompleteness, impossibility, and imperfection.

As a therapist I am only too familiar with the shadows of love. A person comes into therapy with the sincere intention of getting care and cure, then he or she falls in love with the therapist. The very situation—regular meetings, a private room, intimate talk—can be as effective as Isolde's love potion and as intense. The patient feels tormented by the strong emotions that find little if any response in the therapist.

"Why don't you tell me about your life?" a patient will say in despair. "You sit there safe and comfortable, aloof, protected by your professionalism, and I spill my guts. I make myself vulnerable and love you. But you don't love me. I'm one in a string of lovers. You must be a voyeur."

We easily fall into fantasies of love with certain people, especially those in certain professions: teachers, managers, nurses, and secretaries. To the soul this love is real, but in the context of life it doesn't have much relevance. Love is elicited in therapy, in medicine, and in education by the caring conversation, the intimate confessions, and by the listening alone. Listening to another and caring for their welfare can be such a comforting experience that the magic aureole of love descends when no one is looking.

The Greeks told a strange story of dark love. Admetus was a distinguished man who had been granted a special favor by Apollo because he had helped the god in a time of trouble. As a reward, he was given a way to sidestep death. When death came to take him to the underworld, Admetus was allowed to find someone willing to take his place and die for him. He asked his mother and father, both of whom had lived long happy lives, to die in his place. But they refused, offering reasonable excuses. His wife, Alkestis, however, agreed and went off with Death. By coincidence, at this time the hero Herakles happened to be visiting, and when he heard the story he went after Death and wrestled with him. Then a veiled woman appeared from the Underworld, who seemed to be Alkestis rescued by Herakles.

This story, as I read it, tells one of the profound, inexplicable mysteries of love. Love always has a close relation to death. Traditionally the story has been read as the wife's role of giving up her life for her husband. But that interpretation, taken literally, leads to misogyny and superficial submission. I think of the death of Alkestis more like the death of Narcissus in his pool. Love takes us out of life and away from the plans we have made for our lives. Alkestis is an image of the feminine face of the soul whose destiny is to move out of life toward depth, which is imagined as death and underworld. To give oneself over to love and marriage is to say yes to death. Submission entails a loss in life, but there is also a gain for the soul. As the Greeks taught, the psyche is at home in the underworld. Love may seem to offer some benefits for the ego and for life, but soul is fed by love's intimacy with death. The loss of will and control one feels in love may be highly nutritious for the soul.

Still, the deathly side of love is not easy. It offends our upper-world values and expectations, and it contradicts the need to be in charge. We can all be like Admetus' parents when death appears, and find excellent excuses for declining the invitation. After all, I have plans and a comfortable life-style, why should I give into this love that will change it all for good? We can also become heroic and, like Herakles, wrestle what we want from the clutches of death. There may be an Alkestis in my heart willing to submit to the demands of love, but there may also be a Herakles who becomes furious at the idea and fights death with muscle.

Besides, the story is ambivalent and mysterious in its ending. Is this Alkestis returning from down below? Why does she have a veil over her face? Could it be that when we forcefully bring back to life what has been lost through love what we get is only a shade of its former reality? Maybe we can never succeed fully in restoring the soul to life. Maybe she will always be veiled and at least partially shielded from the rigors of actual life. Love demands a submission that is total.

In our therapeutic attempts to make life successful we act like Herakles, rescuing the soul from death. We save a person from depression by getting him involved in life in an active way—exactly what Herakles wants. But then we are faced with a veiled soul, someone who is adapted but also camouflaged, suffering distortion in his soul. Or, when we help a person back into life by means of drugs, what we often see is a person back among the living but with the face of a zombie, not unlike the woman Herakles restores to life. The alternative to this heroic struggle on behalf of life is to find something Alkestislike in us that is willing to go under, to *undergo* whatever fate is asking of the soul.

We think we know what love is about, both theoretically and in an episode in life. But love leans toward the mysterious dark niches of the soul's underworld. Its fulfillment is death—more an ending of what life has been up to this point than the beginning of what we expect to happen. Love takes us to the edge of what we know and have experienced, and thus we are all Alkestis whenever we assent to love and willingly accompany him in the guise of death.

## Communal Love

One of the strongest needs of the soul is for community, but community from the soul point of view is a little different from its social forms. Soul yearns for attachment, for variety in personality, for intimacy and particularity. So it is these qualities in community that the soul seeks out, and not like-mindedness and uniformity.

There are many signs in our society that we lack a sufficiently deep experience of community. There is the energetic search for a community, as people try one church after another, hoping to have their unnamable hunger for community satisfied. They bemoan the breakdown of family and neighborhoods, longing for a past golden age when intimacy could be found at home or on the city block. Loneliness is a major complaint and is responsible for deep-seated emotional pain that leads to despair and a consideration of suicide.

I knew a woman who was gregarious, a good conversationalist, and interested in many things. She was always doing things and going places, but at night, when she could no longer distract herself, the demon of her loneliness appeared, and she couldn't sleep. She was the vice-president of a large corporation, and still she suffered her loneliness at home so intensely that she began having thoughts of suicide.

She always talked about how wonderful people were and how much she enjoyed being surrounded by friends, but it seemed to me that she was insisting too much on this point, as though she only wished it were so. One day she told me a story about visiting an old friend. At the end of their conversation the friend tried to embrace her, but she drew back. It wasn't appropriate, she thought, for this woman to show affection publicly. She wondered if her friend was bisexual and was making a pass.

The story made me think that this woman's loneliness had nothing to do with the number of people in her life and everything to do with a kind of moralistic self-protection. Later she told me another story. She was at a party on a beach with a large group of people. As usual, she was making herself useful, preparing the food and taking people's plates. When the group began involving everyone in songs and skits, she drifted to the back and into the darkness, but someone spotted her and dragged her to the center. She knew she could make an excuse and get away, but something in her let loose and she began to sing a simple song she knew from her childhood. She had never done anything like this before, and she was embarassed, but the group loved it. Afterward she felt she had had a breakthrough in her loneliness. She had come down from her moralism and her ideals of community into a genuine and unprotected experience of it.

The Renaissance humanist Erasmus says in his book *In Praise of Folly* that people are joined in friendship through their foolishness. Community cannot be sustained at too high a level. It thrives in the valleys of soul rather than in the heights of spirit. Bill, a priest we will return to in a later chapter, told me many times about his religious order, where community was discussed as an ideal in books on the religious life and by retreat masters. Yet when Bill looked back on his life as a priest he could think of very few colleagues who had been real friends, and he had always felt lonely in the midst of community life. There was little opportunity for intimacy, he said. You were expected to talk about religion, or perhaps sports, but never about yourself. Bill said that in the midst of his personal struggles, especially when he was suffering the torments of scrupulosity, he would sit among his fellow priests and the only thing he would hear, every day, was, "What about those Yankees!" If you couldn't join in this sports talk, you couldn't be part of the "community."

Loneliness can be the result of an attitude that community is something into which one is received. Many people wait for members of a community to invite them in, and until that happens they are lonely. There may be something of the child here who expects to be taken care of by the family. But a community is not a family. It is a group of people held together by feelings of belonging, and those feelings are not a birthright. "Belonging" is an active verb, something we do positively. In one of his letters Ficino makes the remark "The one guardian of life is love, but to be loved you must love." A person oppressed by loneliness can go out into the world and simply start belonging to it, not by joining organizations, but by living through feelings of relatedness—to other people, to nature, to society, to the world as a whole. Relatedness is a signal of soul. By allowing the sometimes vulnerable feelings of relatedness, soul pours into life and doesn't have to insist on itself symptomatically.

Like all activities of the soul, community has its connection to death and the underworld. Christianity talks about the "community of saints," meaning all people present and past to whom we are related by reason of the human community. From the point of view of the soul, the dead are as much a part of community as the living. In a similar spirit Jung makes a mysterious comment in the prologue to his memoirs: "Other people are established inalienably in my memories only if their names were entered in the scrolls of my destiny from the beginning, so that encountering them was at the same time a kind of recollection." Outward community flourishes when we are in touch with the inner persons who crowd our dreams and waking thoughts. To overcome loneliness, we might consider releasing these inner figures into life, like the one who wants to sing or cuss in anger or is more sensual or more critical or even more needy than "I" would like to admit. To "admit" who I am is to "admit" those people into life, so that the inner community serves as a start for a sense of belonging in life. I "remember" people I met for the first time because I am in touch with the archetypal world of my imagination, and on the basis of that self-knowledge I can love anyone I meet and be loved in return. The roots of community are immeasurably deep, and the process of belonging, dealing actively with loneliness, begins in the depth of the soul.

Love keeps the soul on the track of its fate and keeps consciousness at the edge of the abyss of the infinity that is the range of the soul. This doesn't mean that relationships between people are not important to the soul's loves. Quite the opposite: recognizing the importance of love to the soul, our ordinary human loves are ennobled beyond measure. This family, this friend, this lover, this mate is the manifestation of the motivating force of life itself and is the fountain of love that keeps the soul alive and full. There is no way toward divine love except through the discovery of human intimacy and community. One feeds the other.

Care of the soul, then, requires an openness to love's many forms. It is no accident that so many of the troubles we bring to therapy have their roots or manifestations in love. It may help us, in those times of trouble, to remember that love is not only about relationship, it is also an affair of the soul. Disappointments in love, even betrayals and losses, serve the soul at the very moment they seem in life to be tragedies. The soul is partly in time and partly in eternity. We might remember the part that resides in eternity when we feel despair over the part that is in life.

CHAPTER 5

# *Jealousy and Envy: Healing Poisons*

Even though care of the soul is not about changing, fixing, adjusting, and making better, still we have to find a way to live with our disturbing feelings, such as jealousy and envy. These emotions can be so sickening and corrosive that we don't want to leave them raw, wallowing in them for years and getting nowhere with them. But what can we do short of trying to get rid of them? A clue is to be found in the very distaste we feel for them: anything so difficult to accept must have a special kind of shadow in it, a germ of creativity shrouded in a veil of repulsion. As we have so often found, in matters of the soul the most unworthy pieces turn out to be the most creative. The stone the builders reject becomes the cornerstone.

Both envy and jealousy are common experiences. They are entirely different feelings, one a desire for what another person has, the other fear that the other person will take what we have, but they both have a corrosive effect on the heart. Either emotion can make a person feel ugly. There is nothing noble in either of them. At the same time, a person may feel oddly attached to them. The jealous person takes some pleasure in his suspicions, and the envious person feeds on his desire for what others possess.

Mythology suggests that both envy and jealousy are rooted deeply in the soul. Even the gods become jealous. Euripides' *Hippolytus,* for instance, is based on the myth of a young man who is exclusively devoted to the pure goddess, Artemis. Aphrodite is bitterly upset about his single-mindedness and his disdain for the part of life she tends, chiefly love and sex. Enraged and jealous, Aphrodite causes Hippolytus' stepmother, Phaedra, to fall in love with him. Naturally, all kinds of complications and mayhem ensue: in the end, Hippolytus is trampled to death by his horses, panicked by a giant, bull-shaped wave created in the sea by Aphrodite. This form of demise has a certain poetic justice, since Hippolytus had been more devoted to his horses, animals that reflect his nervous energy and spirit, than to people, especially women.

In Greek tragedy the gods and goddesses address us directly. At the opening of Euripides' play about Hippolytus, Aphrodite confesses, "I stir up trouble for any who ignore me, or belittle me, and who do it out of stubborn pride." Here we find a Freudian observation from the fifth century B.C.—repress sexuality and you are in for trouble. We learn from the goddess's mouth that the deepest point in our sexuality can be disturbed when we—our consciousness and intentionality—do not give it the response it requires. (Artemis, too, has her own feelings of jealousy. Near the end of the play she declares, with reference to Aphrodite, "I will choose some great favorite of hers and drop him with the bend of my bow.")

*Hippolytus* presents a typical format for jealousy—a triangle, in this case two goddesses and a mortal. It hints that although ordinary life is the focus of jealous emotions, great mythic themes are also implicated. We tend to think of jealousy as an emotion we can control with understanding and will, and we try to do our best with it. But in spite of our efforts, the human soul proves to be an arena in which great struggles, far deeper than rational understanding can reach, play themselves out. Jealousy feels so overwhelming because it is more than a surface phenomenon. Whenever it appears, issues and values are being sorted out deep in the soul, and all we can do is try not to identify with the emotions and simply let the struggle work itself out.

## Jealousy

If the sacred arts of tragedy and mythology tell us that the gods are jealous, then we can imagine that there is a necessity to this emotion's fitting into the divine scheme of things. Jealousy is not simply insecurity or emotional instability. If the gods are jealous, then our experience of jealousy is archetypal, not completely explained by relationship or personality or family background. The tension we feel in jealousy may be that of much greater worlds colliding than can be seen by looking only at our personal situations. A first step toward finding the soul in jealousy is to think mythologically, to consider what great context there may be for the intense emotions and profound restructuring that we feel in these times.

The story of Hippolytus gives us a hint about

the purpose of jealousy. Here was a man who routinely and consciously neglected a goddess whose task it is to foster an extremely important dimension of human life—love, sex, beauty, and the body. It's all right, the goddess declares, to be devoted to Artemistic purity and self-sufficiency, but desire for another is also valid and important. Aphrodite's jealous anger and the young man's undoing arise because he neglects her necessity. His monotheistic focus on one divine mystery—moral purity and gender exclusiveness—abuses another. Hippolytus' offense is to deny the polytheistic requirements of the soul.

Thinking mythologically, we might imagine our own pain, paranoid suspicions, and jealous rages as the complaint of a god who is receiving insufficient attention. We may be like Hippolytus, sincerely and honestly devoted to principles that we consider absolute, while, unknown to us, other different, seemingly incompatible demands are also coming our way. Hippolytus' haughty purity and vitriolic hatred of women can be seen as his refusal to open himself to a world *other* than that which he has come to love and admire. In the end he is destroyed by the very animals who represent his self-sufficient spirit. His high-minded monotheism kills him. He is too pure, too simple, too resistant to the tensions that exist from the complex demands that life places on the heart.

When jealousy stirs, often a complicated, subtle person is revealed to be also a purist and moralist. Jealousy is demanding surrender to a new claim on the soul, while in defense the individual has taken refuge in moralism. Still, we have to keep in mind that jealousy is an archetypal tension, a collision of two valid needs—in the case of Hippolytus, the need for purity and the need for intermingling, Artemis and Aphrodite. We don't want to turn against Artemis in our efforts to rid ourselves of jealousy or outwit it. The idea is more to create enough space and summon enough holding power to let these two divinities work out some arrangement for coexistence. That is the point in polytheism, and one of the primary ways to go about caring for the soul.

The name Hippolytus means "horse-loosed." A person caught in this myth is someone whose horses, animals of spirit, are not contained. They have leapt the fences of the corral. They are beautiful but dangerous. You sometimes see this Hippolytus horse-spirit in people, not always literally young, who are fervently devoted to a cult or cause. Their motives and the objects of their devotion are noble and spotless, and their commitment may be inspiring. But their very single-mindedness may reveal something darker—a blindness to other values and sometimes even a sadistic element, a too readily justified show of muscle.

But jealousy, like all emotions tinted with shadow, can be a blessing in disguise, a poison that heals. Euripides' play can be seen as a story about curing Artemistic pride. Hippolytus, rigid and closed, is torn apart; that is, his spiritual neurosis is healed by becoming unraveled. The end appears tragic, but tragedy, even in everyday life, can be a form of valuable restructuring. It is painful and in some ways destructive, but it also puts things in a new order. The only way *out of* jealousy is *through* it. We may have to let jealousy have its way with us and do its job of reorienting fundamental values. Its pain comes, at least in part, from opening up to unexplored territory and letting go of old familiar truths in the face of unknown and threatening new possibilities.

I once worked with a young man who was much like Hippolytus, except that instead of a horse he rode a bicycle. He worked in a fast-food restaurant and was in love with one of his coworkers. He pined for her and, although they did go out on dates now and then, often felt rebuked. When he talked about her, he would begin with loving, indeed adoring, language, but soon he would switch to criticism. He complained about her coldness and her preoccupation with herself. (It's not unusual for a jealous person to feel so altruistic and reasonable about his own life, so clean of the vice of selfishness, that he finds the loved one self-serving.) One day this young man came to say that he had lost control. He had screamed at his girlfriend without mercy and felt he could have hit her if his passion had gone any further.

We were both concerned about the intensity of his rage. One reason a person steeped in a self-image of purity can easily become violent is precisely because he is so blind to that potential within himself. Nevertheless, I didn't want to take a stand against his soul, which at the moment was seething with jealous fantasies. He, however, spoke against his feelings and thoughts: "How can I do these things and feel this way?" he said over and over.

I felt his protestations were simply keeping him innocent. He insisted that he was not someone capable of jealousy and that he had never experienced anything like it before, yet his actions were getting more and more threatening. I wanted to know more about his jealousy. The temptation in the midst of such strong feelings is to think that they are pure emotion. We overlook their content—the ideas, memories, and fantasies that swim in the sea of emotion. I wanted to know, among other things, just who in this person was jealous. Instructed by Euripides, I wondered if there was some altar that he, like Hippolytus, was scorning.

It is not enough to personalize jealousy and speak only of *my* insecurity. To reduce jealousy to an ego fault is to overlook its complexity and also to avoid the deeper soul where jealousy is lodged. If we were to give jealousy an open hearing, we might find out something about its history in our life and maybe in our family, the circumstances that have called it forth at this time, and the myth now in progress. These things are never obvious, and so we tend to focus on the obvious emotions and their superficial interpretations. I wanted to go deeper and see the characters and themes at work in the summary statement "I feel jealous." It's as though in care of the soul we have to write our own tragic drama in order fully to know which myth we are in. This is one way to find imagination in emotion, and soul can be uncovered only through imagination.

"I think she is seeing someone else," he told me the day after he screamed at her.

"What makes you say that?" I asked.

"She wasn't home when I called her, and she said she would be."

"Were you checking up on her?"

"Yes, I can't help it," he said, and tears came into his eyes.

"What do you know about yourself that in your jealousy you are not admitting?"

"I guess that I'm not trustworthy. I'm usually not very faithful in a relationship."

"What would happen if she knew this about you?"

"She'd be free to do whatever she wants."

"You don't want her to be free."

"Of course, in my head I want her to be free. I believe in freedom. I hate smothering relationships. But in my gut I can't let her have an inch of freedom."

"So, your jealousy makes you less tolerant."

"Yes. I can't believe this. It goes against all my values."

"What if you tried to learn something from your jealousy, like some value in being less open? Maybe you need to be less tolerant in life in general."

"There's value in not being open, in being intolerant?"

"I can imagine it," I said. "It looks to me that this very active and influential child in your soul wants complete openness and freedom. That leaves a sense of order and limit in the garbage can of repression, where it stirs and becomes wild and unreasonable, and potentially violent. You keep telling me that it's not like you to be so demanding. Could it be that your capacity to make demands is completely cut off from you and so acts out on its own?"

"I believe in freedom," he said proudly. "It's necessary in a relationship for people to give each other plenty of room."

"Maybe it's time to reevaluate your beliefs. Your rage and suspicions call for some kind of adjustment and reflection. Your jealousy, with or without your conscious consent, is setting limits in your life."

"I become a policeman. That's not like me. And she, she's the criminal. I feel justified punishing her for it."

Jealousy draws out a strange cast of characters—the moralist, the detective, the paranoid, the archconservative. The word *paranoia* is usually taken etymologically to mean knowledge (*noia*) that is "alongside" (*para*)—to be beside oneself, mad. But I prefer to think of it as knowledge that lies outside yourself. These soul figures who pretend to know so much— the moralist and the rest—want to find out what is going on. They assume that something threatening and dangerous is afoot. They are hard on the trail of facts, but they behave as if they don't know any details. If my young man did not identify so strongly with the innocent child, he would know what was going on. His innocence is a manipulation and a blinder. He in fact does know, but by identifying with the innocent one he doesn't have to act from that knowledge.

Paranoid knowing satisfies the masochist who takes delight in being hurt. It is typical in many kinds of masochism to assume the role of innocent child. This may be an apotropaic act. *Apotropaic* refers to magical and ritual ways of warding off evil. By playing the role of innocent, the young man didn't have to enter the complicated world of relationship. He could hide his own loose ways and blame his girlfriend for hers. If he were to approach her as a complicated adult, he would have had to face possible rejection from her, for her own reasons, or have had to deal with the complexity of her nature. Instead, he could retreat into the place of the child where, in an odd paradox, his protection is secured by his being hurt.

The young man's feelings of violence show how split off he is from the power of his knowledge. Blinded by a cloud of innocence, he seems not to know his friend or himself or the complexity of relationships in general. He pleads for simple attention and care. When he doesn't get these things, he feels controlled and toyed with. Then, in place of a more genuine power, violent rage pours out of him.

Paradoxically, if he were to allow his jealousy to work from within like a detective, on behalf of his soul, instead of as a free-wheeling paranoid complex, he would discover many things about himself and about love. If he could let the moralist settle more deeply in his soul, he might find a flexible ethical sensibility that had a place for both tolerance and demand. The paranoid element in his jealousy both keeps the possibility of deeper knowledge within reach but also dissociates itself from will and intentionality. It remains unrealistic and twisted, and yet it is the raw material for wisdom. This symptom is terribly important, but it needs "education"—to be drawn out and studied. It has to become much more sophisticated and be brought to levels beyond violence and empty suspicion.

Over the course of several months of discussion, the raw emotions of jealousy gave rise to many stories, memories, and ideas. We were not looking for a vital clue that would explain it and dispel it. Quite the contrary, these stories gave body to the jealousy, so that it could be more richly present. The idea was to let it reveal itself, to allow it to become more rather than less, and thus lose some of its compulsion. The obsessive side of jealousy seems in part to be a function of its hiddenness, arising when it is not being revealed and given place.

When jealous feelings and images penetrate the heart and mind, a kind of initiation takes place. The jealous person discovers new ways of thinking and a fresh appreciation for the complicated demands of love. It is a baptism by fire into a new religion of the soul. In this sense, as Euripides' drama shows with much art, jealousy serves the soul's polytheism. Its rigid moralism comes right out where it can be seen for what it is and therefore can be tempered in the name of flexibility and exploration of values.

My modern Hippolytus didn't want to grow up and be part of a heterogeneous society. In Euripides, the young man spends his time with his adolescent companions and with his horses. Women are a threat and a contamination—"otherness" personified in an entire gender. My Bicycle Man was exquisitely *puer*—boyishly pure in his own thoughts, but harsh in his behavior. He had the odd numinous quality one finds wherever opposites approach each other. He was pure and brutal, high-minded in his values and ugly in his hatred of woman. His idealist values were so spotless that he didn't see his own shadow of haughtiness and misogyny. Purity had triumphed over his soul, and therefore his soul was profoundly disturbed.

## Hera: Goddess of Jealousy

Aphrodite and Artemis are not the only images of jealousy we find in mythology. All the gods and goddesses are capable of violent rages, but foremost in jealousy is Hera, wife of Zeus. She is always ready to burst into a jealous fit over her husband, an archphilanderer. Throughout history Zeus has been criticized as a great god who is also an unfaithful lover. But mythology, even though it is couched in the imagery of mortal life, is not a literal portrait of human qualities and foibles. We always have to look deep into a myth to discern its necessity and mystery. If we look with a poetic eye, we can see that it makes sense for the governor of the universe to want an erotic attachment with everything in the world.

But what would it be like to be wife to this unbounded desire? In human terms it might be like being the mistress of an insanely inspired artist or a politician graced with the charisma that makes him or her a world leader. How can anyone be wife to a desire of cosmic proportions without always feeling threatened?

It's curious that in Greek mythology the wife of the greatest of the gods is known primarily for her jealousy. She isn't the queen who cares for the suffering of her subjects. She isn't absolute beauty fulfilling absolute power. She is a fitful, outrageously infuriated, betrayed, and violated wife. Hera's rage is as much the color of her jealousy as lust is the tone of Zeus's world governance. It is as though jealousy were as important to the maintenance of life and culture as Zeus's counsel and political power. Mythologically, jealousy is coupled with the forces of governance in life and culture.

Zeus, who settles the fundamental disputes of existence and serves as the original "godfather," lusts after every particular in the world he governs. While his desire goes out to the world, Hera's rage speaks for the home, for family and marriage. Their tension is the yin and yang of home and world, of "us" and "other." He is the extrovert, she the introvert. Erotic creativity is the making of a world, jealousy is the preservation of the hearth and interiority. If we did not become jealous, too many events would take place, too much life would be lived, too many connections made without deepening. Jealousy serves the soul by pressing for limits and reflection.

One of the stumbling blocks for a monotheist approaching a polytheistic religion is the validation one finds everywhere in polytheism of unlikely experiences. In the religion of Hera, one of the great virtues is possessiveness. From her point of view, it is not only all right, it is required that one be outraged at infidelity. My violently jealous young man had not yet discovered the virtue of possessiveness. He felt it as outside himself and foreign to his values, and so his possessiveness was compulsive and overwhelming, hitting him unawares. His desperate desire for fidelity on the part of his girlfriend was compensation for a sense of union that was not terribly deep. He played at intimacy and togetherness, but when these feelings actually came upon him, they felt alien. He didn't know what to do with them.

In a culture that prizes individual freedom and choice, the desire to possess is a piece of shadow, but it is also a real desire. Jealousy is fulfilled in true connection with another person. But this connection makes severe demands. It asks us to love attachment and dependence, to risk the unbearable pain of separation, and to find fulfillment in partnership with another—a traditional attribute of Hera.

At the same time, we must remember that in spite of her possessiveness, Hera is drawn to the god of erotic liberation. She embodies half the dialectic of the attachment and dispersion of desire. She comes into play in the tension between having and not having another. To live this tension is one way of bringing different aspects of ourselves together, the vision that knows we are all individuals and ultimately alone in this life, and the utter dependence we all have upon one another. When some part of us longs for more experience, new people, and starting over, jealousy remembers attachment and feels the unending pain of separations and divorces.

## The Archetypal Wife

In a culture in which women are oppressed and all things feminine are undervalued, "wife" is not as honorable a title as it might be. When this *anima* image has no place in the psyche of men, then wifehood becomes literal dependency, and the woman is given all responsibility for home and children. Men are free of the restraints of home life, but they also suffer a loss, because care of home and family gives back vast amounts of feeling and imagination to the soul. Typically men prefer the adventurous path of business, trade, or career. Of course, the career woman also loses *anima* if she devotes herself to the myth of culture building. Both men and women can look down on the image of wife and be glad to be liberated from her inferiority. In this context, the mythological image of Hera reminds us of the honor due to the wife. Her mythic figure suggests that "wife" is a profound face of the soul.

In Hera, a person is most an individual when he or she is defined in relation to another, even though this idea seems to go against all our modern notions of the value of independence and separateness. In our time it doesn't seem right to find identity in relationship to another. Yet this is the mystery of Hera. She is dependency given dignity and even divinity. In ancient times she was given great honor and was worshiped with deep affection and reverence. When people complain that whenever they get into a relationship they become too dependent, we might see this symptom as a lack of Hera sensibility, and the tonic might be to cultivate an appreciation for deeper union in love and attachment.

It takes special skill and sensitivity for a man or woman to evoke the wife within a relationship. Usually we reduce the archetypal reality to a social role. A woman slips into the role of wife, and the man treats her as being in that role. But there is a vast difference between archetype and role. There are ways that Hera can be drawn into the relationship so that being an attentive and serving partner is vitally present in both people. Or Hera might be evoked as the atmosphere of mutual dependency and identity as a couple. In the spirit of Hera, the couple protects the relationship and values signals of their dependency. For Hera, you make a phone call when you're on a trip or out of town. For Hera, you include your partner in visions of the future.

Feelings of jealousy may well be attached to this dependent element in the partnership. Jealousy is part of the archetype. Hera is loving and jealous. But when the value of true companionship is not taken to heart, Hera leaves the scene, and the relationship is reduced to mere togetherness. Then the individuals split themselves into the independent one who stands for freedom and the "codependent" one, tormented by jealousy. If in a marriage one of the partners is clearly the wife— and it's not always the woman—then Hera is not being honored. If you are faced with symptoms of a troubled marriage, look for her distress.

The marriage that Hera honors so fervently is not only the concrete relationship of man and woman, it is any kind of connection, emotional or cosmic. As Jung says, marriage is always an affair of the soul. Hera may also protect the union of distinct elements within a person or in a society.

People often dream about wives and husbands. If we do not view these dreams as having to do only with actual marriage, then we might be guided by them to contemplate more subtle unions. For example, a man dreams he is in a bar with a woman he finds attractive. She kisses him and he enjoys it, but he keeps looking behind him to see if his wife is looking. In life, this man is happily married, although occasionally he is disturbed when he finds himself attracted to other women. He also dreams once in a while about alcohol. Usually in these dreams he encounters someone who is drunk, and he is repulsed. This man is very straitlaced and formal, and so it isn't surprising to see his dreams opening out into different directions. His awareness of his "wife"—all that he is wedded to—is strong and serves him well. If he followed through on all his attractions, his marriage might be over and his life would certainly be in pieces. On the other hand, the Dionysian and Aphroditic needs of his soul, expressed in the alcohol and sex of his dreams, also claim some attention. This is in fact the major tension of his life at this time: a well-practiced Hera loyalty to his actual wife and to his value system is being challenged by an invitation to experiment and to explore in a more passionate direction.

A woman tells a dream in which her husband and three children are all having a picnic on a green hillside with three unknown red-haired women. The women, she knows somehow in the dream, are her husband's lovers. They also show some erotic attention to the children. The dreamer is watching from a window in their home and is feeling a mixture of pleasure in seeing her family happy and jealousy in relation to the three women.

Again we see the dialectic that is so typical of Hera. The dreamer is enjoying her role as wife and mother in the dream, but she also feels Hera's jealousy at the proximity and erotic tone of the three women. The image of three women is common in dreams and in art—the three graces or the three fates, past, present, and future. Maybe some new fateful, flaming (red) passion—not necessarily a person—is entering the dreamer's soul, giving rise to the familiar tension between new passion and old cherished life structures. At this point the dreamer is in an observer's role, sitting like Hera in her home, watching this new dynamic from a distance.

Our wedded loves are not always human. The poet Wendell Berry makes an interesting confession in one of his books. He says that sometimes when he travels he falls in love with a place and has strong fantasies about moving there, just as a person might entertain erotic thoughts about being with a new spouse. But Berry then speaks from Hera, recommending faithfulness to home. We shouldn't be taken in by these enticements from outside, he advises. Dreams on this theme seem to be less certain about what we *should* do when presented with this tension. They simply present the setting and the feeling of jealousy that maintains the loyalty to home. The tension is between attachment to what is and the promise of a new passion. In order to care for the soul, we may have no choice but to open our hearts wide enough to contain that tension and polytheistically give both needs a hearing.

One more word about Hera: Karl Kerényi, the historian who was a friend of Jung and who developed his own archetypal approach to mythology, makes an intriguing comment in his book, *Zeus and Hera*. Hera was fulfilled, he tells us, in lovemaking. (That word *fulfilled*, by the way, is a special Hera word; other Greek words used as attributes of Hera are related to the word *telos*, which means end or purpose.) Kerényi is saying, then, that it is essential in Hera to find her purpose and fulfillment in sex. It may seem obvious that sex is part of being a wife, but I want to accent the idea that this particular side of sex, the fulfillment of intimacy and companionship, has its divinity. Hera was honored as Zeus's lover. The "Homeric Hymn to Hera" tells us that she and Zeus enjoyed a three-hundred-year honeymoon. Furthermore, Kerényi mentions that Hera renewed her virginity each year in the spring Kanathos, an actual spring where the cult statue of Hera was dipped in an annual ritual, and so she presented herself to Zeus as a girl and was then fulfilled in her sexuality.

In Jungian language, we could say that Hera is part of the *anima* of sex. In the marriage bed, partners can encounter each other as if for the first time, thus enjoying this Hera imagination of renewable virginity. If a relationship honors Hera, it is blessed with the pleasures of experiencing the fulfillment of the sexual bond between the people. The problem is, Hera cannot be evoked without her full nature, including her jealousy and her wifehood, which may at times be accompanied by feelings of inferiority and dependence. To find soul in relationship and in sex, it may be necessary to appreciate the inferior feelings that are part of the "wife" archetype.

The God who brings the disease, it is said, is the one who heals it. This is the "wounding healer" or the "healing wounder." If the disease is jealousy, then the healer could be Hera, who knows jealousy better than anyone. Therefore, we are back where we began. If we want to cure our jealousy, we may have to enter into it homeopathically. Those very qualities that are so pronounced in jealousy—dependency, identity through another, the longing to protect the union—may have to be taken even closer to heart so that Hera can be honored. If jealousy is compulsive and overwhelming, then maybe Hera is complaining of neglect and the fact that the relationship does not have the soulfulness that only she can bring to it. Strangely, perhaps jealousy itself contains the seeds of the fulfillment of both sex and intimacy.

*Envy*

Similar to jealousy in the way it jabs at the heart is envy, one of the seven

deadly sins and clearly serious shadow material. Once again we ask a difficult question:
How do you care for the soul when it is presenting itself in the green ooze of envy? Can
we give this deadly sin an open-minded hearing? Can we perceive what the soul wants
when it wrenches us with longing for what another person has?

Envy can be consuming. It can crowd out
every other thought and emotion with its pun-
gency. It can make a person distracted,
"touched," as we say, aching for the life, position, and possessions of others. My neighbors
have happiness, money, success, children—
why don't I? My friend has a good job, looks,
luck—what's wrong with me? There may be a
good dose of self-pity in envy, but it's the longing that is so bitter.

Although envy may appear to be filled with
ego, it is not fundamentally an ego problem.
Envy eats away at the heart. If anything, the
ego is the object of envy's corrosive power.
No, it is not an excess of ego, it is an activity of
the soul, a painful process in the soul's alchemy. The ego problem is how to respond to
envy, how to react to the sickening wishes it
inspires. In the face of envy, our task—which
should not surprise us by now—is to find out
what it wants.

Compulsions are always made up of two

parts, and envy is no exception. On the one hand, envy is a desire for something, and on the other, it is a resistance to what the heart actually wants. In envy, desire and self-denial work together to create a characteristic sense of frustration and obsessiveness. Although envy feels masochistic—the envious person thinks he's the victim of bad fortune—it also involves strong willfulness in the form of resistance to fate and character. In the thick of envy, one is blind to one's own nature.

Of course, wherever there is obvious masochism, sadism hides nearby. The sadist in envy fights fervently against the deal fate has handed him. He feels deprived and cheated. Because he is so out of touch with the potential value of his own fate, he has elaborate fantasies of others being blessed with good fortune.

The point in caring for the envious soul is not to get rid of the envy, but to be guided back by it into one's own fate. The pain in envy is like pain in the body: it makes us stop and take notice of something that has gone wrong and needs attention. What has gone wrong is that our close-up vision has been blurred. Envy is hyperopia of the soul, an inability to see what is closest to us. We fail to see the necessity and value in our own lives.

I once knew a woman who suffered for years from excruciating, exquisite, unrelenting envy. She worked hard all day at her factory job, trying to make her life better, and then she hid out at night in her house. She couldn't bear to behold what full lives people around her were living. She felt unconsolably lonely and utterly miserable. Over and over she described her friends' happiness in great detail. She knew everything good that happened to them. Whenever word came of some new success or boon to any of her friends, she went into shock, another nail pounded into the chest of envious thoughts she carried with her at all times. Her friends had money, good families, fulfilling work, companionship, and great sex. Listening to her you got the impression that the entire world was blissfully happy, while she alone bore the burden of loneliness and poverty.

The hidden side of masochism is willful tyranny. The misery of this woman's envy veiled her rigidity. Those very friends whom she envied she also judged without mercy. In her own family, she hovered over her two sons, who were in their thirties, and tried to control their every move. She appeared to be selfless in giving her whole life to their welfare and in depriving herself, but she also took pleasure in being in charge of someone else's life. Her envy mirrored her preoccupation with the lives of others and the neglect of her own.

When she came to me for help with her envy, I thought I might invite it in and hear what it had to say. She, of course, claimed she wanted me to find a clever way out of it. But envy is like jealousy in that the person is actually attached to it and would like everyone else to be drawn into it. A person talking about envy is like a religious missionary trying to win converts. Behind the stories of envy is the message: Aren't you as outraged as I am? But, I didn't want to get caught in her sense of outrage. I wanted to know what the envy was doing there and what it had in mind.

It was true that this woman had been brought up in a family that didn't have much money and didn't provide very well for themselves and their children. And yes, her strict religious upbringing had left her with many inhibitions about sex and money and had left her with fixed ideas about sacrificing herself for others. She had two difficult and painful marriages and divorces. But these facts were not enough to account for her overwhelming envy. On the contrary, by reciting this list of plagues at every opportunity, she was rationalizing her state. These convincing arguments were part of her complex. They kept her envy oiled and well polished.

Ironically, this woman's angry explanations for her misfortune distracted her from feeling the pain of her past. Symptoms are often obviously painful, but at the same time they may protect against a deeper pain associated with awareness and facing the fundamental realities of fate. It was as though her envy sucked all that pain into itself and in an odd way kept her from owning her past.

We began our work by slowly going through her many, many stories of deprivation. I watched for ways in which she subtly distanced herself from pain and awareness. For example, she would make excuses for her family. "They didn't know any better. They did their best. Their intentions were good." I tried to go beyond these rationalizations so we could both feel the sadness and emptiness that had been in her past and to acknowledge the limitations and failures on the part of her parents.

In the presence of envy's misery, it is tempting to become a cheerleader. "You can do it. You can have whatever you want. You're as good as anyone else." But that approach falls right into the trap that envy sets up: "I'll try to get my life on the right track, but I know the project is doomed from the very start." The real problem is not the individual's ability to have a good life, it's his capacity not to have one. If we avoid the compensatory move into support and positive thinking, we can learn instead to honor the symptom and let it guide us in close care of the soul. If in envy the person wishes life were better, then maybe it's a good idea to feel that emptiness deeply. Wishes can be fluffy instruments of repression, turning attention to unrealistic and superficial possibilities as a defense against the void that is so painful. It was fairly clear that what this woman was lacking was the capacity to feel her own sense of desolation and emptiness.

Once she began to speak more honestly about her home life and more realistically about her friends, who experienced as much misfortune as anyone might, the whining tone of envy in her voice gave way to something more solid and sober. She could then take more responsibility for her situation, and over time eventually improve it.

In both jealousy and envy, fantasies are potent and utterly captivating, yet they float in an atmosphere somehow removed from actual life. These fantasies are illusions, images kept at bay so they can't touch life directly. But dwelling in an imaginary life is a way of avoiding soul. Soul is always attached to life in some way. As symptoms, jealousy and envy keep life at a safe distance; as invitations to soul, they both offer ways into one's own heart where love and attachment can be reclaimed.

The fact that jealousy and envy are both resistant to reason and to human efforts to erad-icate them is a blessing. They ask us for a deeper diving into the soul, beyond ideas of health and happiness and into mystery. It is the gods who become jealous and envious, and only by touching that deep place of divine ac-tivity can the individual make a response that is transforming, that takes him to an unfamil-iar place where the mythical impulse stirs. Ul-timately, these troublesome emotions offer a path to a life experienced with greater depth, maturity, and flexibility.

Our task is to care for the soul, but it is also true that the soul cares for us. So the phrase "care of the soul" can be heard in two ways. In one sense, we do our best to honor whatever the soul presents to us; in the other, the soul is the subject who does the caring. Even in its pa-thology, and maybe especially then, the soul cares for us by offering a way out of a narrow secularism. Its suffering can only be relieved by the reestablishment of a particular mythical sensibility. Therefore, its suffering initiates a move toward increased spirituality. Ironically, pathology can be a route to soulful religion.

# CHAPTER 6

# The Soul and Power

In the soul, power doesn't work the same way as it does in the ego and will. When we want to accomplish something egoistically, we gather our strength, develop a strategy, and apply every effort. This is the kind of behavior James Hillman describes as heroic or Herculean. He means the word in the bad sense: using brute strength and narrow, rationalistic vision. The power of the soul, in contrast, is more like a great reservoir or, in traditional imagery, like the force of water in a fast-rushing river. It is natural, not manipulated, and stems from an unknown source. Our role with this kind of power is to be an attentive observer noticing how the soul wants to thrust itself into life. It is also our task to find artful means of articulating and structuring that power, taking full responsibility for it, but trusting too that the soul has intentions and necessities that we may understand only partially.

Neither ego-centered will on the one hand nor pure passivity on the other serve the soul. Soul work requires both much reflection and also hard work. Think of all the ancient cultures that poured masses of money, materials, and energy into pyramids, megaliths, temples, and cathedrals on behalf of sacred play or holy imagination. The trick is to find the soulful perspective that feeds action with both passion and imaginal contemplation.

I am reminded here of Jung's constant attempt in both his theory and in his own life to discover the "transcendent function," as he called it, a point of view that embraces the mysterious depths of the soul as well as conscious understanding and intention. This, for Jung, was exactly what *self* means: it is a fulcrum of action and intelligence that feels the weight both of the soul and of the intellect. This is not a mere theoretical construct. It can be, as Jung showed in his own soul work, a way of life. The power that comes from this relocation of the source of action has profound roots and is not destructively caught up in narcissistic motives. The *Tao Te Ching* (ch. 30) says, "The good general achieves his result and that's all; he does not use the occasion to seize strength from it." Tapping the soul's power has nothing to do with the need to fill gaps in the ego or to substitute lamely for its loss of power.

What is the source of this soul power, and how can we tap into it? I believe it often comes from unexpected places. It comes first of all from living close to the heart, and not at odds with it. Therefore, paradoxically, soul power may emerge from failure, depression, and loss. The general rule is that soul appears in the gaps and holes of experience. It is usually tempting to find some subtle way of denying these holes or distancing ourselves from them. But we have all experienced moments when we've lost a job or endured an illness only to find an unexpected inner strength.

Other sources of deep-rooted power are simply concrete peculiarities of personality, or body, or circumstances. One person has a deep resonant voice that takes him places in the world. Another is clever, intelligent in his own way, and imaginative. Some people have a sexual attractiveness that doesn't have to be exploited in order to bring power into life.

Sometimes a young person in need of power

will look to conventional places for it and overlook her own inherent qualities. She tries self-consciously to talk smoothly and to appear comfortable when in fact she's anxious and full of self-doubt. The assumption in some quarters is that if you can effect a "cool" appearance, power is sure to follow. But these crude evocations of strength and confidence inevitably fall apart, and the person is immersed even more deeply in a vat of insecurity.

Writers are taught to "write what you know about." The same advice applies to the quest for the power of the soul: be good at what you're good at. Many of us spend time and energy trying to be something that we are not. But this is a move against soul, because individuality rises out of the soul as water rises out of the depths of the earth. We are who we are because of the special mix that makes up our soul. In spite of its archetypal, universal contents, for each individual the soul is highly idiosyncratic. Power begins in knowing this special soul, which may be entirely different from our fantasies about who we are or who we want to be.

A friend once introduced me to an audience I was about to lecture. "I'm going to tell you," he said to the group, "what Tom isn't. He isn't an artist, he isn't a scholar, he isn't a philosopher, he isn't . . ." I felt somewhat mortified hearing all these things I wasn't. At the time I was teaching at a university and was supposed to give the illusion at least that I was a scholar. Yet I knew I wasn't. My friend's unusual introduction was wise and absolutely correct. Maybe we could all use an emptying out of identity now and then. Considering who we are not, we may find the surprising revelation of who we are. Again, the *Tao Te Ching* (ch. 22), that absolute testament of soulful emptiness, says in words that also echo sayings of Jesus, "When twisted, you'll be upright; when hollowed out, you'll be full."

Soulful emptiness is not anxious. In fact, power pours in when we sustain the feeling of emptiness and withstand temptations to fill it prematurely. We have to contain the void. Too often we lose this pregnant emptiness by reaching for substitutes for power. A tolerance of weakness, you might say, is a prerequisite for the discovery of power, for any exercise of strength motivated by an avoidance of weakness is not genuine power. This is a rule of thumb. The soul has no room in which to present itself if we continually fill all the gaps with bogus activities.

I knew a young man who wanted to be a writer. Something in him urged him to travel and to live the Bohemian life, but he looked around and saw all his peers going to school.

So he decided to overrule his desire for travel and take some college courses. Not surprisingly, he flunked out, and then went on a long trip. It is easy to overlook the obvious, persistent indications of soul, in this case the fantasies and longings for travel, and instead try to manufacture power with demanding and expensive efforts.

## The Logic and Language of the Soul

One of the central difficulties involved in embarking on care of the soul is grasping the nature of the soul's discourse. The intellect works with reasons, logic, analysis, research, equations, and pros and cons. But the soul practices a different kind of math and logic. It presents images that are not immediately intelligible to the reasoning mind. It insinuates, offers fleeting impressions, persuades more with desire than with reasonableness. In order to tap the soul's power, one has to be conversant with its style, and watchful. The soul's indications are many, but they are usually extremely subtle.

Two Sufi stories demonstrate how odd the logic of the soul can appear to the reasoning, heroic mind. In the first, Nasrudin goes to a teacher for music lessons.

"How much do the lessons cost?" he asks.

"Fifteen dollars for the first lesson, ten dollars each after that," says the teacher.

"Fine," Nasrudin replies, "I'll begin with lesson number two."

I don't know if there is a canonical reading of this story, but to me it describes the mercurial wit of the soul from which a great deal of power can arise, as well as the special logic which goes against natural expectations. The alchemists taught that soul work is an *opus contra naturam,* a work against nature. This story is an example of how the soul's understanding of things is "unnatural." In some ways it is like the parable of Jesus in which laborers who arrive to work at the end of the day are paid the same as those who have been at work since sunrise.

The soul doesn't necessarily benefit from long, hard work, or from fairness of any kind. Its effects are achieved more with magic than effort. Just because you have worked a long time and are fair about it doesn't mean you will have the benefits of soul you want. Nor should you enter such work innocently, agreeing to work hard, and then expecting something for your labor. You may have to be like Nasrudin, shrewdly trying to get the most for the least expense. In therapy a person will say,

"I've been at this work for a year. Something should have happened by now." Another will think: "I've chosen a high-priced analyst. I should be getting the very best treatment." This consumer logic, based on fairness and reasonableness, has nothing to do with the way the soul operates and may be the least effective way to seek out its power.

The other Sufi story is more mysterious.

Nuri Bey was a reflective and respected Albanian who married a wife much younger than himself.

One evening when he had returned home earlier than usual, a faithful servant came to him and said, "Your wife, our mistress, is acting suspiciously. She is in her apartments with a huge chest, large enough to hold a man, which belonged to your grandmother. It should contain only a few ancient embroideries. I believe that there may now be much more in it. She will not allow me, your oldest retainer, to look inside."

Nuri went to his wife's room and found her sitting disconsolately beside the massive wooden box.

"Will you show me what is in the chest?" he asked.

"Because of the suspicion of a servant, or because you do not trust me?"

"Would it not be easier just to open it, without thinking about the undertones?" asked Nuri.

"I do not think it possible."

"Is it locked?"

"Yes."

"Where is the key?"

She held it up. "Dismiss the servant and I will give it to you."

The servant was dismissed. The woman handed over the key and herself withdrew, obviously troubled in mind.

Nuri Bey thought for a long time. Then he called four gardeners from his estate. Together they carried the chest by night unopened to a distant part of the grounds, and buried it.

The matter was never referred to again.

This is a captivating and mysterious story. Again, I don't know if there is a canonical reading. To me it shows the soul, typically represented by the woman, as the vessel of mystery. The older man, the *senex,* wants to open this vessel and have the mystery explained. Also, as in the story of the music lesson, there is some shadow in the story, the suggestion that there could be a man in this chest. Or is it that whatever vessel the wife has can hold humanity or a person, as though it were the envelope of the human soul? The wife, again speaking for the soul, inquires into the fantasies of her husband about the chest. But, in typical Hercules fashion, he wants to dismiss the "undertone" and go directly to a literal solution: just open the box.

How many times do we lose an occasion for soul work by leaping ahead to final solutions without pausing to savor the undertones? We are a radically bottom-line society, eager to act and to end tension, and thus we lose opportunities to know ourselves for our motives and our secrets. From the wife's point of view it's simply not possible just to open the chest without taking the undertones into consideration.

But she has the key. Jung says that the *anima* is the face of the soul. In this story she is the one who can open and close the container. The tension centers around whether or not the man will force an opening of the box. Do we need to expose everything that is hidden? Do we need to understand all mysteries? We are used to hearing about the great revelations of science—the discovery of atoms, particles, and DNA—and so quite naturally we think that mysteries are there to be solved. The alternative seems strange, but at the same time it has its own appeal: use our intelligence and skill to preserve the mysteries.

This is a teaching story, because we are taught in the end how to deal with the stuff of the soul. Nuri Bey thinks for a long time. He creates his own inner space with his reflection, and then he is ready for the kind of action that is appropriate for the soul. He calls four gardeners—Jung would have understood the number four here as a symbol of wholeness. They carry the chest at night to a distant place where they bury it and never discuss it again. We think that power comes from understanding and unveiling. But we should know from the story of Oedipus that this approach only goes so far. Oedipus solved the riddle of the sphinx, but then he was blinded, and only afterward slowly came to appreciate the mysteries that are beyond the scope of reason. From the point of view of soul it is just as important, maybe more important, to check the urgency of curiosity and suspicion, to allow certain things to remain distant and buried, to trust one's soul mate or mate soul with things that shouldn't be brought to the light of day.

A man told me once about the woman he was in love with. They had had a quarrel and he had sent a rash, thoughtless letter to her in the heat of his distress. Before the letter arrived by mail, he telephoned her and asked her not to read the letter. She told him later that the letter had arrived and she had torn it up immediately. She had felt enormous curiosity, and on the torn, crinkled paper lying in the waste basket she could see the scribbles of his writing. She confessed she was tempted, but she let it go unread. At that moment, the man told me, he felt they had an unbroken bond between them. Their relationship had been tightened by her reverence. When he told me the story, I thought of Nuri Bey, and the special lesson in the power of soul he learned in his moments of thought when it was decided for him that the chest would remain closed.

Those stories show that power is not always revealed in action. Nuri Bey could easily have overpowered his wife and discovered her secrets, but by preserving her privacy he maintains his power. In general, we keep our power when we protect the power of others.

## Violence and the Need for Power

The word *violence* comes from the Latin word *vis,* meaning "life force." Its very roots suggest that in violence the thrust of life is making itself visible. If that fundamental vitality is not present in the heart, it nevertheless seems to appear distorted by our repressions and compromises, our fears and our narcissistic manipulations.

It would be a mistake to approach violence with any simple idea of getting rid of it. Chances are, if we try to eradicate our violence, we will also cut ourselves off from the deep power that sustains creative life. Besides, psychoanalysis teaches, repression never accomplishes what we want. The repressed always returns in monstrous form. The life current of the soul, *vis,* is like the natural force of plant life, like the grass that grows up through cement and in a relatively short time obliterates grand monuments of culture. If we try taming and boxing in this innate power, it will inevitably find its way into the light.

"Repression of the life force" is a diagnosis I believe would fit most of the emotional problems people present in therapy. These days it is common for therapists to encourage their patients to express their anger, almost as if doing this were a panacea. But I suspect that anger and its expression are only a route into the *force* of life that has become attenuated and difficult for people to feel in our modern society. Renaissance doctors placed both anger and the life force under the aegis of one god, Mars. All people, they taught, have an explosive force ready within them to be unleashed into the world. Simply being oneself—letting one's individuality and unique gifts come forth—is a manifestation of Mars. When we allow ourselves to exist truly and fully, we *sting* the world with our vision and challenge it with our own ways of being.

In entertainment and in politics we sometimes see persons of exceptional talent burst onto the public scene with irrepressible energy and imagination; just being themselves, they stagger us with their brilliance. A metaphor often used for their appearance on the scene is "meteoric." They flash, burn, and streak across our tame and timid world. We say these people have "charisma," a word that means divine favor and gift. Their power is not from the ego. What we see in such people is a divine light burning in their personalities and in their actions.

But throughout human history the expression of individuality has been felt as a threat to the status quo. For all its expressed championing of the individual, our culture in many ways favors conformity. We are pleasantly sedated by the flatness and predictability of modern life. You can travel far and wide and have a difficult time finding a store or restaurant that is even mildly unique. In shopping malls everywhere, in restaurant districts, in movie theaters, you will find the same clothes, the same brand names, the same menus, the same few films, the identical architecture. On the East Coast you can sit in a restaurant seat identical to that you sat in on the West Coast. Yet, as psychoanalysis says, repetition is death. Repetition defends against the rush of individual life. It seeks the deadly peace of a culture that has banished surprise.

So simple a thing as new food can be threatening, and it is well known that fashions in dress can be statements of either conformity or anarchy. Political groups have identified themselves through the length of their hair. Such choices in everyday life have genuine power, and a society concerned about order and smooth functioning may gradually and unconsciously flatten itself out for the apparent good of the whole.

It is not unusual for repressed forces and symptoms eventually to reappear as objects; that is, our fantasy becomes crystallized in a thing that has the power and lure of a fetish. In this sense our nuclear arsenals with their mystery and threat are dark carriers of what has been ignored in the soul. Bombs and missiles give us a constant, daily association with our own destruction. They are reminders that everything cannot be contained and controlled, that as a society we can kill ourselves and obliterate other peoples and the planet itself. This is an unprecedented fetish of power. The Jungian analyst Wolfgang Giergerich has drawn a parallel between the bomb and the "golden calf" of Genesis. Both are idols. Giegerich notes that the calf was actually a bull, an image of unlimited animal power. But, he says, in that mythic moment when Moses destroyed the bull, we banished dark power and set up altars only to the light. Our bombs, then, are a continuation of the ostracized golden calf. Because we have refused to associate ourselves with the darker forces, they have been forced into fetishistic form, where they remain, fascinating and lethal.·

I see a connection, therefore, between our seemingly insoluble violence and our treasured repetitious flatness. The soul, tradition has taught us for centuries, needs the profound and challenging grace of Mars, who reddens everything in his vicinity with the glow of passionate life, brings a creative edge to every action, and sows the seeds of power in every moment and event. When Mars is overlooked and undervalued, he is forced to appear in fetish and in violent behavior. Mars is infinitely greater than personal expression of anger. Creative and destructive, he is life itself poised for struggle.

There is nothing neutral about the soul. It is the seat and the source of life. Either we respond to what the soul presents in its fantasies and desires, or we suffer from this neglect of ourselves. The power of the soul can hurl a person into ecstasy or into depression. It can be creative or destructive, gentle or aggressive. Power incubates within the soul and then makes its influential move into life as the expression of soul. If there is no soulfulness, then there is no true power, and if there is no power, then there can be no true soulfulness.


## Sadomasochism

When the soul's power is neglected, usurped, or toyed with, then we fall into the truly problematical condition of sadomasochism, which can range from being an extreme clinical syndrome to a dynamic at work in the most ordinary, simple transactions. Genuine power, in which there are no tyrants and no literal victims, breaks, in sadomasochism, into two parts: violence and victimization, controller and subject. Sadomasochism, though it may look superficially like genuine strength, is a failure of power. Whenever one person victimizes another, real power has been lost and replaced by a literalistic drama that is dangerous for both parties.

The sadomasochistic splitting of power has the characteristics of all symptomatic behavior: it is literally destructive, and it involves a polarization in which one side of the split is apparent, while the other is hidden. People who turn to violence are visibly controlling; what is less obvious are their weakness and feelings of powerlessness. On the other hand, those who habitually play the victim may be quite unaware of their own more subtle methods of control. This is why issues of power are so difficult to deal with: things are not as they appear to be. Weaklings puff themselves up and try to act strong; tough people hide their vulnerabilities; the rest of us fail to look past the surface. We assume that the fabrications of power all around us are genuine, and we fall victim to them.

As a therapist, I deal with this split every day. A woman came to me once in tears telling me her husband of ten years was having an affair. It was obvious from the beginning that she wanted me to sympathize with her terrible feelings of betrayal, to curse the man, and then to find some way to set him straight. But I kept my distance. From the very first moment I was aware of two things—her exaggerated feelings of victimization and her forcefulness in trying to control me. As she talked, these two aspects became even clearer. She had fallen so far down into the victim role and identified with it so fully that she was completely unaware of her efforts to control both her husband and me. When I pointed this out to her, she told me I was wrong and that she wouldn't come back. I didn't cower in the face of this apparent threat, and eventually we began to sort things out. Within a few weeks her husband ended the affair and some harmony was restored. I was surprised how quickly things settled down, but the woman told me that issues of control had been brought up in previous therapy years ago. She had thought, as so many of us do, that she could "solve" these problems once and for all. Her real strength lay in her ability to check her outrage and look into herself at a time when it was easy to put all the blame on her husband.

## The Dark Angel of Destruction

Violence has a great deal to do with shadow, in particular the shadow of power. For many people born and raised in modern America, innocence—the absence or rejection of shadow—is a strong obstacle to realizing the soul's power. When people talk about power and innocence, they often refer to their religious upbringing, which in one way or another taught them to turn the other cheek and to suffer. David Miller has pointed out that the image of churchgoers as a flock of sheep in a subtle way maintains the notion that to be good is to be weak and submissive.

Another way power is lost is by identifying with the *puer* fantasy that is so strong in the

American psyche. The youthful spirit of idealism, the melting pot, everyone has a chance, all people are equal—these tenets of the American ideal not only cast a dark shadow, they also make power seem undesirable to many people. It gets repressed as shadow material, and as a result many power struggles take place in secret, in an underhanded way.

Dreams frequently present images of dark power in which the dreamer is either the wielder of weapons or their victim. For example, a middle-aged man told me this dream: He was standing outside the door of a bank, waiting for it to be opened. A woman was standing with him, along with a few other people. Suddenly he noticed that two men near him had guns in their pockets. He could see the tips of the handles sticking out, and he saw that the men were slowly sliding them out to go into action. Instinctively he began to run away in panic at the thought of gunshots. He left his friend in the dust, without a care for her, and he woke up feeling guilty about his cowardice.

The man understood his dream as a portrait of his fear of violence. He had great difficulty in the most ordinary confrontations. It would be characteristic of him, he told me, to be overly solicitous about his companion, but in the dream panic overshadowed his altruism, and he made an amazingly speedy retreat. He mentioned other dreams in which he felt panic in the presence of guns, when his only concern was his own protection. In his dreams he never joined battle, and he thought this was a weakness of character.

Sometimes it is useful to understand that dream figures are like angels. They look human, but their world is the realm of imagination, where the natural and moral laws of actual life are suspended. Their actions may be mysterious, not to be taken literally. I saw the two men as dark angels, doing something the dreamer would never think of doing. He was frightened by their guns and ran from them, but maybe he wasn't being cowardly. Flight seems like a sensible response in the presence of guns, especially when you yourself don't have one. We could also see his move away from the woman as something that happens when he senses violence. He is no longer close to the feminine, sensitive world he habitually thinks he should protect.

The dream wasn't just about guns, it also involved robbing a bank. The dream could be seen as a lesson in the necessity of thievery. Sometimes you have to put on a dark mask, carry a weapon on your pocket—in the phallic region and in the female pouch—in order to get along.

Religion is filled with puzzling tales of amoral financial arrangements. As we have seen, Jesus tells the story of the manager who paid the same wages to people who worked for an hour as to those who worked an entire day. The Greeks celebrated the tale of Hermes, who on the first day of his life stole the cattle of his brother Apollo. In order to enjoy the gifts of Hermes, it may be necessary to have our Apollonic values robbed. The story of Nasrudin and the music lesson sounds like an invitation to cheat. In the Gospel story and in countless paintings of the crucifixion, Jesus is shown on a cross between two thieves, one of whom he says will be in heaven with him. This image is sometimes interpreted as the humiliation of Jesus, but the story may also be an elevation of thieving.

Oscar Wilde's letter from prison known as "De Profundis," "from the depths," is an extraordinary example of Romantic theology, and in it he discusses the place of shadow in the image of Jesus:

> The world had always loved the saint as being the nearest possible approach to the perfection of God. Christ, through some divine instinct in him, seems to have always loved the sinner as being the nearest possible approach to the perfection of man. His primary desire was not to reform people any more than his desire was to relieve suffering. . . . But in a

manner not yet understood of the world he regarded sin and suffering as being in themselves
beautiful holy things and modes of perfection.

If we let Oscar Wilde be our guide in the theological understanding of the man's dream,
then we might look at the two gunmen as the
two thieves joined with Jesus. They may be
fallen angels whose job it is to rob banks. They
may be portraying the difficult truth that in order to become wealthy in soul one sometimes
has to steal, forcefully and darkly, from the
reservoir of wealth. It isn't enough to get what
you expect, or work for, or have suffered for.
You may find yourself, as Jesus did, in the
company of thieves and gunmen exactly when
you think you are most innocent, in your pro-
tective mode and close to the woman.

The shadow is a frightening reality. Anyone
who talks glibly about integrating the shadow,
as if you could chum up to shadow the way
you learn a foreign language, doesn't know the
darkness that always qualifies shadow. Fear is
never far removed from power. And genuine
innocence is always to be found in the vicinity
of blood-guilt. The three crosses on Golgotha
do not simply represent the triumph of virtue
over vice. They are a reflection of Christianity's most treasured image, the trinity. They
hint at the great mystery Oscar Wilde points

to: the fact that virtue is never genuine when it sets itself apart from evil. We only sustain violence in our world if we fail to admit its place in our own hearts and identify only with unaffecting innocence.

People frequently tell me dreams of guns and other kinds of weapons. I don't think this is a compensation for innocence in life as much as it is a sign that the soul loves power. Dreams give us a less censored view of the potential of the soul than a person's conscious self-analysis. There are signs in society, too, that the gun is a ritual object. Guns are both banned and adored. A gun is one of the most numinous—mysteriously fascinating and disturbing—objects around us. Those who protest its banishment may be speaking for a rare idol of power that keeps the strength of life, *vis,* before our eyes. A gun is dangerous not only because it threatens our lives, but also because it concretizes and fetishizes our desire for power, keeping power both in sight and also removed from its soulful presence in our daily lives. The presence of the gun in our society is a threat, and we are its victims—a sign that our fetish is working against us. Those old painted cannons that sit in a privileged spot in our towns—there is one down the road from my home in a quiet village—demonstrate the piety with which we honor this holy object, the sacrament of our capacity for murderous power.

It is often said that the gun is a phallic symbol. It is more likely the other way around: the phallus is a gun symbol. We are fascinated by the power of a gun, and it's interesting to note that the word fascinating originally referred to the phallus. But I don't think the gun is as masculine as it would appear to be. The word *gun* comes from the name of a woman, Gunnhilda, whose name in Scandinavian means "war." Another famous gun was called "Big Bertha," suggesting that a gun may be the power of the feminine soul shining forth.

The soul is explosive and powerful. Through its medium of imagination, which is always a prerequisite for action and is the source of meaning, it can accomplish all things. In the strength of its emotions, the soul is a gun, full of potential power and effect. The pen, expressing the soul's passion, is mightier than the sword because the imagination can change the life of a people at their very roots.

If we do not claim the soul's power on our own behalf, we become its victims. We suffer our emotions rather than feel them working for us. We hold our thoughts and passions inward, disconnecting them from life, and then they stir up trouble within, making us feel profoundly unsettled or, it seems, turning into illness. We all know what it feels like to hold anger in our hearts, as it builds and transmutes into corrosive resentment and rage. Even unexpressed love creates a pressure that demands release in some kind of expression.

If violence is the repressed life force showing itself symptomatically, then the cure for violence is care of the soul's power. It is foolish to deny signs of this power—individuality, eccentricity, self-expression, passion—because it cannot be truly repressed. If there is crime in our streets, it is due, from the viewpoint of soul, not just to poverty and difficult living conditions, but to the failure of the soul and its spirit to unveil themselves.

Socrates and Jesus, two teachers of virtue and love, were executed because of the unsettling, threatening power of their souls, which was revealed in their personal lives and in their words. They did not carry guns, yet still they were a threat, because there is nothing more powerful than the revelation of one's own soul. Here is another reason for placing Jesus between two thieves. He *was* a criminal in the eyes of a soul-denying authority. Criminality and transgression, when not acted out in violence, are dark virtues of the heart, necessary for the full presence of an individual on earth.

Only when they are repressed do we find them roaming the streets of a city as incarnations of the rejected shadow.

A soulful life is never without shadow, and some of the soul's power comes from its shadow qualities. If we want to live from our depths—soulfully—then we will have to give up all pretenses to innocence as the shadow grows darker. The chief reward of surrendering innocence, so that the soul may be fully expressed, is an increase of power. In the presence of deep power, life becomes robust and passionate, signs that the soul is engaged and being given expression. Mars, when he is honored, gives a deep red hue to everything we do, quickening our lives with intensity, passion, forcefulness, and courage. When he is neglected, we suffer the onslaughts of uncontained violence. It is important, then, to revere the Marsian spirit and to let the soul burst into life—in creativity, individuality, iconoclasm, and imagination.

# Gifts of Depression

The soul presents itself in a variety of colors, including all the shades of gray, blue, and black. To care for the soul, we must observe the full range of all its colorings, and resist the temptation to approve only of white, red, and orange—the brilliant colors. The "bright" idea of colorizing old black and white movies is consistent with our culture's general rejection of the dark and the gray. In a society that is defended against the tragic sense of life, depression will appear as an enemy, an unredeemable malady; yet in such a society, devoted to light, depression, in compensation, will be unusually strong.

Care of the soul requires our appreciation of these ways it presents itself. Faced with depression, we might ask ourselves, "What is it doing here? Does it have some necessary role to play?" Especially in dealing with depression, a mood close to our feelings of mortality, we must guard against the denial of death that is so easy to slip into. Even further, we may have to develop a taste for the depressed mood, a positive respect for its place in the soul's cycles.

Some feelings and thoughts seem to emerge only in a dark mood. Suppress the mood, and you will suppress those ideas and reflections. Depression may be as important a channel for valuable "negative" feelings, as expressions of affection are for the emotions of love. Feelings of love give birth naturally to gestures of attachment. In the same way, the void and grayness of depression evoke an awareness and articulation of thoughts otherwise hidden behind the screen of lighter moods. Sometimes a person will come to a therapy session in a dark mood. "I shouldn't have come today," he will say. "I'll feel better next week, and we can get on with it." But I'm happy that he came, because together we will hear thoughts and feel his soul in a way not possible in his cheerful moods. Melancholy gives the soul an opportunity to express a side of its nature that is as valid as any other, but is hidden out of our distaste for its darkness and bitterness.

## Saturn's Child

Today we seem to prefer the word *depression* over *sadness* and *melancholy*. Perhaps its Latin form sounds more clinical and serious. But there was a time, five or six hundred years ago, when melancholy was identified with the Roman god Saturn. To be depressed was to be "in Saturn," and a person chronically disposed to melancholy was known as a "child of Saturn." Since depression was identified with the God and the planet named for him, it was associated with other qualities of Saturn. For example, he was known as the "old man," who presided over the golden age. Whenever we talk about the "golden years" or the "good old days," we are calling up this god, who is the patron of the past. The depressed person sometimes thinks that the good times are all past, that there is nothing left for the present or the future. These melancholic thoughts are deeply rooted in Saturn's preference for days gone by, for memory and the sense that time is passing. These thoughts and feelings, sad as they are, favor the soul's desire to be both in time and in eternity, and so in a strange way they can be pleasing.

Sometimes we associate depression with literal aging, but it is more precisely a matter of the soul's aging. Saturn not only brings an affection for the "good old days," he also raises the more substantive idea that life is moving on: we're getting old, experienced, and maybe even wise. A person even in his middle or late thirties will be in conversation and offhandedly recall something that happened twenty years ago. He will stop, shocked. "I've never said that before! Twenty years ago. I'm getting old." This is Saturn's gift of age and experience. Having been identified with youth, the soul now takes on important qualities of age that are positive and helpful. If age is denied, soul becomes lost in an inappropriate clinging to youth.

Depression grants the gift of experience not as a literal fact but as an attitude toward yourself. You get a sense of having lived through something, of being older and wiser. You know that life is suffering, and that knowledge makes a difference. You can't enjoy the bouncy, carefree innocence of youth any longer, a realization that entails both sadness because of the loss, and pleasure in a new feeling of self-acceptance and self-knowledge. This awareness of age has a halo of melancholy around it, but it also enjoys a measure of nobility.

Naturally, there is resistance to this incursion of Saturn that we call depression. It's difficult to let go of youth, because that release requires an acknowledgment of death. I suspect that those of us who opt for eternal youth are setting ourselves up for heavy bouts of depression. We're inviting Saturn to make a house call when we try to delay our service to him. Then Saturn's depression will give its color, depth, and substance to the soul that for one reason or another has dallied long with youth. Saturn weathers and ages a person naturally, the way temperature, winds, and time weather a barn. In Saturn, reflection deepens, thoughts embrace a larger sense of time, and the events of a long lifetime get distilled into a sense of one's essential nature.

In traditional texts, Saturn is characterized as cold and distant, but he has other attributes as well. Medical books called him the god of wisdom and philosophical reflection. In a letter to Giovanni Cavalcanti, a successful statesman and poet, Ficino refers to Saturn as a "unique and divine gift." In the late fifteenth century, Ficino wrote a book warning scholars and studious people in particular to take care not to invite too much Saturn into their souls; because of their sedentary occupations, scholars can easily become severely depressed, he said, and have to find ways to counter their dark moods. But another book could be written about the dangers of living without study and speculation, and without reflecting on our lives. Saturn's moods may be dangerous because of their darkness, but his contributions to the economy of the soul are indispensable. If you allow his depression to visit, you will feel the change in your body, in your muscles, and on your face—some relief from the burden of youthful enthusiasm and the "unbearable lightness of being."

Maybe we could appreciate the role of depression in the economy of the soul more if we could only take away the negative connotations of the word. What if "depression" were simply a state of being, neither good nor bad, something the soul does in its own good time and for its own good reasons? What if it were simply one of the planets that circle the sun? One advantage of using the traditional image of Saturn, in place of the clinical term *depression,* is that then we might see melancholy more as a valid way of being rather than as a problem that needs to be eradicated.

Aging brings out the flavors of a personality.

The individual emerges over time, the way fruit matures and ripens. In the Renaissance view, depression, aging, and individuality all go together: the sadness of growing old is part of becoming an individual. Melancholy thoughts carve out an interior space where wisdom can take up residence.

Saturn was also traditionally identified with the metal lead, giving the soul weight and density, allowing the light, airy elements to coalesce. In this sense, depression is a process that fosters a valuable coagulation of thoughts and emotions. As we age, our ideas, formerly light, rambling, and unrelated to each other, become more densely gathered into values and a philosophy, giving our lives substance and firmness.

Because of its painful emptiness, it is often tempting to look for a way out of depression. But entering into its mood and thoughts can be deeply satisfying. Depression is sometimes described as a condition in which there are no ideas—nothing to hang on to. But maybe we have to broaden our vision and see that feelings of emptiness, the loss of familiar understandings and structures in life, and the vanishing of enthusiasm, even though they seem negative, are elements that can be appropriated and used to give life fresh imagination.

When, as counselors and friends, we are the observers of depression and are challenged to find a way to deal with it in others, we could abandon the monotheistic notion that life always has to be cheerful, and be instructed by melancholy. We could learn from its qualities and follow its lead, becoming more patient in its presence, lowering our excited expectations, taking a watchful attitude as this soul deals with its fate in utter seriousness and heaviness. In our friendship, we could offer it a place of acceptance and containment. Sometimes, of course, depression, like any emotion, can go beyond ordinary limits, becoming a completely debilitating illness. But in extreme cases, too, even in the midst of strong treatments, we can still look for Saturn at the core of depression and find ways to befriend it.

One great anxiety associated with depression is that it will never end, that life will never again be joyful and active. This is one of the feelings that is part of the pattern—the sense of being trapped, forever to be held in the remote haunts of Saturn. In my practice, when I hear this fear I think of it as Saturn's style, as one of the ways he works the soul—by making it feel constrained, with nowhere to go. Traditionally, there is a binding theme in saturnine moods. This anxiety seems to decrease when we stop fighting the saturnine elements that are in the depression, and turn instead toward learning from depression and taking on some of its dark qualities as aspects of personality.

## Insinuations of Death

Saturn is also the reaper, god of the harvest, patron of end-time and its festival, the Saturnalia; accordingly, imagery of death may permeate periods of depression. People of all ages sometimes say from their depression that life is over, that their hopes for the future have proved unfounded. They are disillusioned because the values and understandings by which they have lived for years suddenly make no sense. Cherished truths sink into Saturn's black earth like chaff at harvest time.

Care of the soul requires acceptance of all this dying. The temptation is to champion our familiar ideas about life right up to the last second, but it may be necessary in the end to give them up, to enter into the movement of death. If the symptom is felt as the sense that life is over, and that there's no use in going on, then an affirmative approach to this feeling might be a conscious, artful giving-in to the emotions and thoughts of ending that depression has stirred up. Nicholas of Cusa, certainly one of the most profound theologians of the

Renaissance, tells how he was on a journey, on a ship in fact, when the realization dawned on him in a visionary way that we should acknowledge our ignorance of the most profound things. Discovering that we do not know who God is and what life is all about, he says, is the learning of ignorance, ignorance about the very meaning and value of our lives. This is a starting point for a more grounded, open-ended kind of knowledge that never closes up in fixed opinions. Using his favorite metaphors from geometry, he says that if full knowledge about the very base of our existence could be described as a circle, the best we can do is to arrive at a polygon—something short of sure knowledge.

The emptiness and dissolution of meaning that are often present in depression show how attached we can become to our ways of understanding and explaining our lives. Often our personal philosophies and our values seem to be all too neatly wrapped, leaving little room for mystery. Depression comes along then and opens up a hole. Ancient astrologers imagined Saturn as the most remote planet, far out in cold and empty space. Depression makes holes in our theories and assumptions, but even this painful process can be honored as a necessary and valuable source of healing.

This saturnine truth is evoked by Oscar

Wilde, who, for all his emphasis on fullness of style as a central concern of life, knew the importance of emptying. From the prison cell where he was being punished for his love of a man, he wrote his extraordinary letter, "De Profundis," in which he remarks: "The final mystery is oneself. When one has weighed the sun in the balance, and measured the steps of the moon, and mapped out the seven heavens star by star, there still remains oneself. Who can calculate the orbit of his own soul?" We may have to learn this truth, as Cusa did, that we cannot calculate (notice the mathematical image) the orbit of our own soul. This peculiar kind of education—learning our limits—may not be a conscious effort only; it may come upon us as a captivating mood of depression, at least momentarily wiping out our happiness, and sending us off into fundamental appraisals of our knowledge, our assumptions, and the very purposes of our existence.

In the ancient texts Saturn was sometimes labeled "poisonous." In recommending some positive effects in saturnine moods, I don't want to overlook the terrible pain that they can bring. Nor is it only minor forms of melancholy that offer unique gifts to the soul; long, deep bouts of acute depression can also clear out and restructure the tenets by which life has been lived. The "children of Saturn" traditionally included carpenters, shown in drawings putting together the foundations and skeletons of new houses. In our melancholy, inner construction may be taking place, clearing out the old and putting up the new. Dreams, in fact, often depict construction sites and buildings just going up, suggesting again that the soul is *made:* it is the product of work and inventive effort. Freud pointed out that during bouts of melancholy the outer life may look empty, but at the same time inner work may be taking place at full speed.

## Coming to Terms with Depression

In Jungian language, Saturn may be considered an *animus* figure. The *animus* is a deep part of the psyche that roots ideas and abstraction in the soul. Many people are strong in *anima*—full of imagination, close to life, empathic, and connected to people around them. But these very people may have difficulty moving far enough away from emotional involvement to see what is going on, and to relate their life experiences to their ideas and values. Their experience is "wet," to use another ancient metaphor for the soul, because they are so emotionally involved in life, and so they might benefit from an excursion to the far-off regions of cold, dry Saturn.

This dryness can separate awareness from the moist emotions that are characteristic of close involvement with life. We see this development in old people as they reflect on their past with some distance and detachment. Saturn's point of view, in fact, can sometimes be rather hardhearted and even cruel. In Samuel Beckett's melancholy play *Krapp's Last Tape*, we find a humorous, biting depiction of saturnine reflection. Using a tape recorder, Krapp plays back tapes he has made throughout his life, and listens with considerable gloom to his voices from the past. After one of the tapes, he sits down to make another: "Just listening to that stupid bastard I took myself for thirty years ago, hard to believe I was ever as bad as that. Thank God that's all done with anyway."

These few lines reveal a distance between past and present, as well as a cooler perspective and a deconstruction of values. In most of Beckett's plays we hear characters express their depression and hopelessness, their inability to find any shreds of former meaning; yet they also offer an image of the noble foolishness that is part of a life so riddled with emptiness. In the absolute sadness of these characters, we can grasp a mystery about the human condition. It is not a literal aberration, although it may feel that way, to sudden-ly find meaning and value disappear, and to be overwhelmed with the need for with-drawal and with vague emotions of hopeless-ness. Such feelings have a place and work a kind of magic on the soul.

Krapp, whose name suggests depression's devaluation of human life, shows that cold re-morse and self-judgment do not have to be seen as clinical syndromes, but as a necessary foolishness in human life that actually accom-plishes something for the soul. Professional psychology might try to correct Krapp's self-criticism as a form of neurotic masochism, but Beckett shows that even in its ugliness and foolishness it makes a certain kind of sense.

Krapp playing his tapes and muttering his curses is also an image of ourselves turning our memories over in our minds again and again, in a process of distillation. Over time some-thing essential emerges from this saturnine re-duction—the gold in the sludge. Saturn was sometimes called *sol niger,* the black sun. In his darkness there is to be found a precious brilliance, our essential nature, distilled by de-pression as perhaps the greatest gift of melan-choly.

If we persist in our modern way of treating depression as an illness to be cured only me-chanically and chemically, we may lose the gifts of soul that only depression can provide. In particular, tradition taught that Saturn fixes, darkens, weights, and hardens whatever is in contact with it. If we do away with Saturn's moods, we may find it exhausting trying to keep life bright and warm at all costs. We may be even more overcome then by the increased melancholy called forth by the repression of Saturn, and lose the sharpness and substance of identity that Saturn gives the soul. In other words, symptoms of a loss of Saturn might include a vague sense of identity, the failure to take one's own life seriously, and a general malaise or ennui that is a pale reflection of Saturn's deep, dark moods.

Saturn locates identity deeply in the soul, rather than on the surface of personality. Identity is felt as one's soul finding its weight and measure. We know who we are because we have uncovered the stuff of which we are made. It has been sifted out by depressive thought, "reduced," in the chemical sense, to essence. Months or years focused on death have left a white ghostly residue that is the "I," dry and essential.

Care of the soul asks for a cultivation of the larger world depression represents. When we speak clinically of depression, we think of an emotional or behavioral condition, but when we imagine depression as a visitation by Saturn, then many qualities of his world come into view: the need for isolation, the coagulation of fantasy, the distilling of memory, and accommodation with death, to name only a few.

For the soul, depression is an initiation, a rite of passage. If we think that depression, so empty and dull, is void of imagination, we may overlook its initiatory aspects. We may be imagining imagination itself from a point of view foreign to Saturn; emptiness can be rife with feeling-tone, images of catharsis, and emotions of regret and loss. As a shade of mood, gray can be as interesting and as variegated as it is in black-and-white photography.

If we pathologize depression, treating it as a syndrome in need of cure, then the emotions of Saturn have no place to go except into abnormal behavior and acting out. An alternative would be to invite Saturn in, when he comes knocking, and give him an appropriate place to stay. Some Renaissance gardens had a bower dedicated to Saturn—a dark, shaded, remote place where a person could retire and enter the persona of depression without fear of being disturbed. We could model our attitude and our ways of dealing with depression on this garden. Sometimes people need to withdraw and show their coldness. As friends and counselors, we could provide the emotional space for such feelings, without trying to change them or interpret them. And as a society, we could acknowledge Saturn in our buildings. A house or commercial building could have a room or an actual garden where a person could go to withdraw in order to meditate, think, or just be alone and sit. Modern architecture, when it tries to be cognizant of soul, seems to favor the circle or square where one joins community. But depression has a centrifugal force; it moves away from the center. We often refer to our buildings and institutions as "centers," but Saturn would probably prefer an outpost. Hospitals and schools often have "common rooms," but they could just as easily have "uncommon rooms," places for withdrawal and solitude.

Leaving a television running when no one is watching, or having a radio playing all day long may defend against Saturn's silence. We want to do away with the empty space surrounding that remote planet, but as we fill in those voids, we may be forcing him to assume the role of symptom, to be housed in our clinics and hospitals as a pest, rather than as a healer and teacher—his traditional roles.

Why is it that we fail to appreciate this facet of the soul? One reason is that most of what we know about Saturn comes to us symptomatically. Emptiness appears too late and too literally to have soul in it. In our cities, boarded-up homes and failing businesses signal economic and social "depression." In these "depressed" areas of our cities, decay is cut off from will and conscious participation, appearing only as an external manifestation of a problem or an illness.

We also see depression, economically and emotionally, as literal failure and threat, as a surprise breaking in upon our healthier plans and expectations. What if we were to expect Saturn and his dark, empty spaces to have a place in life? What if we propitiated Saturn by incorporating his values into our way of life? (Propitiate means both to acknowledge and to offer respect as a means of protection.)

We could also honor Saturn by showing more honesty in the face of serious illness. Hospice workers will tell you how much a family can gain when the depressive facts of a terminal illness are discussed openly. We might also take our own illnesses, our visits to the doctor and to the hospital, as reminders of our mortality. We are not caring for the soul in these situations when we protect ourselves from their impact. It isn't necessary to be *only* saturnine in these situations, but a few honest words for the melancholy feelings involved might keep Saturn propitiated.

Because depression is one of the faces of the soul, acknowledging it and bringing it into our relationships fosters intimacy. If we deny or cover up anything that is at home in the soul, then we cannot be fully present to others. Hiding the dark places results in a loss of soul; speaking for them and from them offers a way toward genuine community and intimacy.

## The Healing Powers of Depression

A few years ago, Bill, the priest I mentioned earlier, came to me with a remarkable story. In his sixty-fifth year, thirty years into the priesthood, as a compassionate pastor of a rural church he had given what he thought was perfectly appropriate aid to two of his women parishioners. His bishop, however, thought he had mishandled church funds and used poor judgment in other respects, and so, after a lifetime of respect, he was given two days to pack and leave the diocese.

When he began talking to me about his situation, Bill was quite lively and interested in his experiences. He had taken to group therapy well, where in particular he had found ways to engage some of his anger. He even decided at one point to become a therapist himself, with the idea that he might be able to help his fellow priests. But when he talked about the trouble he had fallen into, he gave me explanations and excuses that seemed naive. About one woman he said, "I was only trying to help her. She needed me. If she hadn't needed my attentions, I wouldn't have given them to her."

I knew I had to look for a way to hold and contain all of Bill's unusual experiences and interpretations without judging them. We spent a great deal of time with his dreams, and quickly he became quite expert at reading their imagery. I also invited him to bring in paintings and drawings that he had been doing in his group therapy. Discussing these images week after week gave us some insight into his nature. By means of this artwork Bill also had a chance to look closely at his family background and some of the key events surrounding his decision to become a priest.

Then a curious thing happened. As the naive explanations for his behavior fell away to be replaced by more substantive thoughts about the larger themes in his life, the tone of his mood darkened. As he expressed more of his anger about the way he had been treated throughout his life as a seminarian and priest, he lost much of his lightness. Meanwhile, he had moved into a home for priests, where he was largely withdrawn. He embraced his solitude and decided not to participate in activities in the home, and gradually, the wounds of his recent experiences deepened into genuine depression.

Now, Bill spoke critically of the church authorities and talked more realistically about his father, who had tried to become a priest and had failed. To some extent Bill thought that he was not cut out by nature to be a priest, that he had taken his father's place, trying to fulfill his father's dreams and not his own.

Bill trusted his depression enough to allow it a central place in his life. In true depressive style he would start every conversation saying: "It's no use. It's all over. I'm too old to have what I want in my life. I made mistakes all along the way, but I can't do anything about it now. All I want to do is stay in my room and read." But he remained in therapy, and every week he spoke from and about his depression.

My therapeutic strategy, if you can call it that, was simply to bring an attitude of acceptance and interest to Bill's depression. I didn't have any clever techniques. I didn't urge him to attend workshops on depression or try guided fantasies to contact the depressed person within. Care of the soul is less heroic than that. I simply tried to appreciate the way his soul was expressing itself at the moment. I observed the slow, subtle shifts in tone and focus that Bill brought in his manner, his words, his dreams, and the imagery of his conversation.

In his depression, when Bill said that he should never have been a priest, I didn't take that statement literally, because I knew how much his priesthood had meant to Bill over the years. But now he was discovering the shadow in his calling. His life as a priest was being deepened, given soul, by new reflection on its limitations. Bill was having to face for the first time the sacrifices he had made in order to be a priest. This was not an absolute disavowal of his priesthood; it was a completion. I noticed that even as he uncovered piece after piece of the sacrifices he had made, and even as he felt intense regret for having become a priest, at the same time he spoke of his loyalty to the church, his continuing interest in theology, and his concern for death and afterlife. In some ways, he was only now discovering the real core of his priesthood. The docile, compulsively helpful priest was dying off, to be replaced by a stronger, more individual, less manipulated man.

From his depressed state, Bill could only see the dying, the ending of a familiar life and the emptying out of long-held values and understandings. But the depression was clearly correcting his naïveté. For most people, their cardinal virtue is also their pivotal fault. Bill's childlike concern for all beings animal, vegetable, and human gave him his compassion and altruistic sensibilities. But his vulnerability also made him the butt of jokes among his fellow priests, who never realized how much he suffered from their teasing. His generosity was unlimited and in a sense had destroyed him. But his depression strengthened him, giving him new firmness and solidity.

By means of his depression, Bill was also better able to see the villains in his life. Previously his naive point of view gave everyone in his experience bland approval. There were neither real heroes nor full-bodied enemies. But in his depression Bill began to feel things much more deeply, and his hostility toward his colleagues came out of him with real grit. "I hope they all die young," he once uttered through his teeth.

Bill would tell me convincingly: "I'm old. Let's face it. I'm seventy. What's left for me? I hate young men. I'm happy when those young turks get sick. Don't tell me I have lots of life left. I don't."

Bill was strongly identified with being an old man. How could I argue with his telling me and himself to face facts and not deny his age? But I believed that this clever statement was a defense against considering other options for identification, and that, paradoxically, it served to keep Bill protected from the lower dimensions of his depression. By giving up at that particular moment, he didn't have to think the thoughts and experience the feelings that were waiting for him in the wings.

One day he told me a dream in which he was going down a steep flight of stairs, then down a second flight; but the latter were too narrow for him and he didn't want to go any farther. Behind him the figure of a woman was urging him on, while he resisted. This was a picture of Bill's state at the time. He was well into a descent, but he was fighting against taking a deeper plunge.

Bill's complaint "I'm an old man; there's nothing left for me" was not really Saturn settling in. Although his statement sounds like an affirmation of age, it is more an attack on age. When he said this I wondered if he had been denied the opportunity to grow up during his many years as a seminarian and priest. He told me that in some ways he had felt like a child the whole time, never worrying about money or survival, never making life decisions, but simply following the orders of his superiors. Now fate had shoved him into a place of profound unsettling and reflection. For the first time he was questioning everything, and now he was growing up at an alarming speed.

"Your dream," I said to him, "about descending a narrow staircase with a woman urging you from behind—I think we might turn to Freud and see it as an attempt at birth."

"I never thought of it that way," he said, interested.

"You seem in your melancholy to be in a bardo state. Do you know what that is?"

"No," he said, "I never heard of it."

"The *Tibetan Book of the Dead* describes that time between incarnations, the period before the next birth into life, as bardo."

"I don't have any taste for the events of life these days."

"That's what I mean," I said. "You don't want to participate in life. You are between lives. The dream may be inviting you to descend into the canal."

"I feel very reluctant in that dream, and I'm disturbed by the woman."

"Aren't we all," I said, thinking how difficult it is to be born into this life again, especially when the first time around was so painful and apparently unsuccessful.

"I'm not ready," he said with understanding and conviction.

"That's all right," I responded. "You know where you are, and it's important to be exactly there. Bardo takes time; it can't be rushed. There's no point in premature birth."

Bill rose to leave and go back to his "cave," as he called his room in the monastery.

"There's nothing else to do, is there?" he asked.

"I don't think so," I said, wishing I could give him some specific hope.

Bill had measured the steps of the moon in his theology classes, and he thought he knew what was good for the soul. But now, having learned from his depression, he was speaking a more solid truth. "I will never again tell another person how to live," he said. "I can only talk to them of their mystery." Like Oscar Wilde in his depression, Bill was finding a greater point of view, a new appreciation for mystery. You would think a priest would be the one person familiar with mystery, but Bill's depression could be seen as a further step in his education in theology.

Eventually Bill's depression lifted, and he took a position in a new city where he worked as both counselor and priest. His period of schooling in Saturn's truths had some effect. He was able to help people look honestly at their lives and their emotions, whereas at a former time he would have tried to talk them out of their dark feelings with purely positive encouragement. He also knew what it was like to be deprived of respect and security, and so he could understand better the discouragement and despair of many people who came to him with tragic stories.

Care of the soul doesn't mean wallowing in the symptom, but it does mean trying to learn from depression what qualities the soul needs. Even further, it attempts to weave those depressive qualities into the fabric of life so that the aesthetics of Saturn—coldness, isolation, darkness, emptiness—makes a contribution to the texture of everyday life. In learning from depression, a person might dress in Saturn's black to mimic his mood. He might go on a trip alone as a response to a saturnine feeling. He might build a grotto in his yard as a place of saturnine retreat. Or, more internally, he might let his depressive thoughts and feelings just be. All of these actions would be a positive response to a visitation of Saturn's depressive emotion. They would be concrete ways to care for the soul in its darker beauty. In so doing, we might find a way into the mystery of this emptiness of the heart. We might also discover that depression has its own angel, a guiding spirit whose job it is to carry the soul away to its remote places where it finds unique insight and enjoys a special vision.

# The Body's Poetics of Illness

The human body is an immense source of imagination, a field on which imagination plays wantonly. The body is the soul presented in its richest and most expressive form. In the body, we see the soul articulated in gesture, dress, movement, shape, physiognomy, temperature, skin eruptions, tics, diseases—in countless expressive forms.

Artists have attempted to convey the expressive powers of the body in many different ways, from odalisques to formal portraits, from Reubens flesh tones to cubist geometries. Modern medicine, on the other hand, is hellbent on cure and has no interest in the body's inherent art. It wants to eradicate all anomalies before there is a chance to read them for their meaning. It abstracts the body into chemistries and anatomies so that the expressive body is hidden behind graphs, charts, numbers, and structural diagrams. Imagine a medical approach more in tune with art, one that is interested in the symbolic and poetic suggestiveness of a disease or a malfunctioning organ.

I had a conversation once with a nutritionist about cholesterol that raised some of these issues. Personally, I have felt a strong resistance to making concern about cholesterol the end-all factor in my relationship to my heart and to food. I told her about my misgivings.

"But cholesterol is a major problem," she said. "People who have had heart problems should especially understand the importance of controlling cholesterol in their diets."

"I don't doubt that cholesterol is a fact," I said, "but I wonder if we take it too factually."

"And the amazing thing is," she went on, "that aspirin can control its bad effects—just one every other day."

"Do you recommend that we all take an aspirin regularly for cholesterol?"

"If you have high cholesterol or if you have had heart problems, yes," she said with conviction.

"Why?" I asked.

"So you live longer," she said.

"So, fighting cholesterol is a move against death."

"Yes."

"Is it a denial of death?" I asked more pointedly. "I remember Ivan Illich's statement that he doesn't want to die of some disease. He wants to die of death."

"Maybe it *is* a denial of death."

"Is it possible," I asked, "to appreciate that we have a problem with cholesterol and yet imagine it differently, so that it isn't another way of wrestling with mortality?"

"I have no idea," she said. "There are certain assumptions we make, and we don't question them."

That is the problem with the body. We have certain assumptions we don't reflect on. If we were to reflect, we might imagine cholesterol differently.

"Could it have anything to do with congested highways?" her psychoanalyst husband offered. "Maybe we don't want congestion anywhere. We crave free passage, on the road and in our arteries."

I appreciated his comment because it took us out of the literal realm of chemistry and treated the symptom as a symbol, a lens through which to see the problem in an altogether different context. This is not to say that congested highways are the *cause* of arterial blockage. Causal thinking usually obstructs imagistic reflection. However, seeing the metaphorical comparison is the beginning of giving the body poetic weight.

Several years ago in Dallas James Hillman gave a lecture on the heart. He was making the point that the current trend to imagine the heart as a mechanical pump or as a muscle is extremely narrow and may be implicated in the widespread occurrence of heart trouble. When we talk this way, we lose sight of soulful images of the heart as the seat of courage and love. Thinking of the heart as an object, we take it for a walk or run it for exercise, but it loses all its metaphoric power and is reduced to a function. As Hillman was saying this, a man sitting in the front of the auditorium stood up. He was wearing a jogging suit and complained loudly that the heart in fact *is* a muscle and has to be kept in shape so we won't have a heart attack.

Hillman's point was that we are attacking the heart when we treat as a mere physical organ what poetry and song for centuries have treated as the seat of affection. It isn't easy for us, so imbued with modern categories of thought, to remember our own biases in this matter. Of course the heart is a pump. That's a fact. Our problem is that we can't see through the thought structures that give value to fact and at the same time treat poetic reflection as nonessential. In a sense, that point of view is itself a failure of heart. We think with our heads and no longer with our hearts.

Hillman's colleague, Robert Sardello, also points out that we give intelligence and power to the brain and then reduce the heart to a muscle. But, he says, the heart has its own intelligence. It knows what to do without orders from the brain. The heart has reasons that may or may not find sympathy from the brain. It has its own style, beating with special force, Sardello notes, in states of passion, as in anger and sex. The brain thinks cool thoughts about cold reality, while the heart thinks in heated rhythms.

The heart is only one of the many organs out of whose functions and shapes metaphoric richness has appeared over time. Historically, soul is to be found in the spleen, the liver, the stomach, the gall bladder, the intestines, the pituitary, and the lungs. Consider our word *schizophrenia* which means "cut off" or "split" phrenes—lungs. Is this mere poetic license, or is it the power of the body in its many varied parts to create a polycentric field for the soul? Hillman and Sardello suggest that it is the function of the body to give us emotions and images proper to its highly articulated organs.

## Symptoms and Disease

Psychoanalysis has made elaborate attempts to chart connections between psychological experience and physical ailments, but generally both psychology and medicine have been reluctant to read these poetic connections. In the fifteenth century, Marsilio Ficino made the observation that Mars dissolves the intestines. Today, with different language but perhaps with the same insight, we think there is a relationship between repressed anger and colitis. On the whole, however, we have only an unsophisticated understanding of the relationship between a particular physical symptom and the emotions.

*Symptom* is close to *symbol*. Etymologically a symbol is two things "thrown together," whereas a symptom is things that "fall together," as if by accident. We think that symptoms appear out of nowhere, and we rarely make the move of "throwing together" the two things: illness and image. Science prefers interpretations that are univocal. One reading is all that is desired. Poetry, on the other hand, never wants to stop interpreting. It doesn't seek an end to meaning. A poetic response to disease may seem inadequate in the context of medical science, because science and art differ radically from the point of interpretation. Therefore, a poetic reading of the body as it expresses itself in illness calls for a new appreciation for the laws of imagination, in particular a willingness to let imagination keep moving into ever newer and deeper insights.

In recent years some have spoken against a metaphoric view of disease because they don't want us "blaming" patients for their physical problems. If cancer is related to a person's way of life, they complain, we will hold the individual responsible for an illness over which he has no control. It is true that blaming a person for his disease only leads to guilt, and no increase in imagination. Yet, in Sardello's words, "The object of therapeutic treatment is to return imagination to the things that have become only physical." Whenever we place blame, we are looking for a scapegoat for a real dislocation which is difficult to find and in which we ourselves, as individuals and as a society, are implicated. Blame is a defensive substitute for an honest examination of life that seeks guidance in our mistakes. Fundamentally it is a way of averting consciousness of error. Sardello recommends that if our hearts are attacking us or if cancer is immersing us in fantasies of death, then we should listen to these symptoms and adjust life accordingly. Rather than blame, we could respond. Listening to the messages of the body is not the same as blaming the patient.

I recently had an experience which in a small way shows the relationship between body and image. I had been feeling a pain in my lower left side. The doctor wasn't sure what it was, but since it didn't worsen over several weeks he suggested watching it closely and not administering any heroic treatments. I agreed completely. Instead, I went to a couple who practice a mild form of massage and who are sensitive to the larger life contexts in which pain presents itself.

It was my first visit, so they asked me some general questions. What do you eat? How is your body doing in general these days? Is there anything going on in your life that you see is related to your pain. If the pain could speak, what might it say?

I appreciated the fact that this session began with a contextualizing of the pain. I found that this simple dialogue had a profound effect on me. It set me in the direction of observing the world surrounding the pain and of listening to its poetics.

Then, as I lay down on the massage table, the two of them, one on each side, began their gentle rubbing. Quickly I fell into deep relaxation. I drifted off to a place in consciousness far from that little room in my little village. My senses were picking up sounds around me, but my attention had sunk into an area sheltered from life.

I felt their hands move along my body, slowly and without much pressure. Then I felt fingers on the place of the pain. I expected to rise from my retreat and to protect myself against their touches. Instead, I remained in that area of distant consciousness.

Suddenly, several large, brightly colored, imposing tigers leapt out of a cage. They were so close that I couldn't see their entire bodies. Their color was more brilliant than anything that could exist in the natural world. They seemed at once playful and ferocious.

One of the massagers said, "How does it feel when I touch you there?"

I said, "Tigers have arrived."

"Speak to them," she said. "Find out what their message is."

I'd love to have found out, but it was obvious

to me these tigers had no interest in speaking English to me. "I don't think they talk," I said.

Even though I was talking to the woman massaging me, the tigers remained playing in the little piece of jungle that had opened up in the dimly lighted room. I didn't make friends with them; they were obviously not about to become pets. But I watched them for quite a while, awed by the strength and brightness of their huge bodies. When the massage was over and the tigers had gone home, I was told that animals frequently make an appearance in that massage room.

I left thinking that I should spend several weeks at least wondering about this visitation. The main things I felt from these tigers were courage, strength, and self-possession, qualities of heart I certainly needed at the time. Not their meaning, but their presence, seemed to give me confidence and strength. Long afterward, when I became aware of that pain again beginning to insinuate itself, I recalled the tigers and drew some courage from them. I also thought I could learn from them to show my true colors, with some brilliance and bravado.

When we bring imagination to the body, we can't expect dictionary-type explanations and clear solutions to problems. A symbol is often defined and treated as though it were a superficial matching of two things, as in dream books that tell you that a snake is always a reference to sex. More profoundly, though, a symbol is the act of throwing together two incongruous things and living in the tension that exists between them, watching the images that emerge from that tension. In this approach to symbol, there is no stopping point, no end to reflection, no single meaning, and no clear instruction on what to do next.

There can be no thesaurus of body imagery. My treatment was less a work to remove pain and more a stimulation of my imagination, so that I could reflect more richly about my body and my life. This is what a symptom is: body and life falling together as if by accident. The response is to contain that coincidence. This could also be a way to read the many androgynous images we find in art and mythology: male and female in one body representing the attempt to contain duality and to live its sometimes grotesque tension. Poetry, whether in literature or in the body, is always demanding that we hold together what seems to belong apart.

This poetical holding, which involves taking the poetic attitude out of the library and into the clinic, leads more deeply into the body and its pain than do measurements and univocal, purely physical interpretations. But it doesn't necessarily offer clarity. Clarity is not one of the gifts of poetry. On the other hand, poetry does provide depth, insight, wisdom, vision, language, and music. We simply don't think about these qualities much when faced with illness.

A sensitive poetic treatment of images sustains intuition, which is more directly related to emotion and behavioral response than a rational interpretation is. As an added benefit, the images remain intact. My tigers, long after my "treatment," are still a source of wonder and insight for me. They haven't been vanquished by a particular message or meaning I have extracted from them. Such intellectual surgery is usually fatal to the animal who comes from that special jungle I had stepped into.

Patricia Berry makes an important point about body and images. Images themselves have body, she says, but we, having become so fact-minded, don't appreciate this subtle body of the imagination. We always want to find some corollary in literal life as a way to give an image body—a dream must be about what happened during the day. A painting is about the painter's life. The pain in my side must be from something I ate. It takes a vivid imagination to realize that images have their own bodies. Those tigers were afire with their orange stripes, and their bodies were massive and heavy. As we allow such images their own physical being, we are less inclined to translate them into abstractions.

Perhaps we are more "into our bodies," as they say, not only when we are exercising or dancing or being massaged, but also when we behold the bodies of imagination. I don't know what the tigers' colors *meant,* nor do I know for sure what the strength of their muscles implied. It seemed important to let them have their bodies, and in that process, because they are created somehow in or out of my imagination, I moved into a close accord with *my* own body, whatever that is.


## Bodily Pleasure

If my colon is in pain because of anxiety, then that organ is not just a piece of biologically functioning flesh. It has some link with consciousness and a particular mode of expression. Sandor Ferenczi, Freud's noted Hungarian colleague, described body parts as having their own "organ eroticism." As I understand him, he meant that each organ has its own private life and, you might say, personality that takes pleasure in its activities. My colon was unhappy, and if I could attend to its complaint I might begin to understand what was making it uneasy, or, so to speak, "dis-easy."

The body's images are like those of dream. Touch my side and out comes a jungle. Many people going to the doctor have their own "cognitive maps" of their bodies, their own imagination of what the body looks like inside and what is going on at the moment in its ill-ness. If we weren't so insistent on univocal meanings, wanting only expert opinions, which are as much fantasy as a patient's thoughts, about what is going on, we might pay more attention to the patient's imagina-tion of the illness. Even hypochondria could be taken seriously as a true expression of the soul's malaise.

Ferenczi's phrase "organ eroticism" suggests that the body's parts not only function, they also take pleasure in what they do. One asks, not is the organ *working,* but is it enjoying it-self. Ferenczi is inviting us to shift the mythic base of our ideas about body organs from per-formance to pleasure. I can imagine interview-ing my kidneys: Are you relaxed? Are you en-joying your activity today? Or am I doing something that is making you depressed?

The word *disease* means "not having your elbows in a relaxed position." "Ease" comes from the Latin *ansatus,* "having handles," or "elbows akimbo"—a relaxed posture, or at least not at work. Dis-ease means no elbows, no elbow room. Ease is a form of pleasure, dis-ease a loss of pleasure. A specialist in disease should begin his questions for diagnosis with issues of pleasure. Are you enjoying life? Where is it not pleasurable? Are you fighting pleasure somewhere or in some part of your body that is seeking pleasure? The history of philosophy demonstrates the remarkable fact that whenever soul is placed at the center of concern, pleasure is one of the most prominent factors discussed.

Also curious is that whenever pleasure is tied to soul in the writings of philosophers, it is not separated from restraint. Epicurus, as we have seen, lived a simple life and taught a philoso-phy of pleasure. Ficino, who in his early years espoused the philosophy of Epicurus explicitly (later he lived it but did not speak about it openly), gave a high place to pleasure, yet he was a vegetarian, ate sparsely, traveled none and treasured friends and books over all other possessions. The motto of his Florentine acad-emy was displayed on a banner that read PLEASURE IN THE PRESENT. In one of his let-ters he give this epicurean advice: "Let your meditation walk no further than pleasure, and even a little behind."

We could imagine disease as not just a physical phenomenon but as a condition of the person and world, as the failure of the body to find its pleasure. Pleasure does not necessarily refer to the gratification of the senses or the frenzied pursuit of new experiences, possessions, or entertainments. The true Epicurean devotes himself or herself to pleasure with attention to soul and therefore doesn't become compulsive about it. If we put Ferenczi's organ eroticism together with Epicurean restraint, we might live in a world in which our ears would not be assaulted all day long by either harsh sounds or Muzak. We think of pollution as chemical poisoning, but the soul can be poisoned through the ear. We might be aware of the value of scents and aromas as well. Ficino recommended a high culture of flowers and spices as a powerful way to ensoul the world.

We might imagine much of our current disease as the body asserting itself in a context of cultural numbing. The stomach takes no pleasure in frozen and powdered foods. The back of the neck complains about polyester. The feet die of boredom for lack of walking in interesting places. The brain is depressed to find itself described as a computer and the heart surely doesn't enjoy being treated as a pump. There isn't much opportunity to exercise the spleen these days, and the liver is no longer the seat of passion. All these noble, richly poetic organs, teeming with meaning and power, have been made into functions.

We are perhaps the only culture to regard the body with such poverty of imagination. Ours is also the only time in our own history to chase the mystery away from the body and from its disease mode of expression. In the sixteenth century, Paracelsus gave doctors the following advice: "The physician should speak of that which is invisible. What is visible should belong to his knowledge, and he should recognize illnesses, just as anyone who is not a physician can recognize them from their symptoms. But this is far from making him a physician; he becomes a physician only when he knows that which is unnamed, invisible, and immaterial, yet has its effect."

These words of Paracelsus would be difficult to apply in the modern medical context, where the invisible that has effect is seen through microscopes and by means of x-rays. Medicine literalizes the invisible. Modern medicine trusts the microscope to reveal the roots of illness, but the microscope doesn't look far enough within. The Paracelsian physician would take into account the invisible factors at work in illness—emotions, thoughts, personal history, relationship, longing, fear, desire, and so on.

In the fifth book of Homer's *Iliad*, we find a

description of wounding that takes us deep into the invisible world. In the midst of raging battle, even the gods are hurt. Aphrodite is struck in the hand, Hera's breast is hit with a three-barbed arrow, and Hades, too, gets an arrow. This book is sometimes called "The Song of the Wounded Gods."

What does it mean when a god is wounded? Jung is often quoted as saying that the gods have now returned to us in our diseases. I would alter that to say that the gods themselves suffer our wounds. It is they who bear the burden of our compulsions, and disease is the expression of their pain and injury. In the medical world, all of our high-tech language sings the song of the wounded gods. In the heroic struggle to be "someone," to make life work and to find happiness, things we do may inflict wounds on something much deeper than "me." The very foundations of existence can be affected, and so disease and illness arise as from some profound, mysterious place, very much as a divine apparition.

Illness is to a large extent rooted in eternal causes. The Christian doctrine of original sin and the Buddhist Four Noble Truths teach that human life is wounded in its essence, and suffering is in the nature of things. We are wounded simply by participating in human life, by being children of Adam and Eve. To think that the proper or natural state is to be without wounds is an illusion. Any medicine motivated by the fantasy of doing away with woundedness is trying to avoid the human condition.

With this larger dimension in mind, we could examine our lives to see how our actions might be offending the very roots of our existence. We could look for self-contradiction and self-alienation. I don't mean to suggest personal guilt for our symptoms, but we could look to our physical problems for guidance in aligning our lives with our natures or, mythologically speaking, with the will of the gods. We could do this as well as a society. If we are killing ourselves by smoking, then what are we trying to accomplish with this activity? If cancer is cell growth gone berserk, then is there a god of growth who is being dishonored by our economic and technological fanaticism about growth? By discerning the divine principle deep in our activities, we might find the "cure" of our illness. The ancient Greeks taught that the god who heals is the same god who brought the disease in the first place.

Looking into the mythology of our illnesses, we could consider them from a religious point of view. The idea is not so much to bring religion to suffering as to see that suffering inspires religion. Our wounds remind us of the gods. If we allow sickness to lead us into wonder about the very base of experience, then our spirituality is strengthened. Accepting that we are wounded, we enter life differently than if our only concern is to overcome the wound. When we respond to the mysterious appearance of an illness, we live with responsibility to fate.

If the gods appear in our diseases, and if the gods are wounded in our Iliadic battles (life's warfare), then it makes no sense to avoid life in order to avoid its wounds. We could find new, deep value in illness, without masochistically indulging in it. We could risk the battle. In our psychological lives, too, we could hold off our palliatives and our techniques for relieving suffering long enough to find the god who has been struck and to reestablish harmony in our relation to that god. Illness offers us a path into the kind of religion that rises directly from participation in the deepest levels of fate and existence.

## Illness's Soul Mate

In his book on Asklepios, the Greek god of medicine, Kerényi reproduces a fascinating ancient sculpture that shows a doctor treating a man's shoulder. In the background, as though in a dream (entirely appropriate to Asklepios, who healed by means of dreams), a snake—the god's animal form—is touching the man's shoulder with its mouth. This gesture was considered particularly effective for healing. The image suggests that the various treatments physicians employ on the physical plane have counterparts in the soul. In dream, healing is often accomplished by an animal form, not by a rational, technical procedure. As reports of dreams often describe, the snake simply bites the person where it hurts. It vaccinates the patient with its immediate, potentially poisonous contact.

We can learn from this image that all illness is stereophonic. It plays out at the level of actual body tissues and also at the level of dream. All illness is meaningful, although its meaning may never be translatable into entirely rational terms. The point is not to understand the cause of the disease and then solve the problem, but to get close enough to the disease to restore the particular religious connection with life at which it hints. We need to feel the teeth of the god within the illness in order to be cured by the disease. In a very real sense, we do not cure diseases, they cure us, by restoring our religious participation in life. If the gods appear in our diseases, it follows that our lives may be too secular and in need of such a visitation.

The following is a dream reported by a sensitive woman trained in the medical professions. She is lying in a bed together with two physicians dressed in white coats. They are talking about a degenerative disease that everyone is going to get. One of the doctors is interested in the fact that in the early stages of the disease, the patient goes deaf. He says that this is an opportunity to experience what it is like to be deaf. The dreamer worries about who is going to take care of the people if everyone has the disease. Then the scene shifts, and the dreamer walks into the office of another doctor. She sees a porcelain figure of a woman on his desk. She picks it up and holds it to her chest. She notices that the doctor has art objects all around his room. She notices in particular an ivory figurine of a woman with gold-leaf hair and dress. She holds the porcelain figure out and sees that an arm has been broken off at the shoulder, and she feels bad.

This dream suggests in several ways the ancient theme of the "wounded healer." The doctors are in bed with the patient. Everyone, including the doctors, will get the disease. One of the doctors even likes the idea of experiencing the symptoms. The patient/dreamer doesn't understand the mysterious truth that illness is unavoidable. How can the problem be treated if everyone is infected? The doctors are not concerned about this issue. They seem to understand and accept the fact that illness is universal.

The dream also shows that whoever cures us has to be "in bed" with our illness. The doctors are not divorcing themselves from the illness, making the patient and her problem something foreign to them. They don't exactly treat it, they become intimate with it, and express the desire to experience it themselves. As a psychotherapist, if I distance myself defensively from the problems my clients bring to me, I force them to carry universal illness while I try to have power over the disease in order to be protected from it. Healing, however, may ask more from the doctor. It may require a willingness to approach the illness as an intimate, as someone interested in the mystery, and as a member of the human community affected by this disease. How often do we talk about alcoholics or drug addicts as if they were not part of our community, as though their problem had absolutely nothing to do with us?

Fortunately for the dreamer, the third doctor is like Paracelsus and Ficino. He has art objects in his office. Obviously he knows that medicine is more an art than a science, and that art plays a role in his practice. I am reminded of Freud's office with its celebrated collection of ancient art pieces. As the traditional medicine of many peoples demonstrates, disease can be treated with images. The patient, for her part, needs to see the images of her healing, just as any of us in distress might look for the stories and images wrapped in our complaints. But she shouldn't bring them too close to her, making them too personal, or they will break apart. We can only approach the gods through poetry, and if disease is the disguise of the gods, then our medicine will have to be full of art and image.

Novalis said, "Every disease is a musical problem. Its cure, a musical solution. The more rapid and complete the solution, the greater the musical talent of the doctor." Many of the ancient physicians I have referred to, such as Robert Fludd and Ficino, were also musicians. They were concerned with the rhythms, tonalities, discords, and concords of the body and the soul. They taught that a doctor, when treating any kind of malady, must know something of the patient's music. What is the tempo of this disease? With what life elements is it in counterpoint? What is the nature of the dissonance that the patient feels as pain and discomfort?

According to Paracelsus, "The disease desires its wife, that is, the medicine. The medicine must be adjusted to the disease, both must be united to form a harmonious whole, just as in the case of man and woman." The dream in which the doctors get into bed with the patient is Paracelsian in tone. The illness is fulfilled and completed by its marriage to treatment. Or, to put it differently, the "wife"—the *anima,* image, story or dream— of the illness is its medicine.

Now, how can this obscure imagery help us with modern practice? Thinking of the Paracelsian wife-medicine, we might place more importance on the stories we tell about our illnesses and the history of our bodies. We might notice dreams that occur at the time of an illness. We could tone down the masculine heroics in the modern practice of medicine and allow some freedom of imagination. A patient, too, could take the attitude of inviting the doctor, figuratively, to get in bed with the illness instead of giving it over to the doctor as to an authority. The bed metaphor, with its erotic connotations, is very different from the metaphors of authority and power that we generally bring to the medical world.

If we were to examine our diseases poetically, we might find a wealth of imagery that could speak to the way we live our lives. Following up on that imagery, we could attune our lives and allow ourselves to be corrected by the disease. That is what I mean when I say that without sickness we wouldn't be cured, physically and psychologically. For example, Sardello looks at imagery in cancer and concludes that its message is that we live in a world where things have lost their body and therefore their individuality. Our response to this disease could be to abandon the mass culture of plastic reproductions and recover a sensitivity to things of quality and imagination. If we attack nature with our polluting methods of manufacturing, and if we let the quality of life fade in the name of speed and efficiency, then symptoms may arise. In Sardello's description of disease, our bodies reflect or participate in the world's body, so that if we harm that outer body, our own bodies will feel the effects. Essentially there is no distinction between the world's body and the human body.

## Body and Soul

The human body in fifteenth-century Florence was an entirely different body from the one you see in the New York of, say, the 1990s. The modern body is an efficient machine that needs to be kept in shape so that its organs will function smoothly and for as long as possible. If something goes wrong with any part, it can be replaced with a mechanical substitute, because that is the way we picture the body—as a machine.

In the Florentine view the human body was a manifestation of the soul. It was possible to entertain a soulless notion of the body, but that was considered an aberration. Such a body was unnaturally split off from soul. We might call it schizoid—lifeless, meaningless and without poetics. But an ensouled body takes its life from the world's body, as Ficino said, "The world lives and breathes, and we can draw its spirit into us." What we do to the world's body, we do to our own. We are not masters of this world, we participate in its life.

When we relate to our bodies as having soul, we attend to their beauty, their poetry and their expressiveness. Our very habit of treating the body as a machine, whose muscles are like pulleys and its organs engines, forces its poetry underground, so that we experience the body as an instrument and see its poetics only in illness. Fortunately, we still have a few institutions that foster an imaginal body. Fashion, for instance, brings a considerable amount of fantasy to the body, although modern dress for men falls quite short in color and variety of styles popular in former times. Cosmetics and perfumery are available to women, and can be an important aspect of cultivating the body's soul.

Exercise could be more soulfully performed by emphasizing fantasy and imagination. Usually we are told how much time to spend at a certain exercise, what heart rate to aim for, and which muscle to focus on for toning. Five hundred years ago Ficino gave somewhat different advice for daily exercise. "You should walk as often as possible among plants that have a wonderful aroma, spending a considerable amount of time every day among such things." His emphasis is on the world and the senses. In a former time, exercise was inseparable from experiencing the world, walking through it, smelling it and feeling it sensually, even as the heart got its massage from the exertion of the walk. Emerson, a great New England walker, wrote in his essay "Nature": "The greatest delight which the fields and woods minister is the suggestion of an occult relation between man and the vegetable. I am not alone and unacknowledged. They nod to me, and I to them." In this Emersonian exercise program, the soul is involved in the perception of an intimacy between human personality and the world's communing body.

If we could loosen the grip we have on the mechanical view of our own bodies and the body of the world, many other possibilities might come to light. We could exercise the nose, the ear, and the skin, not only the muscles. We might listen to the music of wind in the trees, church bells, distant locomotives, crickets and nature's teeming musical silence. We could train our eyes to look with compassion and appreciation. Soul is never far from attachment to particulars; a soulful body exercise would always lead us toward an affectionate relationship to the world. Henry Thoreau, who exercised his body in the context of making a retreat at Walden Pond, writes: "I rejoice that there are owls. Let them do the idiotic and maniacal hooting for men. It is a sound admirably suited to swamps and twilight woods which no day illustrates, suggesting a vast and undeveloped nature which men have not recognized." Body exercise is incomplete if it focuses exclusively on muscle and is motivated by the ideal of a physique unspoiled by fat. What good is a lean body that can't hear Thoreau's owls or return a wave to Emerson's wheat? The ensouled body is in communion with the body of the world and finds its health in that intimacy.

A soul-oriented yoga might go through its many postures and forms of breathing while paying attention to the memories, emotions, and images that arise in conjunction with physical motion and posture. Inner images are as important to the soul in exercise as images from nature and culture are to the person on a walk. Often yoga is performed with the ideal of transcendence. We want to get our bodies trimmed down to match a perfect image of ourselves. Or we want physical or psychic powers that go beyond the normal or what we are accustomed to. Behind the practice of yoga might be a perfectionist fantasy or images of purity. But soul is not about transcendence. Soul-yoga wants more intimacy between consciousness and the soul, between our body and the world's body, and between ourselves and our fellow human beings. It basks in the imagination its methods bring, without expecting images and memories to take it toward any goal of improvement.

We paint the body, photograph it, dance with it, and decorate it with cosmetics, jewelry, clothes, costumes, tattoos, rings, and watches. We know that the body is a world of imagination, and that is the essence of its soul. We might do more for its health by looking seriously at artworks that reveal some of the body's expressiveness than by taking vitamins or doing exercises. An unimagined body is on its way toward disease. In times of sickness we could also consider the body's suffering as the dream of its breakdown.

Our hospitals are generally not equipped to deal with the soul in illness. But it wouldn't take much to change them, because the soul doesn't require expensive technology and highly trained experts. Not long ago a hospital administrator asked me for some ideas about improving the hospital's operations. I recommended a few simple things. Their plan was to let patients read their own charts every day and also be given pamphlets describing the chemical and biological aspects of their diseases. I suggested that rather than being given a chart of temperatures and medications, the patients be encouraged to keep track of their impressions and their emotions during their time in the hospital and, most important, to note their dreams every day. I also recommended setting up an art room where patients could paint, sculpt, and maybe dance their fantasies during treatment. I was thinking more of an art studio than of an art therapy room in the usual sense. I also recommended a time and place where patients could tell stories about their illnesses and hospitalization, certainly not with an expert who would reinforce the technical medical format, but maybe with a real storyteller or someone who would know the importance of letting the soul speak and find its images.

The word *hospital* comes from *hospis*, which means both "stranger" and "host," plus *pito,* meaning "lord" or "powerful one." The hospital is a place where the stranger can find rest, protection, and care. Maybe the disease is the stranger who comes to the hospital, and maybe the actual hospital is only the concrete form of our own capacity to host the alien disease. The Latin *hospis* also means "enemy," and I don't want to lose this shadow element in disease. Illness is an enemy, but we've already lived out that myth with conviction. Now may be the time to see illness as the stranger who needs a place in which to stay and be cared for.

Toward the end of his soulful book *Love's Body,* Norman O. Brown says, "What is always speaking silently is the body." Our task as hospices of our own illness and caretakers of our bodies is to tune up the ear that hears such speech. It is obviously not a literal ear that listens to the body's silent speech, not the actual stethoscope or even the CAT-scan. The technology of this ear is more subtle and more perceptive than any instrument yet invented. It is the ear of the poet, that is, any person who regards the world with imagination. Emerson says that only the poet knows the facts of astronomy, chemistry, and the other sciences, "because he takes them as signs."

We may understand the body as a collection of facts, but if we also grant it its soul, it is an inexhaustible source of "signs." Tending the body in all its physicality, but also with imagination, is an important part of care of the soul. But such a project calls for an approach that is difficult to conjure up in an age of facts—medical poetics. Will the day come when Paracelsus, Ficino, and Emerson will be high on the list of required reading for medical students? When the medical student will make a serious and close study of the body in art? When a visit to the doctor will include a review of the patient's fateful history, dreams, and personal fantasies about the illness?

That day will probably come, because it already has been. The Renaissance therapist Ficino was equipped with a lute on which he could play his patient's distemper into art. Keats made an easy career move from medicine to poetry. Emerson explored the mysteries of illness as a philosopher. The tight hold that the technical fantasy of life has had on modern consciousness appears to be easing in some quarters. Maybe there is a chance that the body will be freed from its identification as a *corpus,* a corpse, and once again feel the flush of soul as it becomes animated by a new appreciation for its own art.

# CHAPTER 9

# The Economics of Soul: Work, Money, Failure, and Creativity

Care of the soul requires ongoing attention to every aspect of life. Essentially it is a cultivation of ordinary things in such a way that soul is nurtured and fostered. Therapy tends to focus on crises or chronic problems. I've never heard anyone come to therapy and say they want to discuss gardening or to examine the soul issues in a house that they're building or to prepare to be a city councilperson. Yet all of these ordinary things have a great deal to do with the condition of the soul. If we do not tend the soul consciously and artfully, then its issues remain largely unconscious, uncultivated, and therefore often problematic.

One of the most unconscious of our daily activities from the perspective of the soul is work and the settings of work—the office, factory, store, studio, or home. I have found in my practice over the years that the conditions of work have at least as much to do with disturbances of soul as marriage and family. Yet it is tempting simply to make adjustments in response to problems at work without recognizing the deep issues involved. Certainly we allow the workplace to be dominated by function and efficiency, thereby leaving us open to the complaints of neglected soul. We could benefit psychologically from a heightened consciousness about the poetry of work—its style, tools, timing, and environment.

Several years ago I gave a lecture on the medieval idea that the world is a book to be read. Monks used the phrase *liber mundi,* the "book of the world," to describe a spiritual kind of literacy. Afterward, a woman, a housewife, who had attended telephoned to ask if I would come to her house, to read it in this way. I had never done such a thing, but in therapy I had been reading dreams and paintings for years, so the idea was appealing.

Together we walked through the rooms, observing them closely, and quietly discussed our impressions. This "reading" was not an analysis or an interpretation. It was more "dreaming the house onward," to paraphrase an expression of Jung's—"dreaming the dream onward." My idea was to see the house's poetry and alphabet, to understand the gestures it was making in its architecture, colors, furnishings, decorations, and the condition it was in at that particular time. The woman was truly devoted to her home and wanted to give housework a place of dignity in her life.

Some of the images that came to us were personal. I heard stories of a former marriage, of children, visitors, and her own childhood. Others had to do with the architecture of the building and with American history, and a few touched on philosophical questions about the very nature of dwelling and shelter.

I remember in particular an immaculate bathroom with smooth tiles and cool colors. The bathroom is a room full of strong imagery and psychological content—bodily waste, cleansing, privacy, cosmetics, clothing, nudity, pipes connected to the underground, and running water. It is a favored setting for many dreams, an indication of its special appeal to the imagination. This bathroom seemed to me unusually orderly and clean, and having agreed to an honest reading of the house, we discussed the efforts my hostess put into keeping this room spotless.

In this reading of her house, I wasn't trying to figure this woman out, or look for something wrong, or come up with some new way for her to live her life. We were simply taking a special look at the house in order to glimpse signs of the soul that lay hidden in the everyday and commonplace. At the end of our tour, we both felt unusually connected to the place and to its things. For my part, I was motivated to reflect on my own home and to think more deeply about the poetics of everyday life.

The home is a place of daily work, whether or not one has an "outside" job. If you were to read your own house, at some point you would find yourself standing before the tools of housework: vacuum cleaner, broom, dust-mop, soaps, sponges, dishpan, hammer, screwdriver. These things are very simple, and yet they are fundamental to the feeling we have of being at home. Jean Lall, an astrologer and therapist from Baltimore, lectures on the soul of housework. She calls housework "a path of contemplation" and says that if we denigrate the work that is to be done around the house every day, from cooking to doing laundry, we lose our attachment to our immediate world. There is also a close relationship, she says, between daily work around the house and responsibility to our natural environment.

I might put it this way: there are gods of the house, and our daily work is a way of acknowledging these home spirits that are so important in sustaining our lives. To them, a scrub brush is a sacramental object, and when we use this implement with care we are giving something to the soul. In this sense, cleaning the bathroom is a form of therapy because there is a correspondence between the actual room and a certain chamber of the heart. The bathroom that appears in our dreams is both the room in our house and a poetic object that describes a space in the soul.

I don't mean to inflate the simple things of life with exaggerated meaning and formality, but we might be reminded of the value to the soul of doing our daily chores attentively and with an eye to detail. We all know that at some level daily work affects character and the overall quality of life, but we usually overlook the way soulfulness can adhere to ordinary housework and the gifts it can bring to the soul. If we let other people do our ordinary work for us, or if we do it ourselves without care, we might be losing something irreplaceable and eventually experience that missing element as a painful sense of loneliness or homelessness.

We can "read" the house of our outside work life in the same way I read that woman's home: examine its environment, look closely at its tools, consider the way time is spent and note the moods and emotions that typically surround the work itself. How you spend your working hours—what you look at, sit on and work with—makes a difference, not only in terms of efficiency but for its effect on your sense of yourself and the direction your imagination takes. Some businesses cover over their soulless conception of work with a veneer of fake walls, plastic plants, and pseudoart. If that is what we give to the workplace in the name of beauty, then that is the measure of soulfulness we will have at our job. Soul cannot be faked without serious consequences. In his poem "The Garden," the poet Andrew Marvell refers to "a green thought in a green shade." Surrounded by plastic ferns, we will be filled with plastic thoughts.

## Work as Opus

In many religious traditions, work is not set off from the precincts of the sacred. It is not "pro-fane"—in front of the temple—it is *in* the temple. In Christian and Zen monasteries, for instance, work is as much a part of the monk's carefully designed life as are prayer, meditation, and liturgy. I learned this when I was a novice in a religious order. A novice is a fledgling monk, learning the ins and outs of the spiritual life of prayer, meditation, study, and . . . work. I recall one day in particular, when I was given the job of pruning apple trees. It was a cold day in Wisconsin, and I was out on a limb sawing away at shoots sticking up on limbs all around me like minarets. I took a minute to rest, hoping the limb wouldn't suddenly break, and asked myself, "Why am I doing this? I'm supposed to be learning prayer, meditation, Latin, and Gregorian chant. But here I am, my hands frostbitten, feeling not terribly secure in the top of a tree, my fingers bloody from an erratic saw blade, doing something I know nothing about." The answer, I already knew, was that work is an important component of the spiritual life. In some monasteries monks file off to work in procession, wearing their long hooded robes and maintaining silence. Monastic writers describe work as a path to holiness.

Formal religion always gives us hints about the depth dimension of anything in daily life, in this case the idea that work is not the secular enterprise the modern world assumes it is. Whether we do it with mindfulness and art, or whether it takes place in unmitigated unconsciousness, work affects the soul profoundly. It is full of imagination and speaks to the soul at many different levels. It may, for example, conjure up certain memories and fantasies that have special significance These may be connected to family myths, traditions, and ideals. Or work may be a means of sorting out issues that have little to do with the work itself. It may be a response to fate. We may find ourselves doing work that has been in the family for generations or working at a job that appeared after a number of coincidences and chance events. In this sense, all work is a vocation, a calling from a place that is the source of meaning and identity, the roots of which lie beyond human intention and interpretation.

Etymology, the examination of the deep imagery and myth that reside within ordinary language, also offers some insight into work. Sometimes we refer to work as an "occupation," an interesting word that means "to be taken and seized." In the past this word had strong sexual connotations. We like to think that we have chosen our work, but it could be more accurate to say that our work has found us. Most people can tell fate-filled stories of how they happen to be in their current "occu-pation." These stories tell how the work came to occupy them, to take residence. Work is a vocation: we are called to it. But we are also loved by our work. It can excite us, comfort us, and make us feel fulfilled, just as a lover can. Soul and the erotic are always together. If our work doesn't have an erotic tone to it, then it probably lacks soul as well.

The technical name for the category of ritu-als that take place in church, such as baptism or the eucharist, is liturgy. It comes from the Greek words *laos* and *ergos,* which together can be translated simply as "ordinary person's work" or "the labor of the laity." The rituals that take place in church are a kind of work, the soul's work: something of the soul is being created in the work of ritual. Still, there is no need to separate that work from the work that goes on "in the world." From a depth point of view, all work is liturgy. Ordinary actions, too, accomplish something for the soul. What takes place in a church or temple is an exem-plar for what happens in the world. Church points out the profound, often hidden nature of worldly activity. We could say, then, that all work is sacred, whether you are building a road, cutting a person's hair, or taking out the garbage.

We can bridge the gap between sacred

church and secular world by occasionally ritualizing the everyday things we do. It isn't necessary to place a cloak of religiosity on everyday work in order to make it sacred; formal
ritual is only a way of reminding ourselves of
the ritual qualities that are in work anyway.
Therefore, like a sacristan who reverences
everything he tends, we might want to buy
tools of satisfying quality—well made, pleasing to look at, and fitted to the hand—and
cleansers that respect the environment. A special table cloth might help ritualize a dinner,
or an office desk of special design or select
woods could transform the workplace into an
arena that has imaginal depth. Often work
spaces are devoid of imagination, so that the
workers are left with a purely secularized feeling that doesn't feed their souls.

Workers assume that their tasks, too, are
purely secular and functional, but even such
ordinary jobs as carpentry, secretarial services, and gardening relate to the soul as much
as to function. In the medieval world, these
forms of work each had a patron god—Saturn, Mercury, and Venus, respectively—indicating that in each case matters of profound
significance to the soul are encountered in
daily work. We could learn from our ancestors
that the familiar tasks involved in an ordinary

job have a presiding god and constitute a liturgy in relation to that god.

Mythology also offers some suggestions for thinking deeply about work. Daedalus, for instance, was known as the ingenious maker of dolls and toys, which came to life when a child played with them. Hephaistos, one of the truly great gods, made furniture and jewelry, among other things, for the other gods. Our own children play with toys as if they were alive, keeping the myth alive. It would make great mythological sense for makers of toys to look deeply into their work and see that Daedalus has a hand in it. If they had a deep sense of the truly magical nature of their product, they could take care of the souls of children with sacred imagination. The same principle holds for all professions and for all forms of labor.

When we think of work, we only consider function, and so the soul elements are left to chance. Where there is no artfulness about life, there is a weakening of soul. It seems to me that the problem with modern manufacturing is not a lack of efficiency, it is a loss of soul.

Not understanding soul, companies look to the work of other cultures and try to mimic their methods. What they don't realize is that method is not the only thing. Another culture may be successful in its manufacturing and business because it is still mindful of the needs of the heart. It may not be enough to copy surface strategies, ignoring the deeper evaluation of feeling and sensibility that gives work grounding in the human heart and not just in the brain.

Another way to enrich the imagination of work is to follow Jung in his work with alchemy. Alchemy was a process in which raw material was placed in a vessel where it was heated, observed closely, heated some more, passed through various operations and observed once again. In the end, the result was an arcane product imagined mysteriously to be gold, the stone of the philosophers, or a potent elixir. In Jung's view, alchemy was a spiritual practice carried out for the benefit of the soul. Its play with chemicals, heat, and distillation was a poetical project in which substances, colors, and other material qualities offered an external imagery for a hidden parallel process of the soul. Just as astrology based its entire symbol system on the bodies of planets, so alchemy found its poetic inspiration in the qualities of chemicals and their interactions.

This process of working the stuff of the soul, objectified in natural materials, the alchemist called the *opus,* that is, "the work." We could imagine our own everyday work alchemically in the same way. The plain concerns of ordinary work are the raw material, the *prima materia,* as the alchemist called it, for working out the soul's matter. We work on the stuff of the soul by means of the things of life. This is an ancient idea espoused by Neoplatonists: ordinary life is the means of entry into higher spiritual activity. Or we could say that at the very moment we are hard at work on some worldly endeavor, we are also working on a different plane. Perhaps without knowing it, we are engaged in the labors of the soul.

We might understand the role of everyday work in the soul by looking more closely at the idea of *opus.* In his book *Psychology and Alchemy,* Jung describes the *opus* as a work of imagination. He is discussing an old alchemical text that tells how to produce the philosophers' stone. The passage says that one should be guided by a true and not a fantastic imagination. Commenting on this idea, Jung says that imagination is "an authentic accomplishment of thought or reflection that does not spin aimless and groundless fantasies into the blue; that is to say, it does not merely play with its object, rather it tries to grasp the inner facts and portray them in images true to their nature. This activity is an *opus,* a work."

We move closer to the soul's work when we go deeper than intellectual abstractions and imaginary fancies that do not well up from the more profound roots of feeling. The more deeply our work stirs imagination and corresponds to images that lie there at the bedrock of identity and fate, the more it will have soul. Work is an attempt to find an adequate alchemy that both wakens and satisfies the very root of being. Most of us put a great deal of time into work, not only because we have to work so many hours to make a living, but because work is central to the soul's *opus*. We are crafting ourselves—individuating, to use the Jungian term. Work is fundamental to the *opus* because the whole point of life is the fabrication of soul.

To put it more simply, the job and the *opus* are related insofar as work is an extension or reflection of yourself. You conclude a successful business transaction, and you feel good about yourself. You build a cherry dining table or sew a star quilt, then you stand back and contemplate it, feeling a surge of pride. These feelings give a hint that the alchemical *opus* is in play. The trouble is, if what we do or make is not up to our standards and does not reflect attention and care when we stand back to look at it the soul suffers. The whole society suffers a wound to soul if we allow ourselves to do bad work.

When it is not possible to feel good about

our work, then soulful pride, so necessary for creativity, turns into narcissism. Pride and narcissism are not the same thing; in a sense, they are opposites. Like Narcissus, we need to be objectified in an image, something outside ourselves. The products of our work are like the image in the pond—a means of loving ourselves. But if those products are not lovable, we are forced into a narcissistic place where we lose sight of the work itself and focus on our own personal needs. Love of the world and our place in it, attained largely by our work, turns into solipsistic craving for love.

Work becomes narcissistic when we cannot love ourselves through objects in the world. This is one of the deeper implications of the Narcissus myth: the flowering of life depends upon finding a reflection of oneself in the world, and one's work is an important place for that kind of reflection. In the language of Neoplatonism, Narcissus discovers love when he finds that his nature is completed in that part of his soul that is outside himself, in the soul of the world. Read in this way, the story suggests that we will never achieve the flowering of our own natures until we find that piece of ourselves, that lovable twin, which lives in the world and *as* the world. Therefore, finding the right work is like discovering your own soul in the world.

In his book *Psychology and Religion: West and East*, Jung says, following alchemical teaching, "The soul is for the most part outside the body." What an extraordinary idea! The modern person is taught to believe that the soul—or whatever language is used for soul—is contained in the brain or is equivalent to mind and is purely and humanly subjective. But if we were to think of the soul as being in the world, then maybe our work would be seen as a truly important aspect of our lives, not only for its literal product but also as a way of caring for the soul.

As we saw in our earlier discussion of the myth, narcissism occurs as a symptom in direct reaction to the failure of the Narcissus myth. Our work takes on narcissistic qualities when it does not serve well as a reflection of self. When that inherent reflection is lost, we become more concerned instead with how our work reflects on our reputations. We seek to repair our painful narcissism in the glow of achievement, and so we become distracted from the soul of the work for its sake. We are tempted to find satisfaction in secondary rewards, such as money, prestige, and the trappings of success.

It's obvious that climbing the ladder of success can easily lead to a loss of soul. An alternative may be to choose a profession or projects with soul in mind. If a potential employer describes all the benefits of a job, we could ask about the soul values. What is the spirit in this workplace? Will I be treated as a person here? Is there a feeling of community? Do people love their work? Is what we are doing and producing worthy of my commitment and long hours? Are there any moral problems in the job or workplace—making things detrimental to people or to the earth, taking excessive profits or contributing to racial and sexist oppression? It is not possible to care for the soul while violating or disregarding one's own moral sensibility.

Narcissus and work are further related because the love that goes out into our work comes back as love of self. Signs of this love and therefore of soul are feelings of attraction, desire, curiosity, involvement, passion, and loyalty in relation to our work. I once counseled a man who worked in an automobile factory. He hated his work. On a team that did spray painting, he was the troubleshooter, clearing up clogged pipes and keeping the chemical mixtures in proper proportion. He was good at what he did, but he experienced his job as an imprisonment. He came to me wondering what had happened in his childhood to make his life so unhappy.

As he talked I noticed that most of his annoyance was focused around his job. So, we discussed his work in detail. Some of his dreams were set on the job site, so we had many occasions to explore the history of his imagination of work, including his childhood fantasies of a life work, his many jobs, his education and training, and his current habits of work. Notice that I was not trying to present him with options or get him to find a better job. I wanted to focus on the place of work in his soul and listen to its complaints about what he was doing. Eventually his reflections on work led him to seek a change. One day he got up enough courage to get a position in sales, which he felt was much better suited to him. Soon many of his "psychological" problems began to disappear. "I love my job," he told me. "I don't mind being criticized for a mistake, and I love to come to work. That other job just wasn't me." The job of troubleshooting spraying operations might have suited another person, but not this man, who had to suffer awhile in his work until he moved into something soulful for him.

To say that a job isn't me is to say that the relationship between work and the soul has fallen down, or, to put it in alchemical language, work and *opus* have no correspondence. When that linkage is present, work is easier and more satisfying because the counterpoint between job and *opus* is harmonious. When the soul is involved, the work is not carried out by the ego alone; it arises from a deeper place and therefore is not deprived of passion, spontaneity, and grace.

In his *Lives of Artists,* Vasari tells a story about the Renaissance sculptor and architect Filippo Brunelleschi. Donatello, Filippo, and other artists were hanging out in Florence when Donatello mentioned a beautiful marble sarcophagus he had seen in the town of Cortona, a good distance away. "Filippo conceived a tremendous desire to see the work," Vasari writes. "So, without changing his shoes or clothes, immediately he headed off for Cortona, examined the sarcophagus, made a sketch of it, and brought it back to Florence before he was missed." Similar stories are told of Bach walking many miles to hear great music and spending late nights copying the works of composers he admired.

Stories of artists' intensive pursuit of their vision and craft are a kind of mythology revealing the archetypal dimensions of soulful work. In our own lives this archetype may appear in a small way, as in a great feeling of satisfaction after spending the morning at the right task. Or it may appear, as it did for the factory worker, in a satisfying career move. One can imagine a radical restructuring of career counseling toward focusing on the soul. Testing would then assess the nature of the *opus* rather than aptitude, and discussion would touch upon issues much deeper than the surface ego concerns of life.


## *Money*

Money and work are, of course, intimately related. By splitting concern for financial profit from the inherent values of work, money can become the focus of a job's narcissism. In other words, pleasure in money can take the place of pleasure in work. Still, we all require money, and money can be an integral part of work without loss of soul. The crucial point is our attitude. In most work there can be a close relationship between caring for the world in which we live (ecology) and caring for the quality of our way of life (economy).

Ecology and economy, both from the Greek *oikos,* have to do with "house" in the broadest sense. Ecology (*logos*) concerns our understanding of the earth as our home and our search for appropriate ways to dwell on it. Economy (*nomos*) is concerned with the ways in which we get along in this world home and with the family of society. Money is simply the coinage of our relationship to the community and environment in which we live. We are paid for our work, and in turn we pay for services and products. We pay our taxes, and the government provides for the basic needs of the community. *Nomos* in economics means law, but not natural law. It is the recognition that community is necessary and that it requires rules of participation. Money is central in our attempts to live a communal life.

But a community is not a wholly rational construction. Each community has a complicated personality, with a varied past and mixed values. It has a soul and so it also has shadow. Money is not just a rational medium of exchange, it also carries the soul of communal life. It has all the complications of soul, and, like sex and disease, it is beyond our powers of control. It can fill us with compelling desire, longing, envy, and greed. The lives of some people are shaped by the lure of money, while others sense the temptation and take an ascetic route, in order to avoid being tainted. Either way, money retains its powerful position in the soul.

A neurotic way of dealing with money can reflect and intensify our other problems. For example, we may split money into fantasies of wealth and poverty. If a person's attitude toward money is essentially a defense against poverty, then this person may never truly experience wealth. The *experience* of wealth is, after all, a subjective thing. For some, to be wealthy is to have credit cards paid off, for others it requires owning a Rolls Royce or two. Wealth cannot be measured by a bank account because it is primarily what we imagine it to be. Ignorant of the soul and its own brand of wealth, we may become giddy in the pursuit of money because we fear literal poverty around the corner.

Once again we can turn to religion to search out some deeper images of wealth and poverty. In religious orders, monks take a vow of poverty, but if you visit monasteries you might be surprised at how often you find beautifully built and furnished buildings on prime real estate. The monks may live simply but not always austerely, and they never have to worry for food and shelter. Monastic poverty is sometimes defined not as a scarcity of money and property but rather as "common ownership." The purpose of the vow is to promote community by owning all things in common.

What if, as a nation, a city, or a neighborhood, to say nothing of the globe, we all took such a vow of poverty? We would not be romanticizing deprivation, we would be striving toward a deep sense of community by feeling ownership of common property. As it is, we divide property literally into public and private. Owners can do anything they want with their private property within the limits of zoning laws, and even these do not always have the welfare of the community in mind. As a public, we may feel no rights or obligations concerning the condition and quality of these buildings and businesses.

If we do not feel any general sense of proprietorship toward the earth, then we can think that it is someone else's responsibility to keep the oceans clean and the air free of poison. The truly wealthy person, however, is the one who "owns" it all—land, air, and sea. At the same time, not splitting wealth and poverty, this wealthy person doesn't own anything. From the perspective of soul, wealth and poverty come together in responsible use and enjoyment of this world, which is only leased to us for the period of our tenure here.

Money is like sex. Some people believe that the more sexual experiences they have, with as many different people as possible, the more fulfilled they will be. But even great quantities of money and sex may not satisfy the craving. The problem lies not in having too much or too little, but in taking money literally, as a fetish rather than as a medium. If wealth is found by rejecting the experience of poverty, then it will never be complete. The soul is nurtured by want as much as by plenty.

When I speak for the soul of poverty, I do not mean one should romanticize poverty as a means of transcending bodily life. Certain forms of spirituality flee the evils of money in favor of transcendence and moral purity. Some people think they should work without receiving any payment. Others like to barter their services, with the intention of avoiding money's shadow. But poverty, like wealth, can be taken too literally, so that the person escaping money stands lonely outside the community that economics helps to sustain. The desire for wealth, a legitimate element in the soul's eros, may be lost, along with its joy; or it is repressed and then sneaks back in awkwardness about money or in behind-the-scenes financial wizardry and hoarding. Religions of all denominations demonstrate a remarkable ability, often covert, to raise and invest money. It is not surprising to hear now and then of a highly regarded religious group or leader suddenly exposed for financial scheming, for when the soul of money is denied, it takes on an added measure of shadow.

Like sex, money is so numinous, so filled with fantasy and emotion and resistant to rational guidance, that although it has much to offer, it can easily swamp the soul and carry consciousness off into compulsion and obsession. We have to distinguish between shadow qualities of money that are part of its soulfulness and symptoms of money gone berserk. Greed, avarice, cheating, and embezzlement are signs that the soul of money has been lost. We act out the need for wealth of soul through its fetish, gathering actual sums of money without regard for morality, rather than entering the communal exchange of money.

It is the nature of money to be exchanged. In fact, we sometimes refer to it as "change." Robert Sardello, who has studied the role of money in the cultural psyche, compares economics to bodily processes. Profit and consumption are like breathing in and out, he says, and money the medium for that vital action in the body of society. When money no longer serves community exchange, it becomes an obstacle to the communal flow. Scheming and greedy manipulation interfere with the natural rhythm of exchange. A group, for instance, announces a fund-raising plan for a public project, and the large cut taken by the organizers is either completely hidden or advertised in extremely small print. Money is notoriously drenched in shadow, but when any individual or group takes that shadow to themselves, soul is lost.

Ideally, money corrupts us all not literally,

but in the alchemical sense. It darkens innocence and continually initiates us into the
gritty realities of financial exchange. It brings
us into hand-to-hand combat in the sacred
warfare of life. It takes us out of innocent
idealism and brings us into the deeper, more
soulful places where power, prestige, and self-
worth are hammered out through sub-
stantial involvement in the making of culture.
Therefore, money can give grounding and
grit to a soul that otherwise might fade in the
soft pastels of innocence.

Dreams of money often hint at its many levels of meaning. Recently I dreamed I was
walking down a dark city street in the early
hours of the morning. A man approached me
and pressed a knife against my back. "Give me
your change," he said. I knew I had two hundred dollars in my right-hand pants pocket
and about fifteen in my left. Cleverly I reached
into my left pocket and gave him everything
that was there. I wondered if he would ask for
more, but he took the small sum and ran off.
On waking, I recalled the dream and thought:
I have a tendency to give myself away. I ruin
my plans sometimes, or overlook my own
needs in order to accommodate others. Then I
feel resentment and anger.

Later that day I had a few minutes to think

about the dream further. First impressions about your own dreams are often one-sided and shallow. My first thought represented my usual sense of myself, as giving away too much. So I tried to look at the actual dream. Maybe the ego in the dream was too clever. I deceived and cheated the man who was stealing from me. The dark street, a strong image in the dream, was asking me for change. I had noticed in the dream the careful use of that word *change*. Was I being asked to change my ways? To engage in the exchange of the city's darkness? To give something of real value to my own needy shadow side? Is there a flip side to my tendency to give myself away? Do I also hold back my wealth with a false sense of cleverness, with too much thought? In the dream, without hesitating I found a way to outwit the dark street with my duplicity—my *two* pockets.

This dream, I think, gave me needed instruction in the economics of the soul. Money is its coinage and may take the form of passion, energy, talent, or commitment. Like many people, I may hoard my talents, my soul money, for fear of the shadowy streets of embodied life. I may divide my resources, hoarding the greater share while at the same time being prepared to lose small quantities. As is often the case, my dream invited me to consider aspects of my character that I'd prefer to keep hidden and unexamined.

With regard to money's shadow, it's important to be neither moralistic nor literal. For example, the pleasure of hoarding can be seen as an archetypal quality of money itself, which becomes soul-denying only when it is the only way we deal with money, or when we use it for purely personal reasons. One of the things one does with money is to gather it together and hold it: this is the "breathing in" in Sardello's image. If shadow is not acknowledged, however, the hoarding may be carried out with feelings of guilt, a sign that we are trying to do two things at once—enjoy money's hoarding shadow and yet maintain innocence.

A corporation making large profits may feel the weight in its pockets and decide to give some away. It has two choices. Its gift could bring it more deeply into community, where its power and responsibility would be properly placed. Or the company might try to outwit its guilt in some clever scheme in which it seems to give away its profits but actually makes more in tax benefits. In the first case, money quite naturally buys a way into community. In the second case, a corporation or an individual may think they are getting away with something by manipulating communal economics, but in fact there is a loss of soul and their money becomes a fetish giving rise to pathological symptoms. When a society becomes corrupted by money's shadow, that society falls apart; whereas a society that owns up to its financial shadow can be nurtured.

In the medieval world, the job of counting money and keeping it secure was understood to be the province of Saturn, god of depression, tightness, anality, and profound vision. Saturn resides in the little act of counting money at the teller's window or in stashing a wad of cash into a purse or wallet. These gestures, important to the soul, are ways in which money rites are observed in everyday life. The way we fashion cash, checks, and bank accounts also shows the divine spark of Saturn in ordinary monetary transactions. A crisp bill as a birthday gift or the first dollar made by a business framed in glass demonstrate that cash itself is honored and is worthy to be enshrined. Hoarding, too, has its rituals—whether money is stuffed under a mattress or in a Swiss bank account.

The relationship between money and work carries so much fantasy that it is both a burden and an extraordinary opportunity. Many of the problems associated with work center on money. We don't make enough. We feel we are worth more than we are making. We don't ask for the amount we deserve. Money is our only concern. Our fathers will be proud of us only when we have made as much as they have or more. We will feel part of adult society only when we have all the hallmarks of wealth and financial security. As a result of such feelings, we respond to money either apotropaically—shunning its power—or compulsively. An alternative is to *enter into* the particular fantasies that money gives us and see what messages they might offer. If we think we need to make a lot of money in order to justify our existence, for example, then maybe there is a truth there. We may need to be more immersed in communal, concrete life in order to feel the soulfulness contained in that fantasy. The only mistake would be to take that fantasy too literally. We could end up with millions of dollars and still wonder when we are going to grow up.

## Failure in Work

One perhaps surprising source of potential soul in our work is failure. The dark cloud of failure that shadows our earnest efforts is to some extent an antidote for overly high expectations. Our ambition for success and perfection in work drives us on, while worries about failure keep us tied to the soul in the work. When ideas of perfection dive downward into the lower region of the soul, out of that gesture of incarnation comes human achievement. We may feel crushed by failure, but our lofty aims may need some spoiling if they are to play a creative role in human life. Perfection belongs to an imaginary world. According to traditional teaching, it is the life-embedded soul, not soaring spirit, that defines humanity.

Christianity offers a profound image of this gesture of descent. Artists have painted hundreds of versions of the Annunciation, the moment when the Holy Spirit in the form of a bird in a shower of golden light makes the lowly woman, Mary, pregnant with a divine child. This mystery is remembered every time an idea is brought into life. First we are inspired, and then we search out ways to give body to our inspirations.

Ordinary failures in work are an inevitable part of the descent of the spirit into human limitation. Failure is a mystery, not a problem. Of course this means not that we should try to fail, or take masochistic delight in mistakes, but that we could see the mystery of incarnation at play whenever our work doesn't measure up to our expectations. If we could understand the feelings of inferiority and humbling occasioned by failure as meaningful in their own right, then we might incorporate failure into our work so that it doesn't literally devastate us.

According to the alchemists, *mortificatio,* which means "making death," is an important part of the *opus*. Jung explains that mortifications in life are necessary before eternal factors can be manifested. A person is expressing this mystery when he realizes, "It's a good thing after all that I didn't get that job I wanted." For all its simplicity, such a statement penetrates beneath human intention and desire and captures the gist of the mystery of failure. In moments of mortification, you may discover that human intention and ambition are not always the best guides in life and work.

If we do not grasp this alchemy of failure, then we stand a good chance of never succeeding. Comprehending the mystery in failure and acknowledging its necessity—the way it works alchemically on the soul—allows us to see through our inabilities and not overly identify with them. Being literally undone by failure is akin to the "negative narcissism" we examined earlier. It's a negative way of denying the divine or the mysterious a role in human effort. The narcissist says, "I'm a failure. I can't do anything right." But indulgence in failure, wallowing in it rather than letting it affect the heart, is a subtle defense against the corrosive action that is essential to it and that fosters soul. By appreciating failure with imagination, we reconnect it to success. Without the connection, work falls into grand narcissistic fantasies of success and dismal feelings of failure. But as a mystery, failure is not mine, it is an element in the work I am doing.

## Creativity with Soul

Creativity, another potential source of soul in our work lives, is much romanticized. Usually we imagine creativity from the *puer* point of view, investing it with idealism and lofty fantasies of exceptional achievement. In this sense, most work is not creative. It is ordinary, repetitious, and democratic.

But if we were to bring our very idea of creativity down to earth it would not have to be reserved for exceptional individuals or identified with brilliance. In ordinary life creativity means making something for the soul out of every experience. Sometimes we can shape experience into meaningfulness playfully and inventively. At other times, simply holding experience in memory and in reflection allows it to incubate and reveal some of its imagination.

Creativity may assume many different forms. It might at times be saturnine, so that a bout with depression, for example, might be understood as a particularly creative time. Brooding generates its own style of awareness and its own brand of insight, and out of depressive moods important elements of culture and personality can emerge. Jung says that in his long period of falling apart, a "state of disorientation," as he called it, he conceived (an Annunciation word) some of his fundamental psychological insights. At other times, creativity can be imagined Aphroditically, as arising out of sexual interest and desire. Certainly Marilyn Monroe was creative in her own way.

Creativity finds its soul when it embraces its shadow. The artist's block, for instance, is a well-known part of the creative process: inspiration stops and the writer is faced with an intractable empty page. Everyone, not only artists, recognizes that evaporation of ideas. A mother may enjoy raising her children for months or years, every day thinking up new ideas for them. Then one day the inspiration leaves and emptiness takes over. If we could see how our blank spots are a part of our creativity, we might not so quickly exclude this aspect of work from our humble lives.

Igor Stravinsky, perhaps the greatest composer of our century, was a hard worker who saw his music less as personal expression and more as an object to be invented and worked. "The workmanship was much better in Bach's time than it is now," he once said in an interview. "One had first to be a craftsman. Now we have only 'talent.' We do not have the absorption in detail, the burying of oneself in craftsmanship to be resurrected a great musician." He was suspicious of the artist as a pure channel of inspiration. "Should the impossible happen," he said in his Harvard University lectures, "and my work suddenly be given to me in a perfectly completed form, I should be embarrassed and nonplussed by it, as by a hoax."

Creative work can be exciting, inspiring, and godlike, but it is also quotidian, humdrum, and full of anxieties, frustrations, dead ends, mistakes, and failures. It can be carried on by a person who has none of the soaring Icarus wishes to abandon the dark shadows of the labyrinth in favor of the bright sunshine. It can be free of narcissism and focus on the problems the material world furnishes anyone who wants to make something of it. Creativity is, foremost, being in the world soulfully, for the only thing we truly make, whether in the arts, in culture, or at home, is soul.

Nicholas of Cusa, and Coleridge after him,

described human creativity as a participation in the act of God creating the cosmos. God creates the cosmos, we create the microcosmos, the "human world," in Cusa's words. As we do our daily work, make our homes and marriages, raise our children, and fabricate a culture, we are all being creative. Entering our fate with generous attentiveness and care, we enjoy a soulful kind of creativity that may or may not have the brilliance of the work of great artists.

The ultimate work, then, is an engagement with soul, responding to the demands of fate and tending the details of life as it presents itself. We may get to a point where our external labors and the *opus* of the soul are one and the same, inseparable. Then the satisfactions of our work will be deep and long lasting, undone neither by failures nor by flashes of success.

# SPIRITUAL
# PRACTICE AND
# PSYCHOLOGICAL
# DEPTH

---

*Recognize what is before your eyes, and what is hidden will be revealed to you.*

THE GOSPEL OF THOMAS

# CHAPTER 10

# The Need for Myth, Ritual, and a Spiritual Life

I have been emphasizing the soul's need for vernacular life—its relationship to a local place and culture. It has a preference for details and particulars, intimacy and involvement, attachment and rootedness. Like an animal, the soul feeds on whatever life grows in its immediate environment. To the soul, the ordinary is sacred and the everyday is the primary source of religion. But there is another side to this issue. The soul also needs spirituality, and as Ficino advises, a particular kind of spirituality: one that is not at odds with the everyday and the lowly.

In the modern world we tend to separate psychology from religion. We like to think that emotional problems have to do with the family, childhood, and trauma—with personal life but not with spirituality. We don't diagnose an emotional seizure as "loss of religious sensibility" or "lack of spiritual awareness." Yet it is obvious that the soul, seat of the deepest emotions, can benefit greatly from the gifts of a vivid spiritual life and can suffer when it is deprived of them. The soul, for example, needs an articulated worldview, a carefully worked out scheme of values, and a sense of relatedness to the whole. It needs a myth of immortality and an attitude toward death. It also thrives on spirituality that is not so transcendent, such as the spirit of family, arising from traditions and values that have been part of the family for generations.

Spirituality doesn't arrive fully formed without effort. Religions around the world demonstrate that spiritual life requires constant attention and a subtle, often beautiful technology by which spiritual principles and understandings are kept alive. For good reason we go to church, temple, or mosque regularly and at appointed times: it's easy for consciousness to become lodged in the material world and to forget the spiritual. Sacred technology is largely aimed at helping us remain conscious of spiritual ideas and values.

Earlier I introduced a client of mine who had trouble with food and who told me a dream of old women cooking up a hearty outdoor meal. Although this dream was relevant to the young woman's physical problems with food, I thought it also spoke to the hunger in her soul for primordial femininity. By eating the food cooked by the women, she would absorb their spirit; the dream was a female version of the male Last Supper. In another dream related to food, she discovered that her esophagus was made of plastic and wasn't long enough to reach her stomach.

This extraordinary image is a perfect description of one of the main problems of the modern world: our means of connecting to our inner work do not reach deep enough. The esophagus is an excellent image of one of the soul's chief functions: to transfer material of the outside world into the interior. But in this dream it is made of an unnatural substance that stands for the superficiality of our age, plastic. And if this soul function is plastic, then we will not be fed well. We will feel the need of a more genuine means of bringing outer experience deep inside us.

Just as the mind digests ideas and produces intelligence, the soul feeds on life and digests it, creating wisdom and character out of the fodder of experience. Renaissance Neoplatonists said that the outer world serves as a means of deep spirituality and that the transformation of ordinary experience into the stuff of soul is all-important. If the link between life experience and deep imagination is inadequate, then we are left with a division between life and soul, and such a division will always manifest itself in symptoms.

A person starving herself anorectically evokes in her food rituals vestigial forms of religious practice. Her disdain for her body and her asceticism in denying herself food represent pseudoreligion and symptomatic spirituality. A degree of asceticism is a necessary part of spirituality, but a symptomatic, compulsive approach to the ascetic life only shows how far we are from true religious feeling. As society's symptom, anorexia could be trying to teach us that we need a more genuine spiritual life where restraint has a place, but not as neurosis. If our spirituality is like a plastic esophagus, then we are starving ourselves, not fasting in a sacred sense.

In many religions, food is a powerful metaphor. Communion, union with divinity, is accomplished by means of food. Taking food into the body is a ritual way of absorbing the god into oneself. In this context, the woman's dream is especially poignant, since her plastic esophagus interferes with the rite of communion.

All eating is communion, feeding the soul as well as the body. Our cultural habit of eating "fast food" reflects our current belief that all we need to take into ourselves, both literally and figuratively, is plain food, not food of real substance and not the imagination of real dining. In another, less literal sphere, we appropriate information in "sound bites," another food image, instead of taking life in, digesting it, and making it part of us. Most of our science, physical and social, operates as if there were no interior life, or at least assumes that the interior life has little or nothing to do with the outside world. If the interior life is acknowledged, it is considered secondary, something to tend to once we have taken care of the real concerns of business or daily life. Culturally we have a plastic esophagus, suited perhaps to fast food and fast living, but not conducive to soul, which thrives only when life is taken in in a long, slow process of digestion and absorption.

## Psychological Modernism

Professional psychology has created a catalogue of disorders, known as the DSM-III, which is used by doctors and insurance companies to help diagnose and standardize problems of emotional life and behavior with precision. For example, there is a category called "adjustment disorders." The problem is that adjusting to life, while perhaps sane to all outward appearances, may sometimes be detrimental to the soul. One day I would like to make up my own DSM-III with a list of "disorders" I have seen in my practice. For example, I would want to include the diagnosis "psychological modernism," an uncritical acceptance of the values of the modern world. It includes blind faith in technology, inordinate attachment to material gadgets and conveniences, uncritical acceptance of the march of scientific progress, devotion to the electronic media, and a life-style dictated by advertising. This orientation toward life also tends toward a mechanistic and rationalistic understanding of matters of the heart.

In this modernist syndrome, technology becomes the root metaphor for dealing with psychological problems. A modern person comes into therapy and says, "Look, I don't want any long-term analysis. If something is broken, let's fix it. Tell me what I have to do, and I'll do it." Such a person is rejecting out of hand the possibility that the source of a problem in a relationship, for example, may be a weak sense of values or failure to come to grips with mortality. There is no model for this kind of thinking in modern life, where almost no time is given to reflection and where the assumption is that the psyche has spare parts, an owner's manual, and well-trained mechanics called therapists. Philosophy lies at the base of every life problem, but it takes soul to reflect on one's own life with genuine philosophical seriousness.

The modernist syndrome urges people to buy the latest electronic gear and to be plugged in to news, entertainment, and up-to-the-minute weather reports. It's vitally important not to miss out on anything. I've seen some extreme examples, like one man who spends most of his day in front of several television monitors keeping track of events from around the world. He doesn't need all this information professionally, but he feels his life would be empty if he let any gaps appear in his grasp of the news. A woman who manages a computer firm knows the very latest chemical and mechanical medical treatments, and she can tell you the side effects of whatever pill you are taking; yet in private she feels overwhelmed by her failure to get her life on track and settled. Her sickness is not amenable to the literal medications she knows so well, because her ennui is a soul malady.

There sometimes seems to be an inverse relationship between information and wisdom. We are showered with information about living healthfully, but we have largely lost our sense of the body's wisdom. We can tune in to news reports and know what is happening in every corner of the world, but we don't seem to have much wisdom in dealing with these world problems. We have many demanding academic programs in professional psychology, and states often have rigid requirements for the practice of psychotherapy, and yet there is undoubtedly a severe dearth of wisdom about the mysteries of the soul.

The modernist syndrome also tends to literalize everything it touches. For example, ancient philosophers and theologians taught that the world is a cosmic animal, a unified organism with its own living body and soul. Today we literalize that philosophy in the idea of the global village. The world soul today is created not by a demiurge or semi-divine creator as in ancient times, but by fiber optics. In the rural area where I live you can see huge television reception dishes in the backyards of small homes, keeping villagers and country folk tuned into every entertainment and sports event on the earth. We have a spiritual longing for community and relatedness and for a cosmic vision, but we go after them with literal hardware instead of with sensitivity of the heart. We want to know all about peoples from far away places, but we don't want to feel emotionally connected to them. Our passion for anthropological knowledge is paradoxically xenophobic. Therefore, our many studies of world cultures are soulless, replacing the common bonding of humanity and its shared wisdom with bites of information that have no way of getting into us deeply, of nourishing and transforming our sense of ourselves. Soul, of course, has been extracted from the beginning because we conceive education to be about skills and information, not about depth of feeling and imagination.

## Retreat from the Modern World

In the past, people concerned with soul often dealt with these problems of the modern world, which to some degree have long been with us, by seeking out a place of retreat. Jung provides a remarkable example of a person attuned to the soul who adjusted his life not to social reality, but to his feelings of longing and restlessness. In his memoirs he tells how he built a stone tower as a dwelling for himself. It began as a primitive structure and over many years grew into something more complicated. He says he didn't have an overall plan in mind from the beginning, but he found out that every four years he added to the building. Significantly, to Jung the number four symbolized wholeness. In the end this tower became a sacred space, a place for his soul work where he could paint on the walls, write his dreams, think his thoughts, enjoy his memories, and record his visions. The title of his memoirs, *Memories, Dreams, Reflections,* reveals the kind of work he accomplished in his tower retreat.

"I have done without electricity," he writes, "and tend the fireplace and stove myself. Evenings, I light the old lamps. There is no running water, and I pump the water from the well. I chop the wood and cook the food. These simple acts make man simple; and how difficult it is to be simple."

The story of Jung's tower gives us several hints about how to care for the soul, especially when it is threatened by modern life. Whereas psychotherapy generally focuses on isolated personality problems and searches for specific solutions to them, care of the soul concentrates on the everyday conditions of life. If an emotional problem presents itself, the real issue may not be some single trauma or troubled relationship. Maybe the issue is a life set up in such a way that soul is neglected habitually. Problems are part of every human life, and they do not necessarily wither the soul. The soul suffers more from the everyday conditions of life when they do not nourish it with the solid experiences it craves.

Jung's tower was a personal temple for his spiritual life. Any of us could follow his example and dedicate a room or even a corner of the house for soul work. Jung's tower helped him create a certain kind of space where he could concretely feel his personal lifetime stretched at both ends, reflectively back into the past and prophetically into the future. His tower was a concrete work of imagination that gave him an exit from modern culture. It is one thing to wish for a way beyond the limits of modernism and another to find an effective means of establishing such an awareness; an effective technology of the soul can be crucial.

Jung remarked that in his tower he felt close to his ancestors—another traditional concern of spirituality. "In the winter of 1955–56," he writes, "I chiseled the names of my paternal ancestors on three stone tablets and placed them in the courtyard of the Tower. I painted the ceiling with motifs from my own and my wife's arms. When I was working on the stone tablets, I became aware of the fateful links between me and my ancestors. I feel very strongly that I am under the influence of things or questions which were left incomplete and unanswered by my parents and grandparents and more distant ancestors."

This remarkable passage demonstrates how much Jung's inner and outer worlds were in fruitful dialogue with each other. For him, to care for the soul meant building, painting, and carving. His tower stands as the embodiment of his inner urgency for simplicity and eternity. The tower is like a fragment from a dream externalized, an "objective correlative," to use T. S. Eliot's phrase, of the inner imagination. Even in his professional writing, Jung took the lead from his soul, as when he launched into an extensive and demanding study of alchemy after a dream pointed him in that direction.

Care of the soul asks us to observe its needs continually, to give them our wholehearted attention. Imagine advising someone with many signs of neglect of soul to build an annex on his house for soul work. It may seem strange or even crazy to do something so expensive and so external to deal with our psychological complaints. Yet it is obvious that soul is not going to be healed solely by means of one hour of interior retreat in the midst of an active modern life. Our retreat from the world may have to be more serious and more constantly present in our lives than a weekly counseling visit or an occasional camping trip.

Getting away from the world has always been part of the spiritual life. Monks secluded themselves in monasteries, ascetics went into the desert, Native American initiates go off on vision quests. Jung's architectural retreat is another version of this archetypal theme—withdrawal from the world. I am not recommending going off to a monastery as a way of dealing with the modernist syndrome that so seriously threatens the life of the soul. Retreat itself can either be soulful or escapist. Some concrete, physical expression of retreat, however, could be the beginning of a spiritual life that would nourish the soul. It could take the modest form of a drawer where dreams and thoughts are kept. It could consist of five minutes in the morning dedicated to writing down the night's dream or to reflect on the day ahead. It might be the decision to take a walk through the woods instead of touring the shopping mall. It might be keeping the television set in a closet, so that watching it becomes a special occasion. It could be the purchase of a piece of sacred art that helps focus attention on spirituality. I know a neighborhood where a man leads a small group doing t'ai chi every morning in a small park.

These are modest forms of retreat that serve the spiritual needs of the soul. Spirituality need not be grandiose in its ceremonials. Indeed, the soul might benefit most when its spiritual life is performed in the context it favors—ordinary daily vernacular life. But spirituality does demand attention, mindfulness, regularity, and devotion. It asks for some small measure of withdrawal from a world set up to ignore soul.

Socially we could also recognize the value of retreat in a public way. Parks and gardens could be protected at all costs by a city sensitive to the need of the soul for retreat. Public buildings could have places where workers and visitors could retreat momentarily as part of their care of soul. It was said that in the war Vietnamese refugees abandoned their homes with nothing in their hands but their little shrines. We could easily give more attention to the objects that focus our spirituality and keep it constant. But nothing we do along these lines will be meaningful unless we value soulfulness for its own sake.

## The Rediscovery of Spirituality

Another aspect of modern life is a loss of formal religious practice in many people's lives, which is not only a threat to spirituality as such, but also deprives the soul of valuable symbolic and reflective experience. Care of the soul might include a recovery of formal religion in a way that is both intellectually and emotionally satisfying. One obvious potential source of spiritual renewal is the religious tradition in which we were brought up.

Some people are fortunate in that their childhood tradition is still relevant and lively to them, but others have to search. Many modern people feel detached from their family's religious tradition because it was a painful experience for them or it seems just too naive and simple-minded. Even for these people, though, there is a way that the inherited religion may still be a source of renewed spirituality: anyone can become a "reformer," a Luther or a Buddha, in relation to their own family religion.

When we look at the history of world religions, in almost every case we see a living tradition. The fundamental insights of every tradition are ever subjected to fresh imagination in a series of "reformations," and what might otherwise be a dead tradition becomes the base of a continually renewing spiritual sensibility. The process is not unlike the work of Jesus, who made a new law out of the old by replacing the commandments of Mount Sinai with the softer beatitudes of his own Sermon on the Mount, or the many reformations within Judaism itself. It is like the emergence of Zen out of Taoism and Buddhism. An individual's life may reflect this cultural dynamic in religion, going through various phases, experiencing conflicting allegiances and convictions and surviving radical reforms and reinterpretations.

My own experience bears witness to this pattern of religious reformation. I was brought up in a fervent Irish-Catholic family. I'm sure I was in first grade when the nuns decided I was good material for the priesthood. I did what I was told and got good grades. I became an altar boy, which placed me in close contact with the priests. Often in my grade school years I served as an altar boy at funerals and then ate breakfast with the priest before riding to the cemetery. I was being prepared in subtle ways, and it seemed only natural to leave home at thirteen to enter a prep seminary.

I spent many years then singing Gregorian

chant, meditating, and studying theology. I lived the religious life happily, not too worried about celibacy or not having a bank account. Following the will of my superiors was the most difficult thing. But my studies in theology were quite progressive. I was reading Paul Tillich and Teilhard de Chardin more passionately than the typical seminary textbooks. My own theological views were reformed so much, in fact, during my last years of study that shortly before I was to be ordained I decided it was time for a major change. It was the late sixties and revolutionary thought was in the air. I left the seminary with the thought that I would never again regard religion and the priesthood with such devotion.

Not long afterward, I had an odd experience. I had been working in a chemical laboratory for the summer. I wore a white lab coat and mixed concoctions according to coded formulas I was given, but I knew nothing about what I was doing. Around me, however, were true chemists. One evening, at the end of the work day, a brilliant young chemist whom I didn't know well walked with me to the train station. We strolled along the tracks and talked about a variety of things. I told him about my seminary training and the new secularism I was enjoying.

He stopped and looked at me closely. "You are always going to do the work of a priest," he said in a strange prophetic tone.

"But I was never actually a priest," I explained.

"No matter, " he said. "You will always do the work of a priest."

I didn't know what he was getting at. He was a modern, no-nonsense scientist, yet he was talking like a psychic.

"I don't understand," I said, standing on the tracks. "I've given up on the idea of priesthood. I don't feel any ambivalence. I'm glad to be starting a new life in a new world."

"Don't forget what I'm saying today," he said, and then he changed the subject. I didn't forget.

As the years go by I understand his meaning more and more, although it's still a mystery. After that summer in the lab I went on to study music, but I felt something missing in those old musical scores I had to transcribe by the hour. I wandered for a year or so and then found myself getting a degree in a theology department of a nearby college. One day a professor approached me and suggested that I get a Ph.D. in religion. "But I don't want to study formal religion any longer," I explained patiently.

"I know a place," he said, "Syracuse University, where you can study it the way you want to, with the arts and psychology all woven into it." Three years later I had my degree in religion, and I wondered then if this was what the chemist had in mind. It wasn't the priesthood, but it was close.

Now I find myself a practicing therapist writing about transforming psychotherapy by recovering a religious tradition called care of the soul—which originally was the work of a curate or priest. Even though my current work has nothing explicitly to do with the established church, it is deeply rooted in that tradition. Catholicism is being shaped and lived, for better or worse, in this so-called lapsed—I might say radically reformed—Catholic. The teachings I grew up with and studied intensely have now been refined, tuned and adjusted in a personal reformation that I by no means planned, but that apparently is being accomplished. Those teachings are the ultimate source of my own spirituality.

## Everyday Sacredness

There are two ways of thinking about church and religion. One is that we go to church in order to be in the presence of the holy, to learn and to have our lives influenced by that presence. The other is that church teaches us directly and symbolically to see the sacred dimension of everyday life. In this latter sense, religion is an "art of memory," a way of sustaining mindfulness about the religion that is inherent in everything we do. For some, religion is a Sunday affair, and they risk dividing life into the holy Sabbath and the secular week. For others, religion is a week-long observance that is inspired and sustained on the Sabbath. It is not insignificant that in our language each day of the week is dedicated to a god or goddess, from Saturn's Saturday to Thursday's Thor to Monday's Moon. In other languages the dedication is equally clear, as in Italian, where Friday is *venerdi*, the day of Venus.

In her extraordinary book, *Ordinarily Sacred*, Lynda Sexson teaches us how to catch the appearance of the sacred in the most ordinary objects and circumstances. She tells the story of an old man who showed her a china cabinet filled with items related to his deceased wife. This was a sacred box, she says, in the tradition of the Ark of the Covenant and the Christian tabernacle. In this sense, a box of special letters or other objects kept in the attic is a tabernacle, a container of holy things. Emily Dickinson's forty-nine ribboned packets of poems, carefully written and stored, are true holy writings, preserved, appropriately, with ritual bindings. We can all create sacred books and boxes—a volume of dreams, a heart-felt diary, a notebook of thoughts, a particularly meaningful album of photographs—and thus in a small but significant way can make the everyday sacred. This kind of spirituality, so ordinary and close to home, is especially nourishing to the soul. Without this lowly incorporation of the sacred into life, religion can become so far removed from the human situation as to be irrelevant. People can be extremely religious in a formal way and yet profess values in everyday life that are thoroughly secular.

An appreciation for vernacular spirituality is important because without it our idealization of the holy, making it precious and too removed from life, can actually obstruct a genuine sensitivity to what is sacred. Churchgoing can become a mere aesthetic experience or, psychologically, even a defense against the power of the holy. Formal religion, so powerful and influential in the establishment of values and principles, always lies on a cusp between the divine and the demonic. Religion is never neutral. It justifies and inflames the emotions of a holy war, and it fosters profound guilt about love and sex. The Latin word *sacer,* the root of *sacred,* means both "holy"

and "taboo," so close is the relationship between the holy and the forbidden.

I once worked with a woman who had a dose
of psychological modernism. She was a fashion model whose profession was keeping her
at a distance from her deep desires, and at
twenty-nine she was feeling over the hill. I noticed in our first few conversations that she referred several times to her advanced age. No
one wants to hire a model who has a wrinkle
or a gray hair, she said. So here was our first
problem. Her career was alienating her from
her body and from her aging.

Growing old is one of the ways the soul
nudges itself into attention to the spiritual aspect of life. The body's changes teach us about
fate, time, nature, mortality, and character.
Aging forces us to decide what is important in
life. This woman was in a profession that encouraged her to sidestep or work against that
natural process, and the resulting division was
invading both her work and her more private
sense of herself.

She also wanted to have a baby, but she
didn't know how she could work pregnancy
into her hectic schedule and travels. She said
she might be able to get a month free, but she
couldn't see how she could get more time. She
also had to keep her thoughts about having a

baby to herself. She was afraid her agent might get wind of it and drop her.

She had been brought up in a Jewish family, but going to temple as a child had never meant much to her. Now she had no knowledge about her religion nor any emotional loyalty to it. Her focus was on her work and she loved the quick-paced life it gave her. In short, she was a jet-setter, and her soul made itself felt only in vague longings for a more satisfying life, a better marriage, and a baby.

She came to me with a simple goal: "I want a better life. I want to do something about the feeling of emptiness I have every morning when I get up. Help me."

"Do you ever dream?" I asked her. I find that a person cut off from inner thoughts and feelings, caught up in a fast external life, simply cannot get very far when they try to understand themselves consciously. People usually confuse self-understanding with rational analysis. Most of us like to take verbal tests that tell us who we are or we get caught up in the latest psychological fad, but these methods tend to inhibit self-knowledge by shrinking our complexity to a simplistic formula.

Dreams are different. They are a person's own mythology and imagery. They are not easy to understand, but that very fact makes them a good starting point for reflection. As we study our dreams over a period of time, we begin to see patterns and recurring images that offer deeper insight than any standardized test or instant self-analysis can approximate.

"I dream all the time," my client said to me. Then she told me the dream she had had that morning. She was sitting in a restaurant in New York, staring at a plate of food on the table in front of her. She took her fork and lifted white crêpes that were on the plate, and underneath she found two fresh green peas. That was the entire dream.

Sometimes dreams are like Japanese haiku or short lyric poems. You have to sit with them the way you would with a miniature painting or a little piece of verse. A restaurant may seem like such an ordinary setting that we might pass it by. But, as we have seen, it is clear how important and how richly symbolic food is to the soul. Psychological symptoms, too, often manifest themselves in weight gain or loss, in allergies to various foods, or in idiosyncratic eating habits.

The word *restaurant* itself is suggestive. It means "restore" and goes back further to the word *stauros,* a stake planted in the ground to help tie things down. Being in a restaurant is not the same as eating dinner at home. For this person in particular a restaurant was a reminder of the difficulty she had in making a home. She was always on the road, always eating in restaurants.

We also considered the simple poetry of the dream. She had to use a fork to lift up the large, flat, not terribly nutritious crêpes in order to find a more nourishing food, the peas. Tiny as they are, peas offer green sustenance. They were like little green jewels of nutrition hidden by a blanket of white. The color green also suggests hope and growth. We talked about blankets of white in her life, things she considered flat and uninteresting that might cover over some hopeful new possibilities. Her first thought was the drudgery of housework. A baby, of course, wouldn't solve that problem. She said she also felt a general malaise, a pale sheet of dreariness in her moods, and yet she had the sense that there was life buried under that flatness.

This pea dream reminded me of another I had heard years before, in which a man was in a restaurant and ordered a steak; instead he was served a large platter of beans. That dream sounded like a Zen story to me and led me to reflect for a long time on the value of plain pedestrian food, especially when we consciously order up something more special. Life has a way of plopping extreme ordinariness in front of us when we are entertaining exotic gourmet daydreams.

A few months after the pea dream, the model came to tell me that she was pregnant. Ah, I thought, were those peas wrapped in crêpes also an image of what was going on in her body?

"Being pregnant is having an effect on me," she said. "My job isn't the only thing in life now. And those worries about getting old are letting up. I don't get it. And what really has me worried is that I'm reading serious books, for God's sake!"

Her spiritual development had begun. Spirituality is not only expressed in the eloquent language of the world's great religions. Out of her pregnancy, this woman began to develop a philosophy of life, no small spiritual achievement. She was entering her fate and seeing her life through the processes of her body in a way she had never known before. These were all beginnings—two orbs of green under a white pancake.

I once heard a story about D. T. Suzuki, the early exponent of Zen in the West. He was sitting at a table with a number of distinguished scholars. A man at his side kept asking him questions. Suzuki ate his dinner patiently and said nothing. The man, who obviously had never read a Zen story, then asked: "How would you sum up Zen for a Westerner like me?" With unusual vigor in his voice, Suzuki looked him in the eye and said: "Eat!"

Spirituality is seeded, germinates, sprouts and blossoms in the mundane. It is to be found and nurtured in the smallest of daily activities. Like Lynda Sexson's china cabinet, the spirituality that feeds the soul and ultimately heals our psychological wounds may be found in those sacred objects that dress themselves in the accoutrements of the ordinary.

## Myth

In the farcical play *The Frogs,* by Aristophanes, the god Dionysus makes a journey to Hades in order to bring back one of the dead poets. The city is languishing under poor poetry, and the best solution appears to be to resurrect one of the old successful practitioners of the art. In the underworld, Dionysus judges a competition between Aeschylus and Euripides, in the end inviting Aeschylus to save the city from its dearth of poetic depth. Euripides is disqualified for demonstrating his supposed profundity with the line "When we hold the mistrusted trustworthy, and the trustworthy mistrust"—a piece of gibberish that can be heard in any time and place that has lost its soul.

Our current cultural situation fits the pattern of *The Frogs* quite closely. We have lost a certain depth in the way we understand our experiences, using language that is often doubletalk and shallow, like the offering of Euripides in hell, in order to describe complex and profound aspects of life. We, too, need a return to the depths and a recovery of a lost appreciation for the poetics of ordinary life. What would we come up with if we sent an ambassador to the depths to find an adequate language and a poetic form equal to our complicated lives? Like the Greek tragedians and philosophers, we could do no better than to revive a sense of myth.

A myth is a sacred story set in a time and place outside history, describing in fictional form the fundamental truths of nature and human life. Mythology gives body to the invisible and eternal factors that are always part of life but don't appear in a literal, factual story. Most of the time, when we tell a story about our lives, we couch it in purely human terms. When was the last time you talked about monsters, angels, or demons when you were describing some strongly felt experience? Myth reaches beyond the personal to express an imagery reflective of archetypal issues that shape every human life.

When we are trying to understand our problems and our suffering, we look for a story that will be revealing. Our surface explanations usually show their shortcomings; they don't satisfy. And so we turn to family themes. Although we take stories of childhood and family literally, I think our recourse to this past is a way of reaching for myth, for the story that is deep enough to express the profound feelings we have in the present. When we discussed the family, I tried to show that memories of mother and father and other family members are acts of imagination, and not just memories. When we talk about what our fathers did or did not do, we are recalling our own actual past and at the same time describing our need for an eternal father, anyone who can play the role of protector and guide, authority and validator. Our memories of the family are a significant part of the mythology by which we live.

In the past few years, a great deal of literature has appeared on the subject of mythology. The strong public response, I believe, has to do with our need for depth and substance in the way we imagine our experience. Mythology from around the world vividly explores the fundamental patterns and themes of human life as you find them anywhere on the globe. The imagery may be specific to the cultures in which the mythology arises, but the issues are universal. This is one of the values of mythology—its way of cutting through personal differences in order to get to the great themes of human experience.

Mythology, for example, often presents a cosmology, a description of how the world came to be and how it is governed. It is important to be oriented, to have some imagination of the physical universe in which we live. That is why many mythologists have noted that even modern science, for all its factual validity, also gives us a cosmology, a mythology in a true sense of the word.

Myth has the connotation of falsehood, as when we judge that an assumption about the way things are is "only" a myth. Myth may seem to be a flight of fancy because its imagery is often fantastic, with many gods and devils or impossible acts and unreal settings. But the fantastic elements in mythology are essential to the genre; they take us away from the realistic particulars of life to invisible factors that are nonetheless real.

Because myth reaches so far in its description of universal ways in which human life plays itself out, it can be an indispensable guide in our self-understanding. Lacking an adequate poetic understanding, like Dionysus in *The Frogs* we are forced to make a journey to the underworld. That journey is not always pleasant. Neurosis and psychosis could be described as the dark form of such a descent, but there is also a lighter version. We could do what Dionysus does, without the dangerous trip to the netherworld: we could resurrect mythmakers of the past by recovering an appreciation for mythologies from around the world.

Mythology is not the same as myth. Mythology is a collection of stories that attempt to portray the myths, the deep patterns, that we live in our ordinary lives. Just as stories of our childhood and family evoke the myths that we live as adults, so cultural mythologies evoke mythic patterns that we may trace in modern life. A mythology from a foreign culture can still help us imagine factors we are dealing with at the deepest levels every day. Mythology teaches us how to imagine more profoundly than sociological or psychological categories allow. This, by the way, is one reason I am cautious about psychological interpretations of mythology: we don't want to reduce the mysteries contained in myth to modern language and concepts that are already insufficient for investigations into our experience.

By reading mythology, we learn how to think more deeply and imagistically. Our current mythology, which we take as literal and not as myth, is a worldview made up of facts, information, and scientific explanations. In this context, the stories and teachings of religion seem to be wholly other, concerned with another world, and so we run up against many conflicts between religion and science. Perhaps if we understood the scientific perspective as a mythology, we might be able to consider other mythologies at the same time.

Myth is always a way of imagining; it is not concerned essentially with fact, except that facts can be the starting point for a mythological story. I remember well a guide in Ireland pointing to a rough gap in a mountain ridge and explaining that it was caused by the Devil taking a giant bite out of the land. Mythology often begins with physical evidence, but then uses it as a springboard for fictions, the truth of which concerns human life and values rather than the physical world that spawned the story. We get it backward when we try to trace mythologies back to their physical sources, thinking then that we have explained the myth.

The same principle holds when we try to explain our current feelings and behavior as *caused by* events that happened in the past. Mythological thinking doesn't look for literal causes but rather for more insightful imagining. It considers the past, but the past as myth is different from the past as fact. As myth, the stories we tell about our lives suggest themes and figures that are operative in the present. If we go so far back in time as to be out of history altogether, to Olympus or Eden, then we touch upon the bedrock themes that are the foundation of human existence.

The depth of myth is one of its characteristics that make it a useful means for bringing soul into life. As we have seen, soul is at home in a sense of time that reaches beyond the limits of ordinary human life. The soul is interested in eternal issues, even as it is embedded in the particulars of ordinary life. This, the interpenetration of time and eternity, is one of the great mysteries explored by many religions and is itself the subject of many mythologies.

Contemporary authors who attempt psychological readings of myth are performing a service that is ancient. Our own Western history is filled with literature that explores contemporary meanings of traditional myths. It is important in that effort, however, not to shrink mythology to our own concepts.

Rather, mythology could enlarge our psychological thinking to include the mysteries at work in human life that will never be fully explained. Mythology can bring soul to our psychological thinking only if we allow the myths to stimulate our imaginations, not if we translate them into modern psychology.

Mythology can also teach us to perceive the myths we are living every day and to observe those that are particularly ours as individuals. It isn't necessary to label all our deep, mythic stories with Greek or Roman names. Mythology is an aid to seeing our myths, but each of us has our own special demons and divine figures, our own other-world landscapes and struggles. Jung advised us to turn to traditional mythology in order to *amplify,* to see more clearly and hear more sharply the themes that are special to us. But the important thing is to realize that, although life seems to be a matter of literal causes and effects, in fact we are living out deep stories, often unconsciously.

We are condemned to live out what we cannot imagine. We can be caught in myth, not knowing that we are acting as a character in a drama. Soul work involves an effort toward increasing awareness of these myths that form the foundation of our lives, for if we become familiar with the characters and themes that are central to our myths, we can be free from their compulsions and the blindness that comes upon us when we are caught up in them. Again, we can see the importance of imaginal practices such as journals, dream work, poetry, painting, and therapy aimed at exploring images in dream and life. These methods keep us actively engaged in the mythologies that are the stuff of our own lives.

The frog chorus in Aristophanes' drama offers a good image for a way of life accommodated to myth. They are amphibious creatures who can live both on the surface and in the depths. In the play, they are able to guide Dionysus and his party to the underworld. In order to enjoy the soulfulness of mythic life, we need this amphibious ability that allows us to know and visit our own deep strata where meaning and values truly are formed.

The frogs tell Dionysus, when he complains about their croaking, that they are loved by Pan, Apollo, and the Muses—those deities who value music and lyrics and who underlie a poetic sensibility in human life. Without poetic awareness, myth turns into rigid fundamentalism, a defensive attitude toward our personal stories. But with the help of the Muses, myth can give depth, insight, and wisdom to everyday life.

# Ritual

Historically, myth and ritual are in tandem. A people tells its stories of creation and of its deities, and then it worships these deities and celebrates its creation in rites. While mythology is a way of telling stories about felt experience that are not literal, ritual is an action that speaks to the mind and heart but doesn't necessarily make sense in a literal context. In church people do not eat bread in order to feed their bodies but to nourish their souls.

If we could grasp this simple idea, that some actions may not have an effect on actual life but speak instead to the soul, and if we could let go of the dominant role of function in so many things we do, then we might give more to the soul every day. A piece of clothing may be useful, but it may also have special meaning in relation to a theme of the soul. It is worth going to a little trouble to make a dinner a ritual by attending to the symbolic suggestiveness of the food and the way it is presented and eaten. Without this added dimension, which requires some thought, it may seem that life goes on smoothly, but slowly soul is weakened and can make its presence known only in symptoms.

It's worth noting that neurosis, and certainly

psychosis, often takes the form of compulsive ritual. We can't stop ourselves eating certain foods, often "junk food," again and again. We can't pull ourselves away from the television set, especially when a program appears that we have grown accustomed to watching. Isn't this a compulsive ritual? People who are severely disturbed chant ritual-sounding words at inappropriate moments or wear exaggerated costumes or wash their hands compulsively. They make gestures with their hands and arms that exaggerate the meanings they want to express. I knew a man who would cross his index fingers whenever he felt the presence of evil, which was several times in an hour, and a woman who would touch her knee at the end of every sentence she spoke.

Could it be that these neurotic rituals appear when imagination has been lost and the soul is no longer cared for? In other words, neurotic rituals could signify a loss of ritual in daily life that, if present, would keep the soul in imagination and away from literalism. Neurosis could be defined as a loss of imagination. We say we "act out," meaning that what should be kept in the realm of image is lived out in life as if it were not poetry. The cure for neurotic ritualism could be the cultivation of a more genuine sense of ritual in our daily life.

Ritual maintains the world's holiness.

Knowing that everything we do, no matter how simple, has a halo of imagination around it and can serve the soul enriches life and makes the things around us more precious, more worthy of our protection and care. As in a dream a small object may assume significant meaning, so in a life that is animated with ritual there are no insignificant things. When traditional cultures carve elaborate faces and bodies on their chairs and tools, they are acknowledging the soul in ordinary things, as well as the fact that simple work is also ritual. When we stamp out our mass-made products with functionality blazoned on them but no sign of imagination, we are denying ritual a role in ordinary affairs. We are chasing away the soul that could animate our lives.

We go to church or temple in order to participate in that strong traditional ritual, but also to learn how to do rituals. Tradition is an important part of ritual because the soul is so much greater in scope than an individual's consciousness. Rituals that are "made up" are not always just right, or, like our own interpretations of our dreams, they may support our pet theories but not the eternal truths. I recall a group of nuns many years ago who decided to sing Easter hymns during the Good Friday services because they thought the focus on Christ's death was too morbid and depressing.

Tradition may have known better the importance of feeling the depth of the Good Friday mood, dark as it is. If we are going to give ritual a more important place in life, it is helpful to be guided by formal religion and tradition.

We may want to seek out a church that is more sensitive to the traditions of ritual than to passing fads, not for the sake of general conservatism but because deep and multifaceted soul is preserved best in traditions that reflect long periods of time. My upbringing was Catholic, and I recall the bones of a saint and a block of stone in the altar, required even if the altar was made of wood. I could take that information about sacred technology home and recognize that it is important to keep some relics of the family in my house. I don't mean their actual bones, but maybe a keepsake, or some photographs or old letters. I might also want something made of stone, as a reminder of the vast time in which soul lives compared to my individual life. I also learned from the church that candles should be made of beeswax and that the choice of bread and wine at a dinner is particularly important.

I remember the sacred book on the altar when I was a boy, the missal for the Mass. It was bound in red leather, and its pages were marked with colorful, broad, tasseled ribbons. The text was large, and the directions for the liturgy were written in red letters that were a stark contrast to the prayers in black. I can even now take a lesson from these particulars, for instance, to keep in mind the importance of rubrics—the red-lettered instructions that tell precisely how to perform a rite. In my own mind I could give attention every day to rubrics, to the special way things ought to be done.

Naturally, what I am suggesting could be taken in a superficial manner. Sometimes people get caught up in rituals that have no soul. They play with rubrics in too light a manner. I'm talking about a deep sense of how things can be accomplished, with style, to evoke a dimension that truly nourishes the soul. I don't recall much sentimentality in the rituals of the Mass when I was a child. Later, I was taught in theology classes that the rituals are effective *ex opere operato,* "from the thing done," rather than because of the intentions of the one performing the rite. Maybe this is a significant difference between genuine ritual and playing at ritualism—the personal intentions and preferences of the one doing the ritual take second place to the traditions and to the ritual that emerges from the materials themselves.

Rubrics cannot arise out of some superficial place. They may be closely tied to the individual's taste and background, but they must also well up from a solid source deep in the person's psyche. Jung's love for his stone carvings was neither sentimental nor experimental. They had an honesty for him and for us who behold them now much later. But that particular form of ritualizing would not be appropriate for everyone.

How interesting it would be if we could turn to priests, ministers, and rabbis in order to get help in finding our own rubrics and our own ritual materials. These spiritual professionals might be better off becoming deeply schooled in such things rather than trained in sociology, business, and psychology, which seem to be the modern preferences. The soul might be cared for better through our developing a deep life of ritual rather than through many years of counseling for personal behavior and relationships. We might even have a better time of it in such soul matters as love and emotion if we had more ritual in our lives and less psychological adjustment. We confuse purely temporal, personal, and immediate issues with deeper and enduring concerns of the soul.

The soul needs an intense, full-bodied spiritual life as much as and in the same way that the body needs food. That is the teaching and imagery of spiritual masters over centuries. There is no reason to question the wisdom of this idea. But these same masters demonstrate that the spiritual life requires careful attention, because it can be dangerous. It's easy to go crazy in the life of the spirit, warring against those who disagree, proselytizing for our own personal attachments rather than expressing our own soulfulness, or taking narcissistic satisfactions in our beliefs rather than finding meaning and pleasure in spirituality that is available to everyone. The history of our century has shown the proclivity of neurotic spirituality toward psychosis and violence. Spirituality is powerful, and therefore has the potential for evil, as well as for good. The soul needs spirit, but our spirituality also needs soul—deep intelligence, a sensitivity to the symbolic and metaphoric life, genuine community, and attachment to the world.

We have no idea yet of the positive contribution that could be made to us individually and socially by a more soulful religion and theology. Our culture is in need of theological reflection that does not advocate a particular tradition, but tends the soul's need for spiritual direction. In order to accomplish this goal, we must gradually bring soul back to religion, following Jung, who wrote in a letter of 1910 to Freud, "What infinite rapture and wantonness lie dormant in our religion. We must bring to fruition its hymn of love."

# CHAPTER 11

# Wedding
# Spirituality
# and Soul

In our spirituality, we reach for consciousness, awareness, and the highest values; in our soulfulness, we endure the most pleasurable and the most exhausting of human experiences and emotions. These two directions make up the fundamental pulse of human life, and to an extent, they have an attraction to each other.

No one needs to be told that we live in a time of materialism and consumerism, of lost values and a shift in ethical standards. We find ourselves tempted to call for a return to old values and ways. It seems that in the past we were more religious as a people and that traditional values had more influence throughout the society. But whether or not that is a blurry, nostalgic view of the past, we want to keep in mind Jung's warning about dealing with present difficulties by wishing for a return to former conditions. He calls this maneuver a "regressive restoration of the persona." Societies can fall into this defensive strategy, attempting to restore what is imagined to be a better condition from the past. The trouble is, memory is always part imagination, and tough times of another era are later unconsciously gilded into the "good old days."

If we can resist this temptation to improve the present by restoring the past, we can start to face our current challenges. It appears to me that we are not a society drifting away from spirituality at all; on the contrary, we are in a certain sense more spiritual than we need to be. The key to lost spirituality and numbing materialism is not merely to intensify our quest for spirituality, but to reimagine it.

In the late 1400s, Ficino wrote in his *Book of Life* that spirit and body, religion and world, spirituality and materialism can all be trapped in a polarizing split: the more compulsively materialist we are, the more neurotic our spirituality will be, and vice versa. In other words, perhaps our madly consumerist society is showing signs of runaway spirituality in its tendencies toward an abstract and intellectualized approach to life. Ficino's recommendation for healing such a split is to establish soul in the middle, between spirit and body, as a way to prevent the two from becoming extreme caricatures of themselves. The cure for materialism, then, would be to find concrete ways of getting soul back into our spiritual practices, our intellectual life, and our emotional and physical engagements with the world.

In the broadest sense, spirituality is an aspect of any attempt to approach or attend to the invisible factors in life and to transcend the personal, concrete, finite particulars of this world. Religion stretches its gaze beyond this life to the time of creation, what the scholar Mircea Eliade called *"in illo tempore,"* that other time outside our own reckoning, the "time" of myth. It also concerns itself with afterlife and with the highest values in this life. This spiritual point of view is necessary for the soul, providing the breadth of vision, the inspiration, and the sense of meaning it needs.

Spirituality is not always specifically religious. Mathematics is spiritual in the broad sense, abstracting from the concrete details of life. A walk through the woods on a sunny fall day can be a spiritual activity, if only because it's a way of getting away from home and routine and being inspired by tall, old trees and the processes of nature, which are far beyond human scale. Spirit, the Platonists said, lifts us out of the confines of human dimensions, and in doing so nourishes the soul.

The pursuit of intellectual and technical knowledge can be undertaken with an excessive fervor or monotheistic single-mindedness sometimes found in the spiritual life. Tracy Kidder's book *The Soul of a New Machine* doesn't really talk about the soul, but it does describe computer inventors and developers as dedicated, self-denying technicians who devote their lives, often to the detriment of their families, to their vision of a technological age. They are "monks of the machine"; caught up in the spirit of their work, like monks of old, they can come to lead an ascetic life in enthusiastic pursuit of a machine that reproduces as much of the natural world as possible in light and electronics. The computer itself, in its refinement of the concrete particulars of life to digital mathematics and light graphics, is, for better or worse, a kind of spiritualization or disembodiment of matter. Medieval monks, too, busied themselves in their own method of sublimating earthly life in intellectual knowledge and reading—copying books and tending to revered libraries.

There are serious drawbacks to the soul in the abstraction of experience. The intellectual attempt to live in a "known" world deprives ordinary life of its unconscious elements, those things we encounter every day but know little about. Jung equates the unconscious with the soul, and so when we try to live fully consciously in an intellectually predictable world, protected from all mysteries and comfortable with conformity, we lose our everyday opportunities for the soulful life. The intellect wants to know; the soul likes to be surprised. Intellect, looking outward, wants enlightenment and the pleasure of a burning enthusiasm. The soul, always drawn inward, seeks contemplation and the more shadowy, mysterious experience of the underworld.

James Hillman has observed that when our spirituality isn't sufficiently profound, it sometimes sneaks out a backdoor and takes on bizarre forms, all kinds of strange enthusiasms. We may go from substantive religious sensibility to cultish devotion. For centuries, for example, astrology was woven into the fabric of literature and religion. Jung wrote an entire volume on astrological factors in Christianity, whose beginnings coincided with the astrological age of Pisces, the fish. A history of sacred art shows astrological themes and images throughout, always connected to the mysteries expressed in dogma and ritual. But today astrology takes its place beside the crossword puzzle in the newspaper. What was once a living mythology that could be included in religious art and theology is now a parlor game. This is one small example of how our spirituality has lost its depth and substance. In other words, in the language of Ficino, it no longer has soul.

## Fundamentalism and Its "Cure"— Polytheism

Often, when spirituality loses its soul it takes on the shadow-form of fundamentalism. I am not referring to any particular groups or sects, but to a point of view that can seize any of us about anything. One way to describe the nature of fundamentalism is through a musical analogy. If you go to a piano and strike a low C rather hard, you will hear, whether you know it or not, a whole series of tones. You hear the "fundamental" note clearly, but it would sound very strange if it didn't also include its overtones—C's and G's and E's and even B-flat. I would define fundamentalism as a defense against the overtones of life, the richness and polytheism of imagination. My students in college were fundamentalists when they objected to discussing the subtle references—the overtones—in a Hemingway novel. A person is being a fundamentalist when he tells me his dream about a snake staring him in the face as it recites passages from the *Song of Songs* is only a carryover of his previous day's experience of finding an earthworm in his backyard.

Here we come upon an important rule, applicable to religious spirituality and to stories, dreams, and pictures of all kinds. The intellect wants a summary meaning—all well and good for the purposeful nature of the mind. But the soul craves depth of reflection, many layers of meaning, nuances without end, references and allusions and prefigurations. All these enrich the texture of an image or story and please the soul by giving it much food for rumination.

Ruminating is one of the chief delights of the soul. Early Christian theologians discussed at length how a biblical text could be read at many levels at once. There were literal meanings and allegorical meanings and anagogical (concerned with death and afterlife) meanings. They typically explained the story of the Exodus, for example, as an allegory about freeing the soul from imprisonment in sin. But this was not the only meaning of the story. This practice suggests an "archetypal" reading of the Bible, regarding its stories not as simplistic moral lessons or statements of belief, but as subtle expressions of the mysteries that form the roots of human life. A miracle story may not be a simple proof of Christ's divinity—the soul has little trouble accepting divinity—but may instead express some unfathomable truth about the ways of the soul. Is there a way that the soul can be fed as if with hundreds of loaves and fishes, although in life there is apparently only one of each? Is there a way that marriage—all weddings take place in Cana—turns water into wine?

From the point of view of soul, the many churches and innumerable understandings of Christianity are its richness, while any attempt to make all churches one may ultimately be a threat to the very life of the religion. It's interesting to remember that the Italian Renaissance received a major spark from a church council convened between the Eastern and Western churches. In the process of setting up the council, imaginative people from many different places met in Florence, and the cross-fertilization of ideas gave rise to yet another perspective on the Christian way of life, this time heavily influenced by exposure to Greek thought and magical practices. Pico della Mirandola, who benefited from conversations occasioned by the council, decided to write a book called *Poetic Theology*. Cosimo di Medici became interested in Egyptian theology of magic.

The infinite inner space of a story, whether from religion or from daily life, is its soul. If we deprive sacred stories of their mystery, we are left with the brittle shell of fact, the literalism of a single meaning. But when we allow a story its soul, we can discover our own depths through it. Fundamentalism tends to idealize and romanticize a story, winnowing out the darker elements of doubt, hopelessness, and emptiness. It protects us from the hard work of finding our own participation in meaning and developing our own subtle moral values. The sacred teaching story, which has the potential of deepening the mystery of our own identity, instead is used defensively in fundamentalism, to spare us the anxiety of being an individual with choice, responsibility, and a continually changing sense of self. The tragedy of fundamentalism in any context is its capacity to freeze life into a solid cube of meaning.

There are many kinds of fundamentalism— Jungian-Freudian, Democrat-Republican, Rock-Blues. One has to do with the way we understand the personal stories we tell. In this age of psychology, for example, many of us convince ourselves that we have certain troubles in our lives because of what happened to us in childhood. We take developmental psychology literally and blame our parents for everything we have become. The situation might change if we could see through those childhood stories, listen to them as myth, grasp their poetry, and hear the eternal mysteries singing through them.

Recently I ran into a small example of the kind of fundamentalism I am talking about. I was sitting in my office when I answered the phone and heard a clear, steady voice say, "Hello, I'm an incest survivor, and I'd like to talk with you."

I was a bit stunned by the abruptness in the way this person identified herself—no name, no conversation, only this two-word category for explaining her life. Of course I realized that this person had suffered a painful experience, and I could appreciate the courage she brought to her admission, like someone struggling with alcohol saying, "I'm John, and I'm an alcoholic." But I was taken as well by the way she *recited* her first utterance to me: "I'm an incest survivor." In those opening words she told me that she was identified with the story of incest. It sounded like a fundamentalist confession of faith. I wondered in those first few moments how, if this woman became a patient, we would deal with both her experience of incest and her fundamentalism. Without denying any of her pain and suffering, would she be able to see through her story of incest? Could she eventually become free to be an individual, rather than the main character in a story from her childhood? Had she accepted a cultural definition of incest as inevitable psychological trauma and so made it into her myth?

I have said that the soul is more interested in particulars than in generalities. That is true of personal identity as well. Identifying with a group or a syndrome or a diagnosis is giving in to an abstraction. Soul provides a strong sense of individuality—personal destiny, special influences and background, and unique stories. In the face of overwhelming need for both emergency and chronic care, the mental health system labels people schizophrenics, alcoholics, and survivors so that it can bring some order to the chaos of life at home and on the street, but each person has a special story to tell, no matter how many common themes it contains.

Therefore, care of the soul for such a person must begin in the simple telling of *her* story. I would want to hear it many times, in fact, in order to grasp its nuances. I thought this woman might benefit from noticing herself in her stories and losing some of her collective, fundamentalist identity. How could she glimpse her own soul while she was busy screening her own mystery with the *idea* of surviving incest? I don't mean to diminish the importance of her experience or even her belief that this event was singularly important in her development. But her story needed to be deepened, perceived in a more complicated manner, and reflected upon from many points of view, not only from the one that said: if you have experienced this, then you will be forever damaged.

We all have fundamentalist stories about ourselves, tales we take literally and believe in devotedly. These stories are usually so familiar that it is difficult to see through them on our own. They are so convincing and believable that they lead to resolutions and axioms that are very much like religious moral principles, except that they have been developed individually. Like the early Christian theologians, we can open up these stories to reveal subtleties, their many layers of meaning, their nuances and contradictions, plot structures, genres, and poetic forms—not so they can be debunked or demythologized, but so they can reveal a much greater range of their meaning and value.

Whether we are talking about religious

stories or our own personal stories, the same problems often appear. What we too often hear are conclusions, a reduction of the rich details of a story to some overarching meaning or moral. In Jungian language, we could say we need to find the *anima* in these stories—their living, breathing soul. Bringing soul to a story entails de-moralizing our images, letting them speak for themselves rather than for an ideology that restricts and slants them from the beginning.

I've heard it said that Catholics don't need psychiatry because they go to confession. I suggest that a person who turns to the Bible as a compendium of insight into the nature of the soul does not need psychology. Generally, psychology is more abstract, less imagistic, more scientific, and less poetic than the Bible, and therefore has less promise for care of the soul. But to look at the Bible for moral certainty, for miraculous proofs of faith, or for avoidance of doubt and the anxiety in making difficult life choices is very different from looking to it for insight. For the fundamentalist, the Bible is something to believe in; for the soul it is a great stimulus for the religious imagination, for searching the heart for its deepest and most exalted possibilities.

One day I expect an "archetypal theology" may show us the *soul* of religious texts from around the world. Now the emphasis is on textual, historical, and structural studies—techno-spiritual issues. A few theologians, notably David Miller, Wolfgang Giegerich, and Lynda Sexson, have brought an archetypal imagination to biblical studies, but there is much more to be done. A book like Job, so loaded with themes and figures familiar to anyone who has had to deal with the question of innocence and suffering, has been opened up imaginatively in many dramatic versions of the story and also in Jung's psychological study. But do we, as a Bible-based society, feel fully the reality of having been chased from Eden? Have we dared to speak with the snake of Paradise as our *in illo tempore* parents did? Do we recognize that snake in our families and in our cities? Is there any relation between it and some of the snakes that appear in our dreams? Do we even seriously consider that our dreams might have something inherently to do with the Bible or the Torah?

The soul's complex means of self-expression is an aspect of its depth and subtlety. When we feel something soulfully, it is sometimes difficult to express that feeling clearly. At a loss for words, we turn to stories and images. Nicholas of Cusa concluded that we often have no alternative but to live with "enigmatic images." Since soul is more concerned with relatedness than intellectual understanding, the knowledge that comes from soul's intimacy with experience is more difficult to articulate than the kind of analysis that can be done at a distance. Soul is also always in process, having, as Heraclitus says, it own principle of movement; so it is difficult to pin down with definition or a fixed meaning. When spirituality loses contact with soul and these values, it can become rigid, simplistic, moralistic, and authoritarian—qualities that betray a loss of soul.

Ingmar Bergman's masterly film *Fanny and Alexander* shows this difference graphically. It contrasts the vitality of family life—colorful relatives, abundant food, festive celebration, mysteries, and shadow—with life under a rigid, authoritarian bishop. The film's mood shifts from fun, intimacy, bawdiness, music, character, belonging, and a warm sense of home to a gray, depressive emphasis on rules, solitude, punishment, fear, emotional distance, violence, and the hope for escape. Obviously, it is not spirituality as such that is presented in the figure of the bishop, but rather a fundamentalist religious spirit cut off from soul. For even the highest and strictest forms of spirituality can coexist with soulfulness. Thomas Merton, who lived in a hermitage, was known for his humor and laughter. St.

Thomas More wore a hairshirt as part of his spiritual practice, yet he was a man of wit, strong family feelings, deep involvement in law and politics, and warm friendship. The problem is never spirituality in itself, which is absolutely necessary for human life, but the narrow fundamentalism that arises when spirituality and soul are split apart.

There are many different kinds of spirituality. The kind with which we are most familiar is the spirituality of transcendence, the lofty quest for the highest vision, universal moral principles, and liberation from many limitations of human life. Play the child's game of making a church with your fingers. "Here's the church and here's the steeple." There you have a simple image of transcendent spirituality. But "open the door and here are all the people," and you see the inner multiplicity of the soul. This is like the statue Plato describes that on the outside is the face of a man, but once opened up contains all the gods.

A tree, an animal, a stream, or a wooded grove can all be the focus of religious attention. The spirituality of a place might be marked with a well or a drawing on the ground or a pile of stones. When we place historical markers on old battlefields or on homes where our ancestors were born or where

George Washington slept, we are performing a genuine spiritual act. We are honoring the special spirit that is attached to a particular place.

Family is also a source and focus of spirituality. In many traditions a home shrine and special photographs honor family members who have passed on. Rites of family gatherings, visits, storytelling, photograph albums, keepsakes, and even tapes of elderly relatives recording their recollections can be spiritual acts that nourish the soul.

Polytheistic religions, which see gods and goddesses everywhere, offer useful guidance toward finding spiritual values in the world. You don't have to *be* a polytheist in order to expand your spirituality in this way. In Renaissance Italy, leading thinkers who were pious and monotheistic in their Christian devotion still turned to Greek polytheism for a wider range of spirituality.

We could learn from the Greeks, for example, to practice a spirituality of Artemis. She was the goddess of the forest, solitude, women giving birth, young girls, and self-containment. Reading her stories and contemplating the many paintings and sculptures of her, we can learn some of the mysteries of nature, both in the world and in ourselves. Through her we can be inspired to explore the mysteries in the ways of animals and plants, or to spend time away and alone, serving the solitude Artemis protects. Just knowing that there is a goddess who strongly protects against intrusion and violation might help nurture that spirit in our own lives and honor it in others.

Polytheism also leads us to find spirituality where we least expect it, such as in an Aphroditic spirituality. We could discover that sex is a source of deep mysteries of the soul and is truly a holy thing, and can be one of the fundamental experiences in the making of soul. Beauty, body, sensuality, cosmetics, adornment, clothes, and jewelry—things we tend to treat in a secular fashion—find religious import in the rites and stories of Aphrodite.

If we can get past various fundamentalist attitudes about the spiritual life, such as attachment to a too simple code of morality, fixed interpretations of stories, and a community in which individual thinking is not prized, then many different ways of being spiritual come into view. We may discover that there are ways to be spiritual that do not counter the soul's needs for body, individuality, imagination, and exploration. Eventually we might find that all emotions, all human activities, and all spheres of life have deep roots in the mysteries of the soul, and therefore are holy.

## The Soul of Formal Religion

Still another way to be spiritual and soulful at the same time is to "hear" the words of formal religion as speaking to and about the soul. Again, Jung gives us an example in his own life. He was fascinated by the dogma of the Assumption of the Virgin Mary, which was proclaimed by the Catholic Church in 1950. No matter that Jung wasn't Catholic. For him this was an important day for the soul, in his words "the most important religious event since the Reformation." It brought woman into the sphere of divinity and signaled a further incarnation of the divine within human life, he thought. He considered the rational arguments for and against the dogma to be almost beside the point. He was more interested in reports of Mary's appearances to children at Lourdes and reportedly to the pope as well. He saw the dogma rising out of a collective need for stronger union between the human and the divine. To him, this dogma was an event of great moment for everyone in the world.

In his writings, Jung drew on many traditions, exploring the implications to the soul of the symbolism of the Catholic Mass, the Chinese image of the Golden Flower, the Tibetan Book of the Dead, the Book of Job, and so on. The danger is that such an approach may psychologize religion and reduce rituals and dogmas to psychological matters. But hearing the soul in religious stories and rites does not have to be reductionistic. Like the Renaissance theologians, we can give the dogmas of our own tradition special status and honor, and at the same time hear them as statements about the soul.

Formal teachings, rites, and stories of religions provide an inexhaustible source for reflection on the mysteries of the soul. For example, consider the story of Jesus standing in the Jordan River to be baptized as he is about to begin his life work. This scene is a portrait of a significant moment in any life: one finds oneself standing in the powerful, streaming currents of time and fate. Catholic teaching says that the water of baptism has to flow: among other things, it represents the stream of events and persons in which the individual finds his place. Heraclitus used the river as an image of life's currents when he said laconically, "Everything flows." We learn from these formal sources how to understand and deal with the soul in special circumstances, and also how to understand similar images when they appear in dreams.

We read the story of Jesus in the river, whether we are Christian or not, and are inspired to make our own baptism. The Jordan is the archetype of our willingness to live fully, to have our own work and mission, and therefore to be blessed, as the Gospel story tells, by a higher father and a protecting spirit. The Renaissance artist Piero della Francesca painted this scene at the Jordan, showing Jesus standing straight in his full dignity, while in the background another man about to be baptized—any of us taking our turn—has his garment almost off, lifted over his head in a posture of exquisite ordinariness. It's an inspiring image of the willingness to step courageously into the river of existence, instead of finding ways to remain safe, dry, and unaffected.

Religious iconography and architecture also show us how spirituality and soul come together. The great cathedrals of Europe portray spirituality in their soaring steeples and tall pointed windows. The steeples vanish in air, like rockets leaving earth for the cosmos. But these cathedrals are also filled with an abundance of color and carvings, sculptures, tombs, crypts, alcoves, chapels, shrines, images, and sanctuaries—all haunts of soul, places of interiority, reflection, imagination, story, and fantasy. The cathedral could be seen as a union of soul and spirit in which both have equal importance and are inherently related to each other.

In religion today there is a tendency to make spirituality relevant through recourse to the social sciences. A more profound union of ordinary life and formal religion might be found in understanding religion as guidance for the soul. Not separating individual and social life from spiritual ideas, we might find more intimate connections between what goes on in church and what happens in the deepest places of the heart. Then we would realize that, more than psychological and sociological relevance, we need rituals carried out with understanding and care, sacred stories told with reverence and discussed with depth, and spiritual guidance that is tutored profoundly in traditional teachings and imagery.

## Ideas with Soul

In the first graduate course in psychology that I taught the students were disturbed to find original writings of Freud and Jung on the reading list. They came to me and complained that the reading was too difficult. These were mature students, already working in the field, and they were intimidated by the original works of major writers. They had been educated for years with textbooks that systematized and summarized the theories of the founding psychologists. But a textbook is a reduction of subtle thought into a simple outline. In the process of streamlining complicated thought, soul is lost. The beauty of the writings of Freud, Jung, Erickson, Klein, and others lies in their complexity, in the inner contradictions that appear from work to work, and in the personal quirks and biases that are everywhere in the original writings and nowhere in the textbooks. You couldn't find quirkier writers than Freud and Jung, and in their personal styles lies the soul of their work.

Once I was asked to sit in on the oral defense of a master's thesis in psychology. I read the quantitative research paper and found one paragraph, on page ninety-five, devoted to "discussion." During the questioning I asked the student why the discussion of her study was so brief. The rest of the committee looked at me with alarm, and later I was told that the discussion was supposed to be at least that short since "speculation" wasn't to be encouraged. The word *speculation* rang out like an obscenity. Whatever was not firmly grounded in quantitative research was considered speculation and had little value in comparison. To me, though, speculation was a good word, a soul word, coming from *speculum*, mirror, an image of reflection and contemplation. This student had fulfilled the spirit, so to speak, of her topic by doing a careful quantitative study, but she had done little for its soul. She could recite the hard details of her research design, but she couldn't reflect on the deeper issues involved in her study, even though she had spent hundreds of hours gathering data and working up her research. She was rewarded for this, while I was considered out of touch with modern methodology. She passed, but I failed.

The intellect often demands proof that it is on solid ground. The thought of the soul finds its grounding in a different way. It likes persuasion, subtle analysis, an inner logic, and elegance. It enjoys the kind of discussion that is never complete, that ends with a desire for further talk or reading. It is content with uncertainty and wonder. Especially in ethical matters, it probes and questions and continues to reflect even after decisions have been made.

The alchemists taught that the wet, sludgy stuff lying at the bottom of the vessel needs to be heated in order to generate some evaporation, sublimation, and condensation. The thick stuff of life sometimes needs to be distilled before it can be explored with imagination. This kind of sublimating is not the defensive flight from instinct and body into rationality. It's a subtle raising of experience into thoughts, images, memories, and theories. Eventually, over a long period of incubation, they condense into a philosophy of life, one that is unique for each person. For a philosophy of life is not an abstract collection of thoughts for their own sake, it is the ripening of conversation and reading into thoughts that are wedded to everyday decisions and analysis. Such ideas become part of our identity and allow us confidence in work and in life decisions. They provide a solid base for further wonder and exploration that reaches, through religion and spiritual practice, into the ineffable mysteries that saturate human experience.

Soul knows the relativity of its claim on truth. It is always in front of a mirror, always in a speculative mode, watching itself discover its developing truth, knowing that subjectivity and imagination are always in play. Truth is not really a soul word; soul is after insight more than truth. Truth is a stopping point asking for commitment and defense. Insight is a fragment of awareness that invites further exploration. Intellect tends to enshrine its truth, while soul hopes that insights will keep coming until some degree of wisdom is achieved.

Wisdom is the marriage of intellect's longing for truth and soul's acceptance of the labyrinthine nature of the human condition.

We are not going to have a soulful spirituality until we begin to think in the ways of soul. If we bring only the intellect's modes of thought to our search for a path or to spiritual practices, then from the very beginning we will be without soul. The bias toward spirit is so strong in modern culture that it will take a profound revolution in the very way we think to give our spiritual lives the depth and subtlety that are the gifts of soul. Therefore, a soul-oriented spirituality begins in a reevaluation of the qualities of soul: subtlety, complexity, ripening, worldliness, incompleteness, ambiguity, wonder.

In therapy I sometimes hear people say they are overwhelmed by feelings and events too complicated to handle. I think to myself, if only this person could think through his values and arrive at some theories about life in general and his own life in particular, that sense of being overwhelmed might be tempered.

Should I be a vegetarian? Is there ever a just war? Will I ever be free of racial prejudice? How far should I go toward responsibility for the environment? How politically active should I be? Moral reflections like these give rise to a philosophy of life that may never have absolute clarity or simplicity. But these soul thoughts can generate a deep-rooted moral sensitivity, different from a straightforward adherence to an established set of principles, but solid and demanding nonetheless.

## *Deepening* Puer *Spirituality*

In our reflections on narcissism we had the opportunity to look at the attitude and point of view that Jungian and archetypal psychology call *puer*. *Puer* is the face of the soul that is boyish, spirited in a way that is perfectly depicted in the image of a male child or young man. But the attitude of the *puer* is not limited to actual boys, to males, to any age group, or even to people. A thing can have a *puer* quality, such as a house that is built more for its narcissistic self-image than for comfort or practicality.

Because the *puer* attitude is so unattached to things worldly, it isn't surprising to find it prevalent in religion and in the spiritual life. For example, there is the story of Icarus. Icarus was the young man who, escaping the labyrinth, put on waxen wings made by his father Daedalus, then flew (despite his father's warnings) too close to the sun and fell tragically to earth.

One way to understand this story is to see it as the *puer* putting on the wings of spirit and becoming birdlike as a way of getting out of labyrinthine life. His escape is excessive, exceeding the range of the human realm, and so the sun sends him plummeting to his death. The story is an image of spirituality carried out in the *puer* mode. Anyone can turn to religion or spiritual practice as a way out of the twists and turns of ordinary living. We feel the confinement, the humdrum of the everyday, and we hope for a way to transcend it all.

I know, from having lived the monastic life myself, how exhilarating that sense of rising above ordinary life can be, with its feelings of purity and unfetteredness; there are moments when I still long for it. I remember also that when I was leaving that life to enter the world for the first time in many years, a friend who was happily married with two children came to try to talk me into staying. It was obvious that he wanted some of that open sky for himself, some relief from the confinements of family life. He couldn't understand how I could let it go. "You're completely free," he said. "No one depends on you."

The vertical movement of the spiritual life is not only freeing, it's also inspiring and, of course, inflating. The feeling of superiority it gives seems worth most of the worldly deprivations required. But the *puer* spirit, so charged with the desire to flee the complexity of the labyrinth, can melt in the heat of its own transcendence. What can only be called a "spiritual neurosis" may develop. I have seen dedicated young men carry self-deprivation too far, suffering the Icarian crash in depressions and obsessions clearly tied to their spiritual aspirations. Some spiritual people effectively leave worldliness behind them, but for others there are dangers in those rarefied airs of spirit. It isn't easy for the high-flying *puer* to remain tethered to soul.

Bellerophon is another boy of myth. He rides the winged horse Pegasus in order to eavesdrop on the conversations of the gods and goddesses, but he falls, too. Here is another *puer* aspect of religion—the desire to know what it is not given to humans to know. Today it is rather common for people "possessed by the spirit" to say, "God told me what to do." They don't mean this in the sense of inner spiritual conversations or in the Jungian sense of active imagination. They mean that they have been chosen—specifically and literally—by God to be trusted with certain secrets. When one hears this kind of admission, one senses the narcissism that gilds the edges of secret religious messages, and one fears the break from earthly life that accompanies this kind of ascent. Of course there is knowledge to be gained from meditative practice, but there is a point where the yearning is excessive, and the resulting collapse may be a severe detachment from life in the world.

Phaethon tries to drive the chariot of the sun across the sky but falls in a fiery crash upon the earth. Acteon, the hunter, wandering into the woods, intrudes on Artemis at her bath and is transformed into a deer. He is then hunted down and killed.

I want to avoid any hint of a moralistic tone in presenting the stories of these mythic young men. Punishment in myth need not be read literally. Rather, the idea is that certain actions elicit specific outcomes. There is karma in *puer* spirituality. The suffering peculiar to each *puer* figure is simply the underside of the pattern. If you let your attention wander, as Acteon did, then you might glimpse wondrous sights hidden to ordinary vision, but you also are going to be changed by your good fortune. The punishments in these stories tell that the soul is *affected* by *puer* movements toward divinity. There is no point in avoiding being affected, but perhaps one should know in advance that spiritual vision comes with a price. The mystical writers, like Teresa of Avila, are adamant in their insistence on good, regular guidance as you go about your spiritual life. Teresa sounds a little like Jung when she warns her fellow sisters to listen closely to the advice of their confessors. If you don't want to be literally transformed into the animal of the goddess you are worshiping, as Acteon was, then you have to allow your visions to work within and upon your heart.

Jesus has many qualities of the *puer*. "My kingdom is not of this world," he says again and again. He is an idealist, preaching a doctrine of brotherly love. He also talks about doing his father's work, sustaining the image of himself as a son. He has a vulnerable childhood, and, much in the manner of another young religious idealist, Gautama Buddha, he is tempted by the devil's invitations to power and wealth, but easily brushes aside these claims of the world. He performs miracles that defy natural law—the longing of every *puer*. And, like the *puer* Hamlet, he carries the burden of his father's spiritual charge. He has a melancholy side, epitomized in his agony in the garden. Finally, of course, Jesus is raised vertically, like the *puer* figures of myth, upon the cross where he is shown to have been beaten and to have bled, a typical suffering endured by the *puer*.

The *puer* in Jesus, and by extension in his religion, is revealed in his distance from his own family. He is told that his mother is looking for him, and he points to the crowd saying, "Here is my mother and father." His relationships with women are not clear, but he is usually shown in the company of several men—a *puer* theme. He is also at odds with the establishment, especially his seniors, the religious leaders and teachers.

The *puer* spirit provides us with fresh vision and necessary idealism. Without it, we would be left with the heavy load of social structures and thinking that isn't adequate for a quickly developing world. At the same time, the *puer* spirit can wound the soul. For example, being so high above ordinary life, whether on wings or horses or chariots, it considers itself invincible. It can be insensitive to the failures and weakness of ordinary mortal life. It is also difficult for people to find intimacy with this *puer* spirit. It can be charming and attractive, but it carries a heavy stick behind its back. There is a concealed sadistic streak in the *puer,* one you would hardly guess is there until it strikes.

There can also be cruelty in the soaring itself. A man once told me a dream in which he was flying a biplane over the farm where he grew up. He could see his family down on the ground in front of the house. They were signaling to him to land and be with them, but he kept flying in circles around them. The *puer* spirit often maintains its distance from the labyrinth of the family. From the soul's point of view, this dream shows a defense against that labyrinth and a choice of pure spirit—air—over descent into the family soul. The family is unhappy and feels the rejection. This theme has its echo in families that try to kidnap and deprogram their children who have joined cults. At issue may be the archetypal struggle of Icarus and Minotaur—the devouring beast at the heart of labyrinthine life that threatens the *puer*. It was said to feed on young men and women.

Once when I was giving a talk on dreams at a spiritualist church, a middle-aged woman in the group told a dream in which she and her family were climbing a mountain. The way was difficult and they had to maneuver over sharp, pointed rocks. At the top, the dreamer found herself hanging onto a thick rope at the end of which dangled her son-in-law, flying high in the air. Even his clothes were puffed up with air. He was "inflated," she said, although she didn't seem to grasp the psychological nuance in the word. She said she was afraid that if she let go of the rope he might fly away and disappear. He himself assured her that he was fine and was having a great time. She noticed that the rope was slack, so it didn't seem in danger of breaking.

I was interested in the dream as a picture of the dreamer's spiritual life. At this time in her life she was making an arduous ascent to the spirit, while at the same time she was a mother fully connected to the world through her family. At the end of her struggle she was identified with the mother who fears for the safety of the son-in-law of her own soul. She was afraid to let that spirit go lest it vanish into the air.

We arrive at another paradox: the grounding one feels is necessary for the spirit may sometimes be best found by letting the spirit have full rein. The son-in-law in the dream wasn't worried, but the dreamer was. He was enjoying his inflation, she was afraid of it. She was willing to make a rocky, painful path toward spirit, but she didn't trust the buoyancy of the spirit itself. At some point, this woman may have to do something even more difficult than all the struggles of meditation, study, and the ascetic life. She may have to let go of the rope and let the spirit find its level. This woman believed in earth; she could handle *its* requirements. But she was afraid of the heights to which her spirit might soar.

Here we have a twist on our theme: one feels a threat to the soul in a runaway spirit, but real harm can be done by a fearful hanging on to a soaring spirit and weighing it down too much with a heavy sense of earthly responsibility. In the dream, the rope was slack: the young man was enjoying a certain level of flight. He wasn't straining to soar higher. The dreamer misread the situation and found herself as a result in unnecessary anguish. The dream supports my impression that we are a people afraid of the heights to which the spirit might take us and so we turn to forms of religion that temper and contain the spirit that potentially could transform our lives. We go to church as much to subdue that spirit as to acknowledge it. Part of preparing spirit for marriage with soul is to let spirit fly and find its airborne pleasures.

According to Meister Eckhart, "As long as you desire to fulfill the will of God and have any hankering after eternity and God, for just so long you are not truly poor." The dreamer couldn't let go of the angel disguised as her son-in-law. She had made her way to the top of the mountain. She had obviously made some real achievements in her spirituality. But at that point she couldn't fathom the mystery of spiritual poverty—letting go of fear, desire, and effort. The man's pants are filled with spirit. They keep him afloat, in a modest ballooning, of human dimensions. He's not in a rocket; he's like a young clown, a spiritual daredevil of an angel.

Spirit gets stuffed into the symptomatic

forms of cults and quackery when we don't allow it its range. In order to solve the problem of the symptomatic *puer*, it isn't necessary to turn to its opposite, the *senex* or "old man." What we can do is take the *puer* seriously, give him attention, let him bend toward the earth by having his own validity and relevance. Our dreamer has a legitimate hunger for spirit. Her attempt to keep it grounded was obviously defensive and fearful. We tend to think that we have to work at keeping spirit within reason, but as the dream shows, spirit can find its own level; it has its own inherent principle of limitation.

## Faith

Faith is a gift of spirit that allows the soul to remain attached to its own unfolding. When faith is soulful, it is always planted in the soil of wonder and questioning. It isn't a defensive and anxious holding on to certain objects of belief, because doubt, as its shadow, can be brought into a faith that is fully mature.

Imagine a trust in yourself, or another person, or in life itself, that doesn't need to be proved and demonstrated, that is able to contain uncertainty. People sometimes put their

trust in a spiritual leader and are terribly betrayed if that person then fails to live up to ideals. But a real trust of faith would be to decide
whether to trust someone, knowing that betrayal is inevitable because life and personality
are never without shadow. The vulnerability
that faith demands could then be matched by
an equal trust in oneself, the feeling that one
can survive the pain of betrayal.

In soul faith there are always at least two figures—the "believer" and the "disbeliever."
Questioning thoughts, drifting away tempo-
rarily from commitments, constant change in
one's understanding of one's faith—to the intellect these may appear to be weaknesses, but
to the soul they are the necessary and creative
shadow which actually strengthens faith by
filling it out and ridding it of its perfectionism.
Both the angel of belief and the devil of doubt
play constructive roles in a full-rounded faith.
The third part of the trinity is life in the flesh
lived with deep trust.

If we don't allow some uncertainty into our
faith as we practice it, we fall victim to neurotic excesses: we may feel superior, or entitled to berate those who have betrayed us, or
we may become cynical about the possibility
of trust. Not owning unfaithfulness, we find it
split off from ourselves and embodied in others. "These other people cannot be trusted."

"This person I put my faith in is despicable, completely untrustworthy." Living only the positive side of faith, the other side creates a nagging paranoid suspicion of others and of the changes life brings.

Also, if we don't acknowledge the shadow side of faith, we tend to romanticize our belief and keep it in fantasy, apart from life. Jung tells about a dream of one of his patients, a theologian. In it the dreamer approaches a lake he had long avoided. As he draws near, a wind stirs the waters and makes ripples. He wakes up terrified. In discussing the dream Jung reminded him of the pool of Bethesda in the Gospel, which was stirred by an angel and became a healing water. But the patient was reluctant to respond. He didn't like that stirring and he didn't see a connection between theology and life. Jung comments that his patient, for all his learning, couldn't see the relevance of the symbolic life of his dreams to the yearnings of his soul. He had the attitude, in Jung's words, that it is "all very well to speak of the Holy Ghost on occasions—but it is not a phenomenon to be experienced." We can verbalize our faith for a lifetime, but it is incomplete without a response. (The word *response*, by the way, is related to a Greek word that means "to pour a libation to the gods.") To respond trustingly to the challenges of life and to the stirring of the soul's waters is to bring faith to completion.

We can keep faith in a bubble of belief so that we don't see it having direct relevance in day-to-day living. I've worked with several people who are very devoted to religion and pride themselves on their faith. But they have no trust in themselves, and they don't entrust themselves to life. In fact, they use their belief system to keep life at a distance. Their belief in religion is absolute, it is the whole of life; but when they are asked to trust a person or a new development in their own lives, they run for cover. Belief can be fixed and unchanging, but faith is almost always a response to the presence of the angel, like the one who stirs the waters. Or it could be the angel who appears to the Virgin Mary and demands absurd faith in his message that she is pregnant with a divine child. *"Fiat mihi,"* she says to the angel, "Let it happen to me even though I don't understand." This angel, Gabriel, appears more often than you might think, telling us that we are pregnant with a new form of life that we should accept and trust.

A cousin of mine who was a nun once confided in me her story of an immense struggle of faith. An early bloomer in spirituality, she had entered the convent young and then spent years living that life enthusiastically. With her unbounded idealism and ever-present intellectual curiosity, she studied the religious life and always sought ways to make it more intense and up to date. But she also had a practical, no-nonsense aspect that tempered her sweetness. Whenever she talked about theology or meditation or education, she would laugh heartily, like a spiritual teacher who always perceives the ironies and absurdities of this life.

That curious mixture of high spirituality and practicality showed itself as well in two passions of hers. She spent many summers getting degrees in science and then taught science courses in various high schools run by her order. But she also studied Zen Buddhism and Eastern meditation practices in a day when ecumenism was frowned upon. Whatever she was doing or talking about, you could feel in her an extraordinary purity of intention and unlimited commitment.

One day she discovered that she had a rare, painful, and fatal disease. Gradually she had to give up her teaching and spend more time just taking care of her body. For several years she suffered intense physical pain and discomfort. She would go from one doctor to the next gathering a few new pieces of information about her unusual condition. At one point, she said, she probably knew more about her disease than any doctor in the country. Characteristically, she arranged her life the best way she could. She studied her illness and developed her own regimens of self-care.

Then, in the midst of her illness, the pain and disruption in her life took their full toll. She lost her faith. This was someone who had spent her entire life cultivating her spirituality and giving herself completely to her religion. She told me that she had become profoundly depressed during one of her hospitalizations. Everything she had believed in collapsed into a deep, dark hole, and she felt that all her previous efforts to live an honest, principled life had been in vain. She called for a priest, but, rather astonishingly, when she told him about her loss of faith, he dashed out of her room. She said she long remembered the image of his back as he hurriedly pushed open the door to get away from her doubt and depression.

She had no choice then but to sink into her black emotion. She had never thought, in all her studies and training in spirituality, that she could have such a crisis of faith. She had expected a continuous ascent in understanding and technique, with maybe a few small surmountable problems here and there. But her fate led her in a different direction, to a place

void of spirit and dominated by utter hopeless-
ness.

She was then led deep inside herself, to the
very edge of the person she knew herself to be,
emptied of all spiritual ambition and all satisfaction in what she had accomplished. She had
no guides, no hints at where to go next. She
had no life in front of her and no one to talk to.
She had read about the Eastern concept of
emptiness, but she didn't know it could feel so
barren.

But, she told me, eventually she discovered a
new kind of faith that rose directly out of her
depressive thoughts and emotions. She was
shocked to feel it stir in that deep, empty pit.
She didn't know what to think of it because it
was so different from the kind of faith she had
been learning about and nurturing all her life.
It was inseparable from her illness and her incapacity. Within this new brand of spirituality,
however, she uncovered a profound peace. She
no longer craved comfort from the hospital
chaplain or anyone else. She said she found it
difficult to describe this new trust she felt, because it was so deep and different from the
faith she had been cultivating in her previous
spiritual practices. There was more individuality in this faith; it was tied closer than could
be imagined to her own identity and to her ill-

ness. She had found what she needed the only way she could—alone. Not long after she told me this story of her loss and recovery of faith, she died peacefully.

There is an economics of the soul by which entry into new areas of thought, emotion, and relationship demands a steep price. Dreams teach this lesson in the imagery of money. The dreamer is told to reach into his pockets and pay the railway conductor or the thief or the shopkeeper. In mythology, the one who journeys to the gate of the underworld is advised to bring some change in order to pay the price of passage. My relative had to pay a high price to the ferryman when she approached his river of forgetfulness. She had to give up her long-held certainties and the joy of her spiritual life. Her former faith had to be emptied before it could be renewed and completed.

There is a Job-like mystery in human suffering and loss that can't be comprehended with reason. It can only be lived in faith. Suffering forces our attention toward places we would normally neglect. The nun's attention had long been focused on her spiritual practice, but then she was forced to look at her own heart without any spiritual props or lenses. She had to learn that faith comes not only from the spiritual life and from high revelations, it also comes as an emanation from the depths, a starkly impersonal reality from the most personal place. She learned, I think, the lesson taught by many mystics: that this necessary dimension of faith is spawned by unknowing. Nicholas of Cusa said we have to be educated into our ignorance or else the full presence of the divine will be kept at bay. We have to arrive at that difficult point where we don't know what is going on or what we can do. That precise point is an opening to true faith.

## The Divine Union

In the midst of everyday struggle we hope for enlightenment and some kind of release. In our prayer and meditation, we hope for a fulfilling ordinary life. Jung always taught that these two, *anima* and *animus,* are capable of a mystical wedding, the *hieros gamos,* a divine union. But it is not an easy marriage to effect. Spirit tends to shoot off on its own in ambition, fanaticism, fundamentalism, and perfectionism. Soul gets stuck in its soupy moods, impossible relationships, and obsessive preoccupations. For the marriage to take place, each has to learn to appreciate the other and to be affected by the other—spirit's lofty aims tempered by the soul's lowly limitations, soul's unconsciousness stirred by ideas and imagination.

The movement toward this union is something to be attempted, worked, and traveled. That is the very idea of soul-making, described by Keats and recommended by Hillman. Soul-making is a journey that takes time, effort, skill, knowledge, intuition, and courage. It is helpful to know that all work with soul is process—alchemy, pilgrimage, and adventure—so that we don't expect instant success or even any kind of finality. All goals and all endings are heuristic, important in their being imagined, but never literally fulfilled.

In spiritual literature the path to God or to perfection is often depicted as an ascent. It may be done in stages, but the goal is apparent, the direction fixed, and the way direct. Images of the soul's path, as we have seen, are quite different. It may be a labyrinth, full of dead-ends with a monster at the end, or an odyssey, in which the goal is clear but the way much longer and more twisted than expected. Odysseus is called *"polytropos,"* a man of many turns—a good word for the path of soul. Demeter must seek her daughter everywhere and finally descend to the underworld before earth can come back to life. There is also the odd path of Tristan, who travels on the sea without oar or rudder, making his way by playing his harp.

Textures, places, and personalities are important on the soul path, which feels more like an initiation into the multiplicity of life than a single-minded assault upon enlightenment. As the soul makes its unsteady way, delayed by obstacles and distracted by all kinds of charms, aimlessness is not overcome. The wish for progress may have to be set aside. In his poem *"Endymion"* Keats describes this soul path exactly:

> But this is human life: the war, the deeds,
> The disappointment, the anxiety,
> Imagination's struggles, far and nigh,
> All human; bearing in themselves this good,
> That they are still the air, the subtle food,
> To make us feel existence.

This is the "goal" of the soul path—to *feel existence;* not to overcome life's struggles and anxieties, but to know life first hand, to exist fully in context. Spiritual practice is sometimes described as walking in the footsteps of another: Jesus is the way, the truth, and the life; the bodhisattva's life models the way. But on the soul's odyssey, or in its labyrinth, the feeling is that no one has ever gone this way before. People in therapy often ask, "Do you know anyone else who's had this experience?" It would be a relief to know that the blind alleys of this soul path are familiar to others. "Do you think I'm on the right track?" someone else will ask.

But the only thing to do is to be where you are at this moment, sometimes looking about in the full light of consciousness, other times standing comfortably in the deep shadows of mystery and the unknown. Odysseus knows he wants to get home, yet he spends years in Circe's bed, developing his soul, on the circular island where all paths go round and round.

It is probably not quite correct to speak of the soul's *path*. It is more a meandering and a wandering. The soul path is marked by neurotic tendencies as well as by high ideals, by ignorance as well as by knowledge, and by daily incarnated life as well as by high levels of consciousness. Therefore, when you call up a friend to talk about the latest mess that has come into your life, you are tending another turn in your polytropic path. The soul becomes greater and deeper through the living out of the messes and the gaps, as my cousin's did during her rediscovery of faith in a tragic illness. To the soul, this is the "negative way" of the mystics, an opening into divinity only made possible by giving up the pursuit of perfection.

Another description of the soul's path can be found in Jung's concept of individuation. I've heard people acquainted with Jung's writings ask one another, "Are you individuated?"—as though individuation were some pinnacle of therapeutic achievement. But individuation is not a goal or destination, it is a process. As the essence of individuation, I would emphasize the sense of being a unique individual, being actively involved in soul work. All my gifts and gaps and efforts coalesce and coagulate—to use alchemical language—into the unique individual I am. Nicholas of Cusa wrote to a man named Giuliano, "All things Giulianize in you." The individual hard at work in the process of soul-making is becoming a microcosm, a "human world." When we allow the great possibilities of life to enter into us, and when we embrace them, then we are most individual. This is the paradox Cusanus described in so many ways. Over a lifetime, however long or short, cosmic humanity and the spiritual ideal are revealed in human flesh, in various degrees of imperfection. Divinity—the body of Christ, the Buddha nature—becomes incarnated in us in all our complexity and in all our foolishness. When the divine shines through ordinary life, it may well appear as madness and we as God's fools.

The best definition of individuation I know is an inspired paragraph in James Hillman's *Myth of Analysis:*

> Transparent Man, who is seen and seen through, foolish, who has nothing left to hide, who has become transparent through self-acceptance; his soul is loved, wholly revealed, wholly existential; he is just what he is, freed from paranoid concealment, from the knowledge of his secrets and his secret knowledge; his transparency serves as a prism for the world and the not-world. For it is impossible reflectively to know thyself; only the last reflection of an obituary may tell the truth, and only God knows our real names.

The path of soul is also the path of the fool, the one without pretense of self-knowledge or individuation or certainly perfection. If on this path we have achieved anything, it is the absolute unknowing Cusanus and other mystics write about, or it is the "negative capability" of John Keats—"being in uncertainties, mysteries, doubts, without any irritable reaching after fact and reason."

As we become transparent, revealed for exactly who we are and not who we wish to be, then the mystery of human life as a whole glistens momentarily in a flash of incarnation. Spirituality emanates from the ordinariness of this human life made transparent by lifelong tending to its nature and fate.

The path of the soul will not allow concealment of the shadow without unfortunate consequences. You don't achieve the goal of the philosophers' stone, the lapis lazuli at the core of your heart, without letting all of human passion into the fray. It takes a lot of material, alchemically, to produce the refinement of the peacock's tail or the treasured gold—other images of the goal. But if you can tolerate the full weight of human possibility as the raw material for an alchemical, soulful life, then at the end of the path you may have a vision within yourself of the lapis and sense the stone idols of Easter Island standing nobly in your soul and the dolmen of Stonehenge marking eons of time in your own lifespan. Then your soul, cared for in courage, will be so solid, so weathered and mysterious, that divinity will emanate from your very being. You will have the spiritual radiance of the holy fool who has dared to live life as it presents itself and to unfold personality with its heavy yet creative dose of imperfection.

Toward the end of *Memories, Dreams, Reflections* Jung writes, "The whole man is challenged and enters the fray with his total reality. Only then can he become whole and only then can God be born."

Spiritual life does not truly advance by being separated either from the soul or from its intimacy with life. God, as well as man, is fulfilled when God humbles himself to take on human flesh. The theological doctrine of incarnation suggests that God validates human imperfection as having mysterious validity and value. Our depressions, jealousies, narcissism, and failures are not at odds with the spiritual life. Indeed, they are essential to it. When tended, they prevent the spirit from zooming off into the ozone of perfectionism and spiritual pride. More important, they provide their own seeds of spiritual sensibility, which complement those that fall from the stars. The ultimate marriage of spirit and soul, *animus* and *anima*, is the wedding of heaven and earth, our highest ideals and ambitions united with our lowliest symptoms and complaints.

# CARE OF THE WORLD'S SOUL

---

*Humility in the artist is his frank acceptance of all experiences, just as Love in the artist is simply that sense of Beauty that reveals to the world its body and its soul.*

OSCAR WILDE

CHAPTER 12

# Beauty and the
# Reanimation
# of Things

Attending a Roman Catholic
Mass recently, I was struck by the translation
of an ancient prayer I knew well from the old
days, when the Mass was sung in Latin. The
exact translation of the prayer from the Latin
is "Lord, only say the word, and my soul shall
be healed." The new English version is: "Lord,
only say the word and I shall be healed." It's a
small difference, but a very telling one: we no
longer make a distinction between soul and
self. It could be tempting to place the idea of
care of the soul in the category of self-

improvement, which is much more of an ego project than is care of the soul. But the soul is not the ego. It is the infinite depth of a person and of a society, comprising all the many mysterious aspects that go together to make up our identity.

The soul exists beyond our personal circumstances and conceptions. The Renaissance magus understood that our soul, the mystery we glimpse when we look deeply into ourselves, is part of a larger soul, the soul of the world, *anima mundi*. This world soul affects each individual thing, whether natural or human-made. You have a soul, the tree in front of your house has a soul, but so too does the car parked under that tree.

To the modern person who may think of the psyche as a chemical apparatus, the body as a machine, and the manufactured world as a marvel of human brainpower and technology, the idea of *anima mundi* might seem strange indeed. The best some forms of psychology can do with our occasional intuitive sensation that all things are alive is to explain the phenomenon as projection, the unconscious endowment of human fantasy onto an "inanimate" object. *Inanimate* means "without *anima*"—no *anima mundi*.

The trouble with the modern explanation that we *project* life and personality onto things is that it lands us deeply in ego: "All life and character comes from me, from how I understand and imagine experience." It is quite a different approach to allow things themselves to have vitality and personality.

In this sense, care of the soul is a step outside the paradigm of modernism, into something entirely different. My own position changes when I grant the world its soul. Then, as the things of the world present themselves vividly, I watch and listen. I respect them because I am not their creator and controller. They have as much personality and independence as I do.

James Hillman and Robert Sardello, both of whom have written extensively about the world soul in our own time, explain that objects express themselves not in language but in their remarkable individuality. An animal reveals its soul in its striking appearance, in its life habits, and in its style. The things of nature similarly show themselves with extraordinary particularity. A river's power and beauty give it an imposing presence. A striking building stands before us as an individual every bit as soulful as we are.

Everyone knows that we can be deeply affected by the things of nature. A certain hill or mountain can offer a deep emotional focus to a person's life or to a family or community. When my great-grandparents settled in upstate New York after emigrating from Ireland, they created a thriving small farm in the countryside. They raised many kinds of animals, sowed fields with a variety of crops, and planted and tended an orchard with great care. The house that they built was graceful to look at from the outside, and inside it was filled with old paintings and photographs. A player piano stood against the wall of a small parlor, and the kitchen served as the main social center. In front of the house were two grand chestnut trees that offered shade and beauty for the family and the many people who visited the farm for over fifty years.

Not long ago I joined up with some cousins and paid a visit to the old homestead, which had been sold to a man who wanted the land only for hunting. We found that the barn had fallen to the ground and was now completely hidden by brush; even the house was no longer visible among the tall grasses that had grown up around its foundation. But a piece of the orchard was still visible, and the chestnut trees had not lost their nobility and kindliness. My cousins and I talked about those trees and some of the people who had sat under them on hot summer days telling tall tales and innumerable stories about the past. I remembered an uncle making a slanted cut on a small twig from the tree, showing me the marks of horse-shoe nails in the cross-section—his explanation of why the tree was called a horse chestnut.

If someone thinking of widening the road or building a new house should ever come to cut down those chestnut trees, it would be a painful loss for me and many members of my family, not just because the trees are symbols of time past, but because they are living beings filled with beauty and surrounded by a huge aura of memory. In a real sense they are part of the family, bound to us as individuals of another species but not another community.

Made things also have soul. We can become attached to them and find meaningfulness in them, along with deeply felt values and warm memories. A neighbor told me he wanted to move to a different town, but his children loved their house so much they wouldn't let him make the move. We know these feelings of attachment to things, but we tend not to take them seriously and allow them to be part of our worldview. What if we took more seriously this capacity of things to be close to us, to reveal their beauty and expressive subjectivity? The result would be a soul-ecology, a responsibility to the things of the world based on appreciation and relatedness rather than on abstract principle. Our felt relationship to things wouldn't allow us to pollute or to perpetuate ugliness. We couldn't let a beautiful ocean bay become a sewer system for shipping and manufacturing because our hearts would protest this violation of soul. We can only treat badly those things whose souls we disregard.

The attachment I am describing is not a sentimentalizing or idealizing of things, but rather a sense of a common life that extends to objects. Because the attachment is superficial, sentimentalizing nature can actually foster abuse of nature. It also seems possible to love the earth intellectually without feeling the emotional relationship; a real relationship with nature has to be fostered by spending time with it, observing it, and being open to its teachings. Any true relationship requires time, a certain vulnerability, and openness to being affected and changed.

A deep ecological sensibility can come only from the deep soul, which thrives in community, in thinking that is not detached from the heart, and in relatedness to particulars. It's a simple idea: if you don't love things in particular, you cannot love the world, because the world doesn't exist except in individual things. *Anima mundi* refers to the soul in each thing, and therefore psychology, as a discipline of the soul, is properly concerned with things. Ultimately, then, the fields of psychology and ecology overlap, because care of the world is a tending to the soul that resides in nature as well as in human beings.

Let's return to the word *ecology*. As we have already seen, *oikos* means "home." Speaking from the point of view of soul, ecology is not earth science, it is *home* science; it has to do with cultivating a sense of home wherever we are, in whatever context. The things of the world are part of our home environment, and so a soulful ecology is rooted in the feeling that this world is our home and that our responsibility to it comes not from obligation or logic but from true affection.

Without a felt connection to things we become numb to the world and lose that important home and family. The homelessness we see on our city streets is a reflection of a deeper homelessness we feel in our hearts. Homeless people embody a deprivation of soul which we all experience to the extent that we live in an inanimate world without the sense of a world soul to connect us to things. We assume that our loneliness has to do with other people, but it also comes from our estrangement from a world that we have depersonalized by our philosophies. We assume that homelessness has to do with economics, when it is more the mirror of the society and culture we have made.

Care for our actual houses, then, however humble, is also care of the soul. No matter how little money we have, we can be mindful of the importance of beauty in our homes. No matter where we live, we live in a neighborhood, and we can cultivate this wider piece of earth, too, as our home, as a place that is integrally bound to the condition of our hearts.

Every home is a microcosm, the archetypal "world" embodied in a house or a plot of land or an apartment. Many traditions acknowledge the archetypal nature of a house with some kind of cosmic ornament—a sun and moon, a band of stars, a dome that obviously reflects the canopy of the sky. In its architecture and ornamentation, Shakespeare's Globe Theatre was the planet in miniature. Each of us lives in the Globe Theatre of our own homes; what happens to us there happens in our entire world.

Marsilio Ficino recommended that we should all have images in our houses that remind us of our relationship to the cosmos. He suggested, for example, that we place either a model of the universe or an astrological painting on the ceiling of our bedroom. Not so long ago we still carved moons into our outhouses.

But now one rarely sees a cosmic architectural motif, except perhaps for a pointed roof, which could function for us as a spire pointing to the heavens, if we did not explain the geometry of our roofs as a solution to drainage problems.

The Zuni Indians of New Mexico express the idea of the cosmic home in their mythology. In their creation story, the location of their village is found by a water strider, a bug; it stretches its body across the continent, and its heart rests at Zuni. We could all tell a similar myth of our own homes, about how they correspond to our beating animal hearts. When the Zuni sing about this Middle Place, they acknowledge the mystery that a real home is always at once a particular place and the entire world. "When it rained at Zuni," they chant, "it would rain all over the earth." This profound conception of our own homes and locales is the basis of a real, soulful ecology. As long as the heart is involved, care of the place will follow.

## The Psychopathology of Things

If things have soul, then they can also suffer and become neurotic: such is the nature of soul. Care of the soul therefore entails looking out for things, noticing where and how they are suffering, seeing their neuroses, and nursing them back to health. Robert Sardello suggests that a building have a resident therapist to take care of it in its suffering. He is not talking about care for the human residents, but for the building itself. His suggestion implies that we don't usually concern ourselves with the state of things, and tolerate much more ugliness and neglect in the things of our society than we should endure. We don't seem to realize how much our own pain reflects the diseases of our things.

In the idea of *anima mundi* there is no separation between our soul and the world soul. If the world is neurotic, we will share in that disorder. If we are depressed, it may be because we are living or working in a depressed building. Old illustrations, like the charts of the seventeenth-century magus Robert Fludd, show God tuning the great musical instrument of creation. On the strings of this great world guitar are angels, humans, and things. We all vibrate sympathetically like different octaves of the same tone, our human hearts pulsing in the same rhythms as those of the material and spiritual worlds. We participate in the fate and condition of our objects, just as they participate in ours.

The question Sardello asks, in the spirit of

*anima mundi,* is a challenging one: Is the cancer that afflicts our human bodies essentially the same as the cancer we see corroding our cities? Is our personal health and the health of the world one and the same? We tend to think that the world is our enemy, that it is full of poisons that attack us, seeding us with illness and death. But if the world soul and our own souls are one, then as we neglect and abuse the things of the world, we are at the same time abusing ourselves. If we are to attempt to develop a sound practice of ecology, we need to tend our own inner pollutions at the same time, and if we are to attempt to clean up our personal lives through therapy or some other method, we will need at the same time to tend to the neuroses of the world and to the suffering of things.

Care of the soul requires that we have an eye and an ear for the world's suffering. In many American cities, streets and open spaces are littered with abandoned refuse—old tires, appliances, furniture, paper, garbage, rusty automobiles. Houses are boarded up, windows are smashed, wood is rotting, weeds have grown wild. We behold such a scene and think, the solution is to solve the problem of poverty. But why not feel for the things themselves. We are seeing things in a suffering condition—sick, broken, and dying. The disease before us is our failure in relation to the world. What is it in us that can allow the things of the world to become so distressed and to show so many symptoms without a nursing response from us? What are we doing when we treat things so badly?

The trashed-out areas of our cities, the billboards on our highways that prevent us from seeing nature's beauty, the thoughtless destruction of buildings that have memory and a long past, and the construction of cheap housing and commercial buildings—these and countless other soulless ways of dealing with things indicate anger, a rage at the world itself. When our citizens spray-paint a trolley or subway or a bridge or a sidewalk, clearly they are not just angry at society. They are raging at things. If we are going to understand our relationship with the things of the world, we have to find some insight into this anger, because at a certain level those people who are desecrating our public places are doing a job for us. We are implicated in their acting out.

Why does our culture seem so angry at things? Why do we take out our frustrations upon the very things that could potentially make our world into a satisfying and comforting home? One answer may be that when we are cut off from soul and its sensitivity to great spans of time and even timeless elements, we long pain-fully for an ideal future and for immortality. Things have a different lifespan than humans; they can outlast many generations. Old build-ings remind us of a past we were not part of. If we are identified with ego, then those past times are an affront to our desire for im-mortality. Henry Ford, a pioneer in efficient manufacturing, is supposed to have said that history is bunk. If our life efforts are directed toward making a new world, toward growth and constant improvement, then the past will be the enemy, a reminder of death.

Concentration on growth and change erodes appreciation for the eternal realities, those parts of the self that transcend the limits of ego. But soul loves the past and doesn't merely learn from history, it thrives on the stories and vestiges of what has been. Prophecy, described by Plato and the Renaissance Platonists as one of the powers of soul, is a vision of life that em-braces past, present, and future in a way that transcends ordinary awareness. But once we shift attention to care for the soul rather than the ego, we have a way out of the bias of mod-ernism, of living only for the day. A soul sen-sibility awakens an appreciation for old ways and ancient wisdom, for buildings that hold in their architecture and design the tastes and style of another era. Soul loves the past and doesn't merely learn from history, it feeds on the stories and vestiges of what was.

We are also angry at things that we feel no longer serve us. Many of the rusting objects that pollute our city streets are outmoded or no longer functioning tools. If we define a thing only in terms of its function, when it no longer functions we have no feeling for it. We discard it without a proper burial. And yet old things eventually reveal that they hold a great deal of soul. I live among many small old New England farms and frequently see, for example, an old horse-drawn rake sitting beautifully in a pasture, or an old barn leaning into the wind, or the shell of a once stately house transformed now into a splendid ruin. These bits of evidence of past times seem literally to glow with soul.

J. B. Jackson, a historian of landscapes, makes a crucial point about such things in his essay "The Necessity for Ruins." Things in decay, he says, express a theology of birth, death, and redemption. In other words, our things, like us, have to die. We pretend to make things that will last forever, but we know that everything has a definite lifespan. I wonder if the trash that litters our cities and even the countryside isn't part of our attempts to outsmart death. We don't want things to die, and we are angry at them if they do—if they no longer function. In our anger, we don't give them a decent burial. Yet their presence is a literal, inescapable reminder of decay. We don't honor the past, and so it presents itself with the face of our own anger, without human form and imagination. We fail to remember the days before us, and so the things of those days lie cluttering our city streets. Jackson points out that a monument is etymologically a "reminder." Our trash is a reminder—not yet healed by imagination—of the past we have neglected.

The fundamental principle in care of the soul is that soul needs tending. If we do not tend to things in their suffering and decay, assuming that because they are not human, things don't suffer, then their death will press against us as literal and symptomatic. Their illness will appear to be human because, not believing that objects, too, can suffer breakdown, we will take that suffering upon ourselves.

When things die to function, they can resurrect as images of history; and history is good food for the soul. We decorate our homes with antiques as a way of capturing soul, and museums are a focal point in our cities. In a world that denies death, vitality, too, may fade, for death and life are two sides of one coin. Or death may appear in literal form. Our trash, for instance, has become so haunting and demonic that we can no longer bury it. Its capacity to poison our world is becoming clearer, especially as we make things that have no death baked into them from the beginning. When we design things to be immortal, we are literalizing resurrection and immortality; when their usefulness has passed, things just won't go away. In an old movie starring Alec Guinness, *The Man in the White Suit,* a man invents a white suit that will never soil and never wear out. At first it seems like a triumph of technology and a gift to humankind. But soon it is revealed that this eternal suit is a curse, depriving workers of their livelihood and the process of manufacturing (which means, after all, working by hand) of its soul.

Ruins, like the old farm equipment in my neighbor's pastures, show us that something remains of beauty in a thing when its function has departed. Soul is then revealed, as though it had been hidden for years under well-oiled functioning. Soul is not about function, it is about beauty and form and memory. When the artist Merit Oppenheim got the crazy idea to line her teacup with fur, she was shocked to find her inspiration was thought to be a major artistic event. But she had found an elegant way to reveal the personality of the cup by eclipsing its function. Her revolutionary act was a breakthrough to soul, achieved by penetrating our dominant, blinding myth of use.

Things suffer, as a person would, when they are reduced to their functions. Care of the world soul, therefore, requires that we see things less for what they can do and more for what they are. Art helps us in this by reframing things in an aesthetic context, whether it is Oppenheim's teacup lined with fur or Warhol's soup can painted on canvas or Albrecht Dürer's shoes and haystacks articulated with Zenlike immediacy. In order to care for the soul of things, therefore, we must pay attention to form as well as function, to decay as well as invention, and to quality as well as efficiency.

## Beauty, the Face of the Soul

Throughout history we find certain schools of thought, such as the Renaissance Platonists and the Romantic poets, that have focused on the soul. It's interesting to note that these soul-minded writers have emphasized certain common themes. Relatedness, particularity, imagination, mortality, and pleasure are among them; another is beauty.

In a world where soul is neglected, beauty is placed last on its list of priorities. In the intellect-oriented curricula of our schools, for instance, science and math are considered important studies, because they allow further advances in technology. If there is a slash in funding, the arts are the first to go, even before athletics. The clear implication is that the arts are dispensable: we can't live without technology, but we can live without beauty.

This assumption that beauty is an accessory, and dispensable, shows that we don't understand the importance of giving the soul what it needs. The soul is nurtured by beauty. What food is to the body, arresting, complex, and pleasing images are to the soul. If we have a psychology rooted in a medical view of human behavior and emotional life, then the primary value will be health. But if our idea of psychology is based on the soul, then the goal of our therapeutic efforts will be beauty. I will go so far as to say that if we lack beauty in our lives, we will probably suffer familiar disturbances in the soul—depression, paranoia, meaninglessness, and addiction. The soul craves beauty and in its absence suffers what James Hillman has called "beauty neurosis."

Beauty assists the soul in its own peculiar ways of being. For example, beauty is arresting. For the soul, it is important to be taken out of the rush of practical life for the contemplation of timeless and eternal realities. Tradition named this need of the soul *vacatio*—a vacation from ordinary activity in favor of a moment of reflection and wonder. You may find yourself driving along a highway when you suddenly pass a vista that catches your breath. You stop the car, get out for just a few minutes, and behold the grandeur of nature. This is the arresting power of beauty, and giving in to that sudden longing of the soul is a way of giving it what it needs. Discussions of beauty can sometimes sound ethereal and philosophical, but from the soul viewpoint, beauty is a necessary part of ordinary life. Every day we will find moments when the soul glimpses an occasion for beauty, if only passing a store window and stopping for a second to notice a beautiful ring or an arresting pattern in a dress.

Some scholars say that the Three Graces dancing in a circle in Botticelli's famous painting *Primavera* represent Beauty, Restraint, and Pleasure. According to Renaissance writings, these three are the graces of life. What would a modern equivalent be—technology, information, and communication? The Renaissance graces have to do directly with the soul. Botticelli's painting shows Eros or Desire shooting his flaming arrow at Restraint. The arrow of desire and attachment stops us in our tracks—we are taken by the beauty, and feel its pleasure. Outwardly, of course, nothing is accomplished. We may not buy the ring that has caught our eye, or photograph the vista. The point of the momentary seizure is simply to feed the soul with its preferred diet—a sight that invites contemplation.

For the soul, then, beauty is not defined as pleasantness of form but rather as the quality in things that invites absorption and contemplation. Sōetsu Yanagi, founder of Japan's modern craft movement, defines beauty as that which gives unlimited scope to the imagination; beauty is a source of imagination, he says, that never dries up. A thing so attractive and absorbing may not be pretty or pleasant. It could be ugly, in fact, and yet seize the soul as beautiful in this special sense. James Hillman defines beauty for the soul as things displaying themselves in their individuality. Yanagi's and Hillman's point is that beauty doesn't require prettiness. Some pieces of art are not pleasing to look at, and yet their content and form are arresting and lure the heart into profound imagination.

If we are going to care for the soul, and if we know that the soul is nurtured by beauty, then we will have to understand beauty more

418

deeply and give it a more prominent place in life. Religion has always understood the value of beauty, as we can see in churches and temples, which are never built for purely practical considerations, but always for the imagination. A tall steeple or a rose window are not designed to allow additional seating or better light for reading. They speak to the soul's need for beauty, for love of the building itself as well as its use, for a special opportunity for sacred imagination. Couldn't we learn from our churches and temples, our kivas and mosques, to give attention and funding to this same need in our homes, our commercial buildings, our highways, and our schools?

In a symptomatic way vandalism—which favors schools, cemeteries, and churches—paradoxically draws attention to the sacredness of things. Frequently when we have lost a sense of the sacred, it reappears in a negative form. The work of dark angels is not altogether different from those who wear white. Here, then, is another way to interpret the abuse of things—as an underworld attempt to reestablish their sacredness.

An appreciation for beauty is simply an openness to the power of things to stir the soul. If we can be affected by beauty, then soul is alive and well in us, because the soul's great talent is for being affected. The word *passion* means basically "to be affected," and passion is the essential energy of the soul. The poet Rilke describes this passive power in the imagery of the flower's structure, when he calls it a "muscle of infinite reception." We don't often think of the capacity to be affected as strength and as the work of a powerful muscle, and yet for the soul, as for the flower, this is its toughest work and its main role in our lives.

## Things Reanimated

At different times in our history we have denied soul to classes of beings we have wanted to control. Women, it was once said, have no soul. Slaves, the theological defense of a cruel system declared, have no soul. In our day we assume that things do not have soul, and thus we can do to them what we will. A revival of the doctrine of *anima mundi* would give soul back to the world of nature and artifact.

If we knew in our hearts that things have soul, we could not govern them as conscious subject over inert object. Instead, we would have a mutual relationship of affection, respect, and care. We would be less lonely in a world that is alive with its own kind of soul than we are in a mechanical world we think we need to sustain with our technological efforts. Collectively we are like the burdened individual who thinks he or she has to get up early every morning in order to help the sun rise. This is not all that uncommon a neurotic conception, and it reflects an attitude we all share, in part, as participants in the spirit of the times.

In 1947 Jung wrote to a colleague who had been studying Sanskrit and Indian philosophy that he should pay attention to a dream of his in which a star shines in a forest. "You will find yourself again only in the simple and forgotten things," Jung wrote. "Why not go into the forest for a time, literally? Sometimes a tree tells you more than can be read in books." We can find ourselves in such simple and forgotten things, because, when we disallow soul to the simple things around us, we lose that important source of soul for ourselves. Concretely, a tree can tell us much in the language of its form, texture, age, and color and in the way it presents itself as an individual. But in this expression of itself, it is also showing us the secrets of our own souls, for there is no absolute separation between the world's soul and our own. We are truly the world, and the world is us.

*Anima mundi* is not a mystical philosophy requiring high forms of meditation, nor does it ask for a return to primitive animism. The sophisticated artists, theologians, and merchants of the Renaissance who lived this philosophy, such as Pico della Mirandola, Marsilio Ficino, and Lorenzo di Medici, are good examples for us. In their thought, their personal daily practices, and in the art and architecture they inspired, they cultivated a concrete world full of soul. The beauty of Renaissance art is inseparable from the soul-affirming philosophy that tutored it.

These Renaissance masters taught that we need to cultivate our relationship to the ensouled world through simple daily mindfulness and imaginative practices. They recommended careful exposure to specific kinds of music, art, food, landscapes, cultures, and climate. They were Epicureans of a sort, believing that things are rich in what they can offer the soul, but in order to receive that richness we must learn to enjoy things in moderation and use them with discrimination.

Neoplatonic philosophy taught these Renaissance masters of soul that soul straddles the eternal and the temporal, and that the full blend of these two dimensions gives life depth and vitality. Deep perspective in art reflected this profound perspective in thought. Ficino, a vegetarian, was sparse in his diet, and yet he was a connoisseur of fine wines. The Medicis could exercise their talent for commerce and banking and still recognize the importance of the arts and theology to the soul of their society. The secularism of our age, in contrast, forces religion and theology into a chamber, usually a university or a seminary, isolated from commerce and government. Yet soul requires a theological and artistic vision that influences every part of our lives.

Religion and theology show us the mysteries and the rites that inform every piece of ordinary modern life. Without education in these fields we are mistakenly led to believe that the world is as secular as it appears to our eighteenth-century Enlightenment eyes. As a result of this secular philosophy, the divine is met only in our profound social problems and in our personal psychological and physical illnesses. In the face of drugs and crime, for instance, we feel stupefied. Nothing we do seems to help. We can't understand these problems because the negative spark of the divine is in them—religion revealing itself from the dark side.

Therefore, a revival of the worldview known as *anima mundi* is essential for a renewal of psychology and for genuine care of the soul. In the field of psychology, there have been attempts at alignment with religion, especially as we have tried to learn from Eastern religions the techniques and benefits of meditation and higher levels of consciousness. In theology and religion, it is common these days to find religious professionals training themselves in psychology and the social sciences. These two movements and others like them indicate a new awareness that religion, soul, and the world are profoundly implicated in each other. But we can't pursue that insight and also retain the prevailing worldview according to which the world is dead and subjectivity is limited to a reasoning ego. As so many commentators have pointed out, this bifurcated world is a characteristic of modern Western life that is not found in all cultures. We have created a comfortable and amazingly efficient life-style by means of this division, but we have won our pleasures and conveniences at the cost of soul.

To care for the soul we will need to give up our limited ideas of what psychology is, our attempts to gain rational control over our moods and emotions, our illusion that our consciousness is the only sign of soul in the universe, and our desire for dominance over nature and fabricated things. We will have to expose ourselves to beauty, risking the irrationality it stirs up and the interference it can place in the way of our march toward technological progress. We may have to give up many projects that seem important to modern life, in the name of sacred nature and the need for beautiful things. And we may have to do these things both communally and individually, as part of our effort finally to care for the soul.

There is no necessary enmity between technology and beauty, or between care of the soul and development of culture. Science has as much capacity for soulfulness as do art and religion. But in all these areas we have lived for a long time now as though soul were not a factor and consequently encounter soul only in intractable problems and deep-seated neuroses. For example, we have amazingly efficient cars, but marriage is becoming impossible to sustain. We produce movies and television programs without end, but we have little imagination about living in a peaceful international community. We have many instruments for medicine, but we don't understand except in the most rudimentary ways the relationship between life and disease. Once in our past, in Greek tragedies and comedies, a priest presided over the presentation of drama, indicating that going to the theater was a matter of life and death. Today we place theater and the other arts in the category of entertainment. Imagine opening the Sunday newspaper to the section on movies, music, and other arts, and instead of reading "Entertainment" we found a section called "Care of the Soul." We don't have to lose pleasure and fun in order to give the soul what it needs, but we do have to give it attention and articulation.

As long as we leave care of the soul out of our daily lives we will suffer the loneliness of living in a dead, cold, unrelated world. We can "improve" ourselves to the maximum, and yet we will still feel the alienation inherent in a divided existence. We will continue to exploit nature and our capacity to invent new things, but both will continue to overpower us, if we do not approach them with enough depth and imagination.

The way out of this neurosis is to leave our modern divisions behind and learn from other cultures, from art and religion, and from new movements in philosophy that there is another way to perceive the world. We can replace our modernist psychology with care of the soul, and we can begin building a culture that is sensitive to matters of the heart.

# CHAPTER 13

# The Sacred Arts of Life

We can return now to one of Plato's expressions for care of the soul, *techne tou biou,* the craft of life. Care of the soul requires craft (*techne*)—skill, attention, and art. To live with a high degree of artfulness means to attend to the small things that keep the soul engaged in whatever we are doing, and it is the very heart of soul-making. From some grand overview of life, it may seem that only the big events are ultimately important. But to the soul, the most minute details and the most ordinary activities, carried out with mindfulness and art, have an effect far beyond their apparent insignificance.

Art is not found only in the painter's studio or in the halls of a museum, it also has its place in the store, the shop, the factory, and the home. In fact, when art is reserved as the province of professional artists, a dangerous gulf develops between the fine arts and the everyday arts. The fine arts are elevated and set apart from life, becoming too precious and therefore irrelevant. Having banished art to the museum, we fail to give it a place in ordinary life. One of the most effective forms of repression is to give a thing excessive honor.

Even in our art schools, a technical viewpoint is often dominant. The young painter learns about materials and schools of thought, but not about the soul of his vocation or the deeper significance of the content of his artwork. A voice major in a university music department expects to become an artist, but in her first lesson she is hooked up to an oscilloscope that will measure the parameters of her voice and indicate areas to be improved. The soul makes a quick exit before these purely technical approaches to learning.

The arts are important for all of us, whether or not we ourselves practice a particular discipline. Art, broadly speaking, is that which invites us into contemplation—a rare commodity in modern life. In that moment of contemplation, art intensifies the presence of the world. We see it more vividly and more deeply. The emptiness that many people complain dominates their lives comes in part from a failure to let the world in, to perceive it and engage it fully. Naturally, we'll feel empty if everything we do slides past without sticking. As we have seen, art *arrests* attention, an important service to the soul. Soul cannot thrive in a fast-paced life because being affected, taking things in and chewing on them, requires time.

Living artfully, therefore, might require something as simple as *pausing*. Some people are incapable of being arrested by things because they are always on the move. A common symptom of modern life is that there is no time for thought, or even for letting impressions of a day sink in. Yet it is only when the world enters the heart that it can be made into soul. The vessel in which soul-making takes place is an inner container scooped out by reflection and wonder. There is no doubt that some people could spare themselves the expense and trouble of psychotherapy simply by giving themselves a few minutes each day for quiet reflection. This simple act would provide what is missing in their lives: a period of non-doing that is essential nourishment to the soul.

Akin to pausing, and just as important in care of the soul, is *taking time*. I realize these are extremely simple suggestions, but taken to heart they could transform a life, by allowing soul to enter. Taking time with things, we get to know them more intimately and to feel more genuinely connected to them. One of the symptoms of modern soullessness, an alienation from nature and things as well as from our fellow human beings, might be overcome if we took time with whatever we are dealing with.

Living artfully might require taking the time to buy things with soul for the home. Good linens, a special rug, or a simple teapot can be a source of enrichment not only in our own life, but also in the lives of our children and grandchildren. The soul basks in this extended sense of time. But we can't discover the soul in a thing without first taking time to observe it and be with it for a while. This kind of observation has a quality of intimacy about it; it's not just studying a consumer guide for factual and technical analysis. Surfaces, textures, and feel count as much as efficiency.

Certain things stimulate the imagination more than others, and that very blossoming of fantasy might be a sign of soul. An airline executive once talked to me about the struggle he was having in deciding between two jobs that had opened up for him. One was full of prestige and power, while the other was comfortable but quite ordinary. The first he felt he should consider because it was highly prized among his peers, but his thoughts about it were dry. The second one he imagined all day long. In his mind he had already begun to design his office and set his schedule. From the richness of his imagination of it, it was quite clear that the more lowly job appealed to his soul.

The ordinary arts we practice every day at home are of more importance to the soul than their simplicity might suggest. For example, I can't explain it, but I enjoy doing dishes. I've had an automatic dishwasher in my home for over a year, and I have never used it. What appeals to me, as I think about it, is the reverie induced by going through the ritual of washing, rinsing, and drying. Marie-Louise von Franz, the Swiss Jungian author, observes that weaving and knitting, too, are particularly good for the soul because they encourage reflection and reverie.

I also cherish the opportunity to hang clothes on a line outdoors. The fresh smell, the wet fabrics, the blowing wind, and the drying sun go together to make an experience of nature and culture that is unique and particularly pleasurable for its simplicity. Deborah Hunter, a photographer, made a study several years ago of clothes on a line tossed by the wind. There was an element in these photographs, difficult to name, that touched upon vitality, the deep pleasures of ordinary life, and unseen forces of nature, all of which can be found around the house.

In a book not yet published, Jean Lall, the astrologer, observes that daily life at home is full of epiphanies. "Within our daily experience," she writes, "as keepers of home and gardens the spirits still move and speak if we but attend. They slip in through the cracks, making themselves felt in little breakdowns in appliances, unplanned sproutings in the flowerbeds, and sudden moments of blinding beauty, as where sunlight glances across a newly-waxed table or the wind stirs clean laundry into fresh choreography."

Many of the arts practiced at home are especially nourishing to the soul because they foster contemplation and demand a degree of artfulness, such as arranging flowers, cooking, and making repairs. I have a friend who is taking time over several months to paint a garden scene on a low panel of her dining room wall. Sometimes these ordinary arts bring out the individual, so that when you go into a home you can see the special character of your hosts in a particular aspect of their home.

Attending to the soul in these ordinary things usually leads to a more individual life, if not to an eccentric style. One of the things I love to do on a free afternoon is to visit Sleepy Hollow cemetery in Concord, Massachusetts. On a small, knobby hill deep in the cemetery is Emerson's grave, marked by a large, red-streaked boulder that contrasts with the typical gray rectangular gravestones all around him. Thoreau and Hawthorne lie a short distance away. For any who love Emerson's writing, this place is filled with soul. To me, his remarkable gravestone reflects his love of nature and mirrors both his greatness of soul and the irrepressible eccentricity of his imagination. The particular thrust of nature and the presence of a community of writers buried together make the place truly sacred.

When imagination is allowed to move to deep places, the sacred is revealed. The more different kinds of thoughts we experience around a thing and the deeper our reflections go as we are arrested by its artfulness, the more fully its sacredness can emerge. It follows, then, that living artfully can be a tonic for the secularization of life that characterizes our time. We can, of course, bring religion more closely in tune with ordinary life by immersing ourselves in formal rituals and traditional teachings; but we can also serve religion's soul by discovering the "natural religion" in all things. The route to this discovery is art, both the fine arts and those of everyday life. If we could loosen our grip on the functionality of life and let ourselves be arrested by the imaginal richness that surrounds all objects, natural and human-made, we might ground our secular attitudes in a religious sensibility and give ordinary life soul.

I'm suggesting that we consider sacredness from the point of view of soul rather than spirit. From that angle, the sacred appears when imagination achieves unusual depth and fullness. The Bible, the Koran, Buddhist writings, and ritual books of all religions move us to imagine with exceptional range and depth. They bring us into wonder about the cosmos, about the far reaches of time past and present, and about ultimate values. But in a less formal way, any source of imagination that approaches this richness and depth helps create a religious sensibility. When they expose the deep images and themes that course through human life, so-called secular literature and art serve the religious impulse.

The medieval idea about learning, that theology is the ultimate science and all the others are "ancillary"—in humble service—is, to me, absolutely correct. Every issue, no matter how secular it appears to be, has a sacred dimension. If you press anything far enough, you will come up against either the holy or the demonic. Our secular sciences of physics, sociology, psychology, and the rest stop short of theological categories, thus preserving their scientific "objectivity," but also losing soul. Religious sensibility and soul are inseparable. I'm not saying that any particular religious affiliation or belief is essential to soul, but that a solid, palpable, and intellectually satisfying appreciation of the sacred is a sine qua non of living soulfully.

The theme requires a book of its own, but suffice it to say that theology is of concern for everyone, because our most ordinary experiences touch upon issues of such immense depth that they can only be considered religious. Recall Nicholas of Cusa's observation that God is the minimum as well as the maximum. The small things in everyday life are no less sacred than the great issues of human existence.

Becoming the artists and theologians of our own lives, we can approach the depth that is the domain of soul. When we leave art only to the accomplished painter and the museum, instead of fostering our own artful sensibilities through them, then our lives lose opportunities for soul. The same is true when we leave religion to church on the weekend. Then religion remains on the periphery of life, even if it is an exalted periphery, and life loses opportunities for soul. Fine art, like formal religion, is at times quite lofty, while soul in any context is lower case, ordinary, daily, familial and communal, felt, intimate, attached, engaged, involved, affected, ruminating, stirred, and poetic. The soul of a piece of art is known intimately, not remotely. It is felt, not just understood. So, too, the soul of religion lies in an immediate acquaintance with the angelic and the demonic. It is a daily involvement in mysteries and a personal quest for a corresponding ethic. Without soul, religion's truths and moral principles might be believed in, perhaps, and discussed, but they are not taken truly to heart and lived from the core of one's being.

## Dreams: A Royal Road to Soul

Care of the soul involves "work," in the alchemical sense. It is impossible to care for the soul and live at the same time in unconsciousness. Sometimes soul work is exciting and inspiring, but often it is also challenging, requiring genuine courage. Rarely easy, work with the soul is usually placed squarely in that place we would rather not visit, in that emotion we don't want to feel, and in that understanding we would prefer to do without. The most honest route may be the most difficult to take. It is not easy to visit the place in ourselves that is most challenging and to look straight into the image that gives us the most fright; yet, there, where the work is most intense, is the source of soul.

Since we never want to take up the piece of our emotion that is most in need of attention, I usually recommend to my patients that they give increased awareness to their dreams; for there they will find images that in waking life are very difficult to face. Dreams truly are the mythology of the soul and working with them forms a major piece in the project of making life more artful.

As a visit to any bookstore will demonstrate, there are many approaches to working with dreams. I would like to make a few concrete suggestions about what I consider key attitudes and strategies in dealing with dreams in a manner that preserves their integrity, allows meaning to emerge, and generally serves care of the soul.

Therapeutic work with dreams could be a model for less formal habits of giving dreams a serious place in our ordinary lives. When a person comes to me for an hour of therapy, I like to hear a dream or two early in the session. I don't like to listen to a dream and then immediately reach for an interpretation. It is better to let the dream lead us into new territory than to try to master the dream and figure it out at once. After the dream has been told, we might go on to talk about the person's life, since the therapy is almost always concerned with life situations. I may notice ways in which the dream offers us images and a language for talking about life with depth and imagination. Instead of trying to figure out the dream, we are letting the dream figure us out, allowing the dream to influence and shape our way of imagining. Usually, the main problem with life conundrums is that we don't bring to them enough imagination. We understand our difficulties literally and look for literal solutions, which rarely work precisely because they are part of the problem—lack of imagination. Dreams offer a fresh point of view.

In therapy it's tempting for both therapist and patient to translate a dream into theories and rationalizations that merely support the ideas of the therapist or the problematical attitudes of the patient. It is much better to let the dream interpret us rather than for us to become clever in interpreting the dream in ways most compatible with our existing ideas.

It is my experience that a dream reveals itself to the patient and the therapist slowly, gradually. I hear the dream and usually have a few impressions and ideas come to the surface immediately. But there might also be a great deal of confusion about the imagery. I try to hold back my need to overcome a dream with meaning. I tolerate its mood and let its puzzling imagery confound me, turn me away from my convictions in order to consider *its* mystery. Having patience with dreams is extremely important, and is more effective in the long run than any exercise of knowledge, techniques, and tricks. The dream reveals itself on its own timetable, but it does reveal itself.

It's important to trust your intuitions, which are not the same as your intellectual interpretations. For example, sometimes a person will tell me a dream and immediately recommend a way of understanding it or offer a bias toward one of the characters. A woman, for instance, relates a dream in which she has absent-mindedly left her front door open, allowing a man to sneak into her house. "It was a nightmare," she says, "I think the dream is telling me that I'm not careful enough about keeping myself protected. I'm too open."

You see, I'm given a dream and an interpretation. Even though I have considerable experience working with dreams and have been trained not to buy into whatever idea a patient gives me, I'm sometimes unconsciously affected by the interpretation. It's so reasonable.

Of course, she is too vulnerable and is threatened by an intruder. But then I remember my first rule: trust your intuitions. I wonder if the "accidental" opening in the door might not be a good thing for this person. The opening may allow new personalities to enter her living space. I'm also aware that the unintentional may not be unintended at all: someone else besides the "I" may wish to leave the door open. The crack in the door may be an accident only to the ego.

There is often an apparent collusion between the dream-ego and the waking dreamer. As the dreamer tells the dream, she may slant her story in the direction of the "I" in the dream, thus convincing the listener to take a certain position in relation to the figures in the dream. Therefore, perhaps sometimes too much in compensation, I like to assume a rather perverse attitude when I hear the dream. I make a point of considering an angle different from the dreamer's. To put it more technically, I assume that in the telling of the dream the dreamer may be locked in the same complex as is the dream-ego. If I simply accept what the dreamer tells me, I may get caught in the dreamer's complex, and then I'm of no use. So I say to this dreamer: "Maybe it's not so bad that your usual thought about closing doors failed in this case. Maybe it allowed an entry that will prove to be beneficial. At least we can keep an open mind."

Speaking for other figures in the dream, sometimes against the bias of the dreamer, can open up a perspective on the dream that is extraordinarily revealing. Care of the soul, remember, does not necessarily mean care of the ego. Other characters may need acceptance and understanding. We may need to consider objectionable actions and characters as somehow necessary and even valuable.

A woman who is a writer tells a dream in which she catches a friend of hers smearing crayons all over the dreamer's typewriter. "It was an awful dream," she said, "and I know what it means. My inner child is always interfering with my adult work. If only I could grow up!"

Notice that this person, too, is quick to move toward interpretation. More than that, she wants me to take a certain position in relation to her dream. In a very subtle way, this desire is a defense against the otherness of the dream, its challenge. Soul and ego are often in a struggle which is sometimes mild and sometimes savage. So, I am careful not to assume that she is right about the content of the dream.

"Was your friend in the dream a child?" I ask.

"No, she was an adult. She was the age she is in life."

"Then why do you think she is being childish?"

"Crayons are a childish thing," she says as if stating the obvious.

"Can you tell me something about this friend of yours?" I am trying to break free of her strong views about her dream.

"She's very seductive, always wearing outlandish clothes—you know, bright colors and always low-cut."

"Is it possible," I say, taking a leap on the basis of her association, "that this colorful, sensual woman could be adding color, body, and some positive qualities of the child to your writing?"

"I suppose it's possible," she says, still unconvinced by this affront to her more satisfying interpretation.

One of the things that turned me away from her reading of the dream, apart from the general principle that we should avoid getting caught in the dream ego's complexes, was the negative narcissism in her judgment about the child: she didn't want to accept her own childlike ways. Once we moved away from her attachment to her usual way of thinking about herself, an attitude that strongly colored her own thoughts about the dream, we could go on to consider some truly fresh ideas about her life situation and her personal habits.

I am going into some detail about dreams not only because they give us a great deal of insight into our habits and our nature, but also because the way we relate to our dreams can be indicative of our way of dealing with all kinds of things, including our interpretations of the past, our current situation and problems, and the culture in the larger sense.

For example, another rule of thumb about dreams is that there is never a single, definitive reading. At another time, the same dream might reveal something altogether new. I like to treat dreams as if they were paintings, and paintings as if they were dreams. A Monet landscape might "mean" something different to various people who contemplate it. It might evoke entirely different reactions in the same person at different viewings. Over many years, a good painting will retain its power to mesmerize, satisfy, and evoke new reverie and wonder.

The same is true with dreams. A dream may survive a lifetime of neglect or an onslaught of interpretations and remain an icon and a fertile enigma for years of reflection. The point in working with a dream is never to translate it into a final meaning, but always to give it honor and respect, drawing from it as much meaningfulness and imaginative meditation as possible. Entering a dream should revitalize the imagination, not keep it in fixed and tired habits.

A simple but effective approach in working with images—whether they are from dreams, art, or personal stories—is never to stop listening to them and exploring them. Why do we listen to Bach's *St. Matthew Passion* more than once? Because it is the nature of a work of art, of any image, to reveal itself endlessly, one of the methods I use in therapy and in teaching is to listen to a reading of a dream or a story and say, when it is finished, "All right, let's try that again, differently."

Once a young man came to me with a letter he had written to his sweetheart. It was important to him because it expressed his deep feelings. He said he'd like to read it to me aloud. He read it slowly and expressively. When he was finished, I asked him if he'd read it again, with different emphasis. He did, and in this reading we heard different nuances of meaning. We tried it a third and a fourth time, and each time we learned something new. This little exercise points out the rich, multilayered nature of images of all kinds, and the advantage of never stopping in our exploration of them. The images, dreams, and experiences that are important to us will always have a multitude of possible readings and interpretations, because they are rich with imagination and soul.

I understand that this approach to imagination goes against the part of us that longs for a conclusion and a destination in our search for meaning. This is another reason why *care* of the soul, in contrast to *understanding* the soul, amounts to a new paradigm for our modern way of life. It asks us to make a complete turnaround in our usual efforts to figure things out, suggesting a different set of values and new techniques in which we actually appreciate and enjoy the endless unraveling of meaning, the infinitely rich and deep layering of poetics within the shifting, fluid fabric of experience.

The desire to squeeze a single meaning out of a dream or a work of art or a tale from life is inherently and profoundly Promethean. We want to steal fire from the gods for the sake of humanity. We want to replace divine mystery with human rationality. But this loss of complexity and mystery in our everyday response to life stories entails a loss of soul as well, because soul always manifests itself in mystery and multiplicity.

Dreams themselves often show us the way to understand them: they pull the dreamer deep into a body of water, or down into a pit, or down an elevator to a basement, or down a dark stairway, or deep into an alley. Typically, the dreamer, preferring height and light, is afraid to make the downward move into darkness. When I taught in the university, students frequently told me dreams of going into the library, getting on an elevator, then finding themselves in an ancient basement. The dream is not surprising, given the fact that the life of academia is so much an Apollonic, upper-world, ivory tower affair, and stands as a metaphor for all our attempts at understanding.

A woman who worked for a large appliance corporation once told me a dream in which she and her husband got off an elevator on a lower floor of the building, only to find the entire area under water. Together they floated in the water through hallways and streets until they arrived at a wonderful restaurant where they sat and ate a delicious dinner. This, too, is an image of dreamwork: allowing oneself to move around in the liquid atmosphere of fantasy and finding nourishment there. In dreams, which need never be taken literally or according to the laws of nature, we can breathe in a watery atmosphere. Dreams *are* watery: they resist all efforts to make them fixed and solid. We think we can only survive in the airy realms of thought and reason, but this dreamer found that she could be fed in gourmet style in that thicker atmosphere where imagination and life are fluid.

## The Guiding Daimon

An approach often taken to images is to find a meaning outside the image itself. A cigar in a dream is considered a phallic symbol instead of a cigar. A woman is an anima figure instead of a particular woman. A child is the "child part of myself" instead of simply the child of the dream. We think of imagination as a kind of symbolic thinking, with, as Freud put it, a latent and a manifest meaning. If we could "decipher" the given symbols, to use a popular rationalistic word, we could learn the meaning that is hidden in the image.

But there is another possible way to understand the creations of the dream world. What if there were no hidden meaning, no underlying message? What if we chose to confront images in all their mystery, deciding whether to follow their lead or to struggle with them.

The Greeks referred to the multitude of unnamed spirits that motivate and guide life as daimons. Socrates claimed to have lived his life according to the dictates of his daimon. In more recent times, W. B. Yeats warned that the daimon both inspires and threatens. In the chapter of *Memories, Dreams, Reflections* entitled "Late Thoughts," Jung, too, discusses the daimon. "We know that something unknown, alien, does come our way, just as we know that we do not ourselves *make* a dream or an inspiration, but that it somehow arises of its own accord. What does happen to us in this manner can be said to emanate from mana, from a daimon, a god, or the unconscious." He goes on to say that he prefers the term *the unconscious,* but he might just as well say *daimon.* Daimonic living is a response to the movements of imagination. When Jung was building his tower, workmen delivered a large piece of stone that was the wrong size. He took this "mistake" as the work of his Mercurial daimon and used the stone for one of his most important sculptures, the Bollingen Stone.

In the fifteenth century, Ficino, in *his* book on care of the soul, recommended finding the guardian daimon that is with us from the beginning: "Whoever examines himself thoroughly will find his own daimon." Rilke also regarded the daimon with respect. In his *Letters to a Young Poet* he suggests diving deeply into oneself in order to find one's own nature: "Go into yourself and see how deep the place is from which your life flows." Rilke is giving advice to a young man who wants to know whether he is called to be an artist, but his recommendation applies to anyone who wants to live everyday life with art. The soul wants to be in touch with that deep place from which life flows, without translating its offerings into familiar concepts. The best way to fulfill this desire is to give attention to the images that arise as independent beings from the springs of day-to-day imagination.

One implication of offering respect to the dream world is that we have to re-imagine imagination itself. Instead of seeing it as a particularly creative form of mind work, we could understand it more along Greek mythological lines, as a spring from which autonomous beings arise. Our relationship to it would change as well, from attempting to translate florid fantasy into reasonable terms to observing and entering a veritable world of personalities, geographies, animals, and events—all irreducible to completely understandable or controllable terms.

We would realize that the images of dreams and art are not puzzles to be solved, and that imagination hides its meaningfulness as much as it reveals it. In order to be affected by a dream, it isn't necessary to understand it or even to mine it for meanings. Merely giving our attention to such imagery, granting its autonomy and mystery, goes a long way toward shifting the center of consciousness from understanding to response. To live in the presence of the daimonic is to obey inner laws and urgencies. Cicero said that it is the *animus*—the Latin translation of *daimon*—that accounts for who you are. Ficino warned against living in conflict with the daimon lest you succumb to the worst kind of soul sickness. As an example, he says you should never decide where to live without taking into full consideration the demands of the daimon, which may appear as an intuitive attraction or inhibition.

The source from which life flows is so deep that it is experienced as "other." Speaking in the ancient language of the daimonic helps bring imagination into our very sense of self. Our relationship to the deep source of life becomes interpersonal, a dramatic tension between self and angel. In this dialogue, life also becomes more artful, in some cases even dramatic. We see this in people we label psychotic. Most of their actions are explicitly dramatic. Their deep "others," the personalities who play significant roles in their lives, appear in full dress. Writers talk about the characters of their fiction as people with will and intention. The novelist Margaret Atwood said once in an interview, "If the author gets too bossy, the characters may remind her that, though she is their creator, they are to some extent her creator as well."

Art teaches us to respect imagination as something far beyond human creation and intention. To live our ordinary life artfully is to have this sensibility about the things of daily life, to live more intuitively and to be willing to surrender a measure of our rationality and control in return for the gifts of soul.

## The Soul Arts

Care of the soul may take the form of living in a fully embodied imagination, being an artist at home and at work. You don't have to be a professional in order to bring art into the care of your soul; anyone can have an art studio at home, for instance. Like Jung, Black Elk, and Ficino, we could decorate our homes with images from our dreams and waking fantasy.

One of my own forms of expression is to play the piano in times of strong emotion. I remember well the day Martin Luther King, Jr., was killed. I was so overwhelmed that I went to the piano and played Bach for three hours. The music gave form and voice to my scrambled emotions, without explanations and rational interpretations.

The stuff of the world is there to be made into images that become for us tabernacles of spirituality and containers of mystery. If we don't allow soul its place in our lives, we are forced to encounter these mysteries in fetishes and symptoms, which in a sense are pathological art forms, the gods in our diseases. The example of artists teaches us that every day we can transform ordinary experience into the material of soul—in diaries, poems, drawings, music, letters, watercolors.

In a letter on soul-making to his brother George, Keats describes the process of transforming world into soul with the image of a school: "I will call the world a School instituted for the purpose of teaching little children to read—I will call the human heart the hornbook used in that School—and I will call the child able to read, the Soul made from that school and its hornbook. Do you not see how necessary a World of Pains and troubles is to school an Intelligence and make it a soul?"

As we read our experiences and learn to express them artfully, we are making life more soulful. Our homely arts arrest the flow of life momentarily so that events can be submitted to the alchemy of reflection. In a letter to a friend, we can deepen the impressions of experience and settle them in the heart where they can become the foundation for soul. Our great museums of art are simply a grand model for the more modest museum that is our home. There is no reason not to imagine our own homes as a place where the Muses can do their work of inspiration daily.

Another advantage to the soul of practicing the ordinary arts is the gift they leave for future generations. Tradition says that the soul thrives in a sense of time much greater than that of consciousness. To the soul the past is alive and valuable, and so is the future. As we perform the alchemy of sketching or writing upon our daily experience, we are preserving our thoughts for those who follow us. The community made by art transcends the limits of a personal lifetime, so that we can be instructed in our own soul work by the letters of John Keats to his brother.

In the modern world, in which we live mainly for the moment, it is easy to overlook the taste of the soul for a greater sense of time and a profound notion of community. We tend to give superficial explanations for our actions, to speak in literal terms instead of focusing on the reasons of the heart. A man explaining to me why he was getting a divorce went on and on with minor complaints about his wife. What he didn't say was what was obvious from our other conversations, that his heart was going through a major change. He wanted a new life, but tried to justify all the accompanying pain with superficial reasons. Because he didn't speak deeply about what was going on with him, he was cutting himself off from the soul of his divorce.

But when you read the letters of Keats, Rilke, or other poets you find a passionate search for expression and language adequate to the pleasures and pains of life. We can learn from them the importance to everyone, not just poets, of the effort to translate experience into words and pictures. The point of art is not simply to express ourselves, but to create an external, concrete form in which the soul of our lives can be evoked and contained.

Children paint every day and love to show their works on walls and refrigerator doors. But as we become adults, we abandon this important soul task of childhood. We assume, I suppose, that children are just learning motor coordination and alphabets. But maybe they are doing something more fundamental: finding forms that reflect what is going on in their souls. When we grow up and begin to think of the art gallery as much more advanced than the refrigerator door, we lose an important ritual of childhood, giving it away to the professional artist. We are then left with mere rational reasons for our lives, feelings of emptiness and confusion, expensive visits to a psycho-therapist, and a compulsive attachment to pseudoimages, such as shallow television programs. When our own images no longer have a home, a personal museum, we drown our sense of loss in pale substitutes, trashy novels or formulaic movies.

As the poets and painters of centuries have tried to tell us, art is not about the expression of talent or the making of pretty things. It is about the preservation and containment of soul. It is about arresting life and making it available for contemplation. Art captures the eternal in the everyday, and it is the eternal that feeds soul—the whole world in a grain of sand.

Leonardo da Vinci asks an interesting question in one of his notebooks: "Why does the eye see a thing more clearly in dreams than the imagination when awake?" One answer is that the eye of the soul perceives the eternal realities so important to the heart. In waking life, most of us see only with our physical eyes, even though we could, with some effort of imagination, glimpse fragments of eternity in the most ordinary passing events. Dream teaches us to look with that other eye, the eye that in waking life belongs to the artist, to each of us as artist.

When we see pain on a tortured person's face, we might glimpse for a second the image of Jesus crucified, a reality that artists for centuries have shown in infinite variation and detail and one that enters the lives of all of us at one time or another. We might look at a woman in a jewelry shop with the eyes of D. H. Lawrence, who saw Aphrodite in the body of the woman washing her clothes in a river. We might see a Cézanne still life in a momentary glance at our own kitchen table. When a summer breeze blows through an open window as we sit reading in a rare half-hour of quiet, we might recall one of the hundreds of annunciations painters have given us, reminding us that it is the habit of angels to visit in moments of silent reading.

A soul-centered understanding of art sees the interpenetration of poetic image and ordinary life. Art shows us what is already there in the ordinary, but without art we live under the illusion that there is only time, and not eternity. As we practice our daily arts, if only in the composing of a heart-felt letter, we are unearthing the eternal from within ordinary time, engaging in the special qualities, themes, and circumstances of the soul. Soul thrives as we jot down a thought in our diary or note a dream, and give body to a slight influx of eternity. Our notebooks then truly become our own private gospels and sutras, our holy books, and our simple paintings truly serve as icons, every bit as significant in the work of our own soul as the wonderful icons of the Eastern churches are for their congregations.

Care of the soul is not a project of self-improvement nor a way of being released from the troubles and pains of human existence. It is not at all concerned with living properly or with emotional health. These are the concerns of temporal, heroic, Promethean life. Care of the soul touches another dimension, in no way separate from life, but not identical either with the problem solving that occupies so much of our consciousness. We care for the soul solely by honoring its expressions, by giving it time and opportunity to reveal itself, and by living life in a way that fosters the depth, interiority, and quality in which it flourishes. Soul is its own purpose and end.

To the soul, memory is more important than planning, art more compelling than reason, and love more fulfilling than understanding. We know we are well on the way toward soul when we feel attachment to the world and the people around us and when we live as much from the heart as from the head. We know soul is being cared for when our pleasures feel deeper than usual, when we can let go of the need to be free of complexity and confusion, and when compassion takes the place of distrust and fear. Soul is interested in the differences among cultures and individuals, and within ourselves it wants to be expressed in uniqueness if not in outright eccentricity.

Therefore, when in the midst of my confusion and my stumbling attempts to live a transparent life, *I* am the fool, and not everyone around me, then I know I am discovering the power of the soul to make a life interesting. Ultimately, care of the soul results in an individual "I" I never would have planned for or maybe even wanted. By caring for the soul faithfully, every day, we step out of the way and let our full genius emerge. Soul coalesces into the mysterious philosophers' stone, that rich, solid core of personality the alchemists sought, or it opens into the peacock's tail—a revelation of the soul's colors and a display of its dappled brilliance.

# NOTES

P. *17, the great sixteenth-century physician, Paracelsus:* Paracelsus (1493–1541) was a pious, highly influential physician who leaned into the future with his modern medical experiments and into the past with his philosophical dependence upon alchemy and astrology. In his own lifetime, because of his ground-breaking insights into medicine, he was known as the "Luther of physicians." Today he may seem obscure because of the rich cosmic matrix out of which he works, but an appreciative and open mind will find much of value in his writings. *Paracelsus: Selected Writings*, ed. Jolande Jacobi, trans. Norbert Guterman, Bollingen Series XXVIII (Princeton, N.J.: Princeton University Press, 1979), p. 49.

P. *30, the Renaissance doctor Paracelsus:* *Paracelsus: Selected Writings*, p. 63. Paracelsus had read Marsilio Ficino, who taught that the universe is an animal, graced with body, soul, and spirit. Paracelsus applied Ficino's idea to medicine, requiring a true physician to know the world's body, not as an abstraction, but as a living, individual entity. He advises physicians, for instance, to "give heed to the region in which the patient lives ... for one country is different from another; its earth is different, as are its stones, wines, bread, meat, and everything that grows and thrives in a specific region...." A physician should be a "cosmographer and geographer" (*Paracelsus: Selected Writings*, p. 59).

P. *113, Rilke again refers:* Rainer Maria Rilke, *Sonnets to Orpheus,* trans. M. D. Herter Norton (New York: W. W. Norton & Company, Inc., 1942, I,9), p. 33. The "cure" of narcissism is the discovery of the "dual realm" (*Doppelbereich*) of the visible and the invisible. Our symptoms, in this Rilkean philosophy, become invisible not by disappearing altogether, but by being transformed into their "next-deepest" invisible existence. As Rilke says later in the same letter, "All the worlds of the universe are plunging into the invisible as into their next-deepest reality; some stars have an immediate waxing and waning in the infinite consciousness of the Angel,—others are dependent on beings that slowly and laboriously transform them, in whose terrors and raptures they attain their next invisible realisation." Rainer Maria Rilke, *Duino Elegies.* Translation, introduction, and commentary by J. B. Leishman and Stephen Spender (New York: W. W. Norton & Company, Inc., 1967), pp. 129–30.

P. *118, Ficino says, "What is human love?":* Plato's *Symposium* was a literary drinking-party at which guests addressed the nature of love. Ficino, a devoted follower of Plato, imitated the *Symposium* at his own literary banquet, the *Convivium.* In a letter to a Florentine nobleman, Bernardo Bembo, Ficino spells out the requirements for a good convivium, concluding: "To what end is all this written about the convivium? Simply, that we who live separated lives, though not without vixation, may live together in happiness as one." *The Letters of Marsilio Ficino,* vol. 2, trans. Language Department of the School of Economic Science (London: Shepheard-Walwyn, 1978), p. 54. See also, Marsilio Ficino, *Commentary on Plato's Symposium on Love,* trans. Sears Jayne (Dallas: Spring Publications, 1985), p. 130.

P. 199, *Oscar Wilde's letter from prison:* This part of *De Profundis* offers an example of "Romantic theology," an approach to spirituality that recognizes beauty in the soul's tendency toward evil and is profoundly motivated toward compassion for human fallibility. Oscar Wilde, *De Profundis and Other Writings* (New York: Penguin Books, 1973), p. 178.

P. 248, *Paracelsus gave doctors the following advice:* *Paracelsus: Selected Writings,* pp. 63–64.

P. 256, *According to Paracelsus:* *Paracelsus: Selected Writings,* p. 74.

P. 259, *Ficino gave somewhat different advice:* *Marsilio Ficino: The Book of Life,* trans. Charles Boer (Irving, Tx.: Spring Publications, 1980), pp. 96, 116.

P. 260, *at Walden Pond, writes:* Henry David Thoreau, *Walden* (New York: The Library of America, 1985), p. 422. "Communing with nature" doesn't have to be a mystical, suprasensory activity; it may require no more than listening to the sounds sung by birds and insects everywhere. This "world music," or *musica mundana* as the ancients called it, is a prime expression of the world soul.

P. 263, *Norman O. Brown says:* By treating psycho-analysis as poetry, Norman O. Brown has taught us how to see Rilke's dual realm of the visible and the invisible in culture. Paradoxically, the more poetically we regard experience, the more our bodies are engaged. "To recover the world of silence, of symbolism," he writes, "is to recover the human body.... The true meanings of words are bodily meanings, carnal knowledge; and the bodily meanings are the un-spoken meanings." Norman O. Brown, *Love's Body* (New York: Vintage Books, 1966), p. 265.

P. 394, *Jung writes:* C. G. Jung, *Memories, Dreams, Reflections,* trans. Richard and Clara Winston (New York: Vintage Books, 1963), p. 337. In a letter of December 27, 1958, Jung makes it clear that his notions of integration of the personality and individuation do not imply perfection. "I cannot possibly tell you what a man who has enjoyed complete self-realization looks like, and what becomes of him. I never have seen one, and if I did see one I could not understand him because I myself would not be completely inte-grated.... I had to help innumerable people to get a bit more conscious about themselves and to consider the fact that they consist of many different components, light and dark." C. G. Jung, *Letters,* selected and edited by Gerhard Adler in collaboration with Aniela Jaffé, trans. R. F. C. Hull, Bollingen Series XCV:2 (Princeton, N. J.: Princeton University Press, 1975), vol. 2, p. 474.

P. 448, *to find one's own nature:* Rainer Maria Rilke, *Letters to a Young Poet,* trans. Stephen Mitchell (New York: Random House, 1984), p. 9.

P. 451, *said once in an interview:* "Who Created Whom? Characters that Talk Back," *New York Times Book Review,* May 31, 1987, p. 36.

# SUGGESTIONS FOR FURTHER READING

Ficino, Marsilio. *Marsilio Ficino: The Book of Life*. Translated by Charles Boer. Dallas: Spring Publications, 1980.

An excellent translation of a fifteenth-century book. Because of its antique style, it is not easy to follow, but taken a little at a time, and thought of metaphorically, it offers many good suggestions for care of the soul.

Hillman, James. *A Blue Fire: Selected Writings by James Hillman*. Edited by Thomas Moore. New York: Harper & Row, 1989.

This anthology of James Hillman's writings provides an overview of his thinking. An introduction to the book summarizes Hillman's "archetypal psychology," and brief introductions to each chapter guide the reader through his ideas. Hillman is the foremost spokesperson today for a soul-oriented psychology.

*The Homeric Hymns*. Translated by Charles Boer. 5th ed. Dallas: Spring Publications, 1991.

A readable, poetic, beautiful translation of hymns that tell the stories and offer praise to Hera, Aphrodite, Hermes, Demeter, and many other gods and goddesses of the Greeks.

Jung, C. G. *Memories, Dreams, Reflections.* Edited by Aniela Jaffé and translated by Richard and Clara Winston. New York: Pantheon Books, 1973.

I think it is best to approach Jung for the first time through his memoirs and "late thoughts." This is a unique "autobiography," telling the story of a soul rather than a life.

Kerényi, Karl. *The Gods of the Greeks.* Translated by Norman Cameron. London: Thames and Hudson, 1974.

This book has long been my choice as a source for Greek mythological stories and characters. Well-documented, it remains close to classical sources and yet conveys the stories with charm and wit.

Rilke, Rainer Maria. *Letters to a Young Poet.* Translated by Stephen Mitchell. New York: Random House, 1984.

Rilke is an important source for care of the soul because his own perceptions are extraordinarily profound and subtle, and they are presented in his prose and poetry with all the paradox in language and meaning they deserve.

Sardello, Robert. *Facing the World with Soul.* Hudson, N.Y.: Lindisfarne Press, 1991.

This book contains Sardello's fascinating work on soul in the world, as well as his unique approach to spirituality. He constantly surprises with the freshness of his approach to such common themes as economics, things, architecture, medicine, and herpes.

Sexson, Lynda. *Ordinarily Sacred.* New York: Crossroad, 1982.

Lynda Sexson offers a theology of everyday experience in this enchanting book that shows how the religious traditions of the world lie slightly concealed in the details and commonplaces of ordinary life.

Wilde, Oscar. *De Profundis and Other Writings.* New York: Penguin Books, 1973.

Wilde's notorious light wit turned dark in this long reflection affected by his experience of prison. For me, its importance lies in its Romantic reading of Christianity. Wilde may sound heretical, but it is always good to read heresies for the counterpoint they give orthodoxy, allowing us to hear the full music in any religion or philosophy.

Yanagi, Sōetsu. *The Unknown Craftsman: A Japanese Insight into Beauty.* Adapted by Bernard Leach. Rev. ed. New York: Kodansha International, 1989.

This book is full of insights into the nature of art, beauty, and craft. Like the other books I am recommending, it is not a straightforward simplification of these difficult subjects. It is not even fully coherent, yet it keeps the grounding soul in an area that too easily floats off into abstractions and idealizations.

If you have enjoyed
this book in large print
and would like to
receive more information
on other books
of interest,
please write to:

Beth Walker
Walker and Company
720 Fifth Avenue
New York, New York 10019